Steve Goodwin

Dream Golf

Dream Golf

The Making of Bandon Dunes

STEPHEN GOODWIN

Revised and Expanded

ALGONQUIN BOOKS OF CHAPEL HILL   2010

Published by

ALGONQUIN BOOKS OF CHAPEL HILL

Post Office Box 2225

Chapel Hill, North Carolina 27515-2225

a division of

WORKMAN PUBLISHING

225 Varick Street

New York, New York 10014

Updated and expanded edition, Algonquin Books of Chapel Hill, June 2010.
First edition published by Algonquin Books of Chapel Hill in 2006.
Printed in the United States of America.
Published simultaneously in Canada by Thomas Allen & Son Limited.
Design by Anne Winslow.

Excerpt on p. 309 reprinted with permission of *Golfweek*.

The Library of Congress has catalogued a previous edition as follows:
Goodwin, Stephen.
   Dream golf : the making of Bandon Dunes / Stephen Goodwin.—1st ed.
   p. cm.
   ISBN 978-1-56512-530-8
   1. Golf courses—Oregon—Design and construction—Case
studies.   2. Keiser, Mike.   I. Title.
GV982.O74G66 2006
796.352'068795—dc22   2005055589   .

ISBN 978-1-56512-981-8 (revised and expanded edition)

10 9 8 7 6 5 4 3 2 1

For my son, Nick,
with the hope that many golf adventures are out there
waiting for you

Contents

Introduction

EVER SINCE IT OPENED IN 1999, Bandon Dunes has been one of *the* stories in golf, an improbable tale that got better with each telling. On a remote stretch of the Pacific Coast, at the edge of beyond, a golf course had appeared—and not just an ordinary course, but a seaside course of great drama, purity, and beauty. Early visitors to the place came back with stars in their eyes, claiming to have discovered a true American links.

Golfweek ranked Bandon Dunes as a Top 100 course before it had officially opened. *Golf Magazine* had never run a picture of a golf course on its cover—but it ran a picture of Bandon Dunes. Sober, thoughtful golf writers declared the place to be inspirational, comparing it to Pebble Beach in California, and Ballybunion, the fabled Irish links.

Standing joke: What's the difference between Bandon Dunes and Ballybunion? Answer: It's easier to get to Ballybunion.

Golfers wanted to know everything they could learn about this place that seemed to defy all conventional wisdom. From the point of view of the golf industry, Mike Keiser, the owner and developer, had done everything backward. He'd built a resort that was nowhere near any kind of "market." He'd built a golf course that was deliberately and proudly designed not as a contemporary course, but as a "throwback." He'd ignored advice to hire a name architect and chosen, instead, a young, unknown, inexperienced Scotsman, David Kidd.

He had also decreed that the course would be for walkers only. He kept it free of carts, cart paths, and real estate. He was never tempted to make the course private; he wanted it to be open to the public and to be priced so that locals could enjoy it.

People warned him that he was throwing his money away, but Mike Keiser trusted his dream. He believed that other golfers were searching for the same things that he sought in a golf experience—and he was right.

Bandon Dunes touched a nerve. The course soared into the upper reaches of the course rankings, and then, in 2001, its sister course, Pacific Dunes— designed by Tom Doak, a youthful and controversial American golf course architect—opened to even more glowing reviews. It was another links course, and, some said, was more authentic, more beautiful, and more captivating than the first.

With two courses, Bandon Dunes—a name that came to encompass the resort itself as well as the original course—moved into select company. "The list of golf sites that can claim dynamic-duo status is short," wrote Jamie Diaz, one of the most respected writers in golf, in *Travel and Leisure Golf*. His list was a roster of golf's holy places: the Monterey Peninsula, with Pebble Beach and Cypress Point; Shinnecock Hills and National Golf Links; the two tracks at Winged Foot; Olympic Lake and Ocean; Ballybunion Old and New; St. Andrews Old and New; Pinehurst Nos. 2 and 8.

How did Bandon Dunes and Pacific Dunes rate in this elite company? "I'm convinced," Diaz wrote, "it won't be long before Bandon and Pacific— given their public accessibility, unspoiled environment, dramatic setting, thoughtful design and true golf spirit—are considered the best tandem of courses in the world."

The best in the world. Strong words, especially considering that all the other places listed by Diaz have been steeped in tradition. Golf is not a sport that readily embraces the new, but reserves judgment and comes to decisions in its own sweet time. Was it possible that a pair of brand-new courses in Bandon, Oregon, could eclipse the time-honored favorites?

Yes, it was. Visitors to Bandon experienced a classic *coup de foudre,* a blow of passion, love at first sight This was the kind of golf of which people dreamed, golf that lifted the spirits and brought a renewal of gusto and energy. At the rim of the continent, against the colossal sweep of the Pacific Ocean, people seemed to rediscover the game, and to remember what made it so majestic and exhilarating. Bandon hadn't been the site of any notable tournament, nor was it associated with any of the big names in golf; it had won its place by a kind of popular acclamation. Not to stretch the point too far, but Bandon seemed almost like a shrine where something miraculous was said to have occurred, a remote place to which pilgrims found their way, hoping to partake of the mystery, hoping to breathe in the sacred energy.

The Bandon story kept evolving, and so did the place. A third course, Bandon Trails, designed by Ben Crenshaw and Bill Coore, opened in 2005. A few of its holes were located in high dunes, but most of the golf course was routed through meadow and dense forest, opening new vistas and revealing new dimensions of the property. Golf writers hailed Bandon Trails as another treasure, and Bandon Dunes moved into an even more exalted category.

The story still wasn't over. The buzz that had surrounded Bandon Dunes for a decade kicked up a notch with the announcement of a fourth course, Old Macdonald, opening in 2010. The course was conceived as a tribute to Charles Blair Macdonald, and the name, with its playful twist, served notice that the course would be inspired by classic principles of design — but would not be a solemn lecture in golf history. It also signaled that Mike Keiser was willing to vary the pattern. Instead of turning to a designer for an original course, he'd named Tom Doak and Jim Urbina as codesigners of Old Mac, and complemented them with an advisory panel. The goal was still an original course, but this was a much more collaborative arrangement. And since the idea had originated with him, Mike Keiser had edged a little more into the spotlight.

Golfers are recharged at Bandon. In the course of writing this book, I spent a lot of time there, and I saw how many people came up to Mike Keiser to thank him for building the golf courses. They were strangers, but they wanted to let him know how much they'd enjoyed playing at Bandon Dunes, and they wanted to express more than mere enjoyment: They wanted him to know that their experience had *mattered*.

Mike responds to these strangers sincerely and graciously, but he always seems slightly embarrassed to be recognized as the owner of the place. He doesn't have an ounce of pretension in him. He is the visionary who had the imagination, the patience, the money, the sheer guts to bring this place into being, and he knows what he has created. He doesn't crow about it, but his feelings do show themselves every now and then, as they did one day at Bandon Dunes while Mike played a round with an old friend. I was tagging along, and at the 12th hole, a par 3, we had to wait for a few minutes while the group ahead played out.

The ocean was glittering in the afternoon sun, and Mike was talking about the storms that lashed this stretch of the coast in the 1850s. The huge waves had washed away the deposits of gold-laden black sands on the local beaches, putting an end to Bandon's brief gold rush.

"They say we're due for more big storms," Mike said. "Sometimes I wonder how much of the golf course it might take away. That would be a tough call for a golf course owner, wouldn't it? Suppose you were offered a choice: You could save your golf course or your life. Which would you do?"

Then he gave a small, self-conscious laugh, knowing he'd revealed the depth of his attachment to the place he'd created. Mike, the practical businessman, had said in so many words that Bandon Dunes was his legacy.

This book is about Mike Keiser and his pursuit of a dream. It is about the golf courses at Bandon and the men who designed and built them—men who had dreams of their own, dreams that converged with Mike's. It is about the way that these golf courses built on a remote stretch of the Pacific Coast were able to capture golf's ancient magic.

Part One

A Man with a Program

1 | Soul Work

Deep down, I wanted to build something that would last.
I wanted to build a golf course that people would be playing
five hundred years from now. —MIKE KEISER

IN 1985, MIKE KEISER acquired sixty acres of wooded sand dunes in New Buffalo, Michigan. His immediate goal was to prevent a developer from building condos across the road from the lakefront home where Mike and his wife, Lindy, spent weekends with their young children. New Buffalo is a resort town on the southeastern tip of Lake Michigan, a ninety-minute drive from downtown Chicago; for the Keisers—who lived and worked in the city—the place seemed idyllic and remote, the perfect place to escape for quiet, unhurried family weekends. Mike regarded the acquisition of the sixty acres as a "defensive" purchase.

As a partner in a flourishing company, Mike was able to pay cash for the sixty acres. He and Lindy were cofounders of Recycled Paper Greetings (along with his college roommate, Phil Friedmann), and they had seen their enterprise expand from a tiny start-up, with offices in their two-room apartment, into a business that was generating annual sales of roughly $100 million. Launched on Earth Day in 1971, Recycled Paper Greetings was known for its environmental awareness and its witty, irreverent greeting cards. From the start, RPG's cards had offered an alternative to the more traditional, sentimental greeting cards produced by Hallmark, and the company quickly grew into the third largest in the industry. Still privately owned, RPG has been a bold, gutsy, original venture, and it made Mike Keiser a rich man. It also taught him to trust his business instincts.

Those sixty acres of sand dunes gave Mike a kid-with-a-new-toy feeling. He'd been considering various golf investments, and he was serious enough to have looked hard at a large tract of land near Washington, D.C., as a potential golf course site. Now, with a chunk of property to fuel his imagination, he was like, say, Ben Hogan with his first golf club: He'd come into the possession of something that brought his long-simmering interest to a full, rolling boil.

At first, he treated the property as a family playground, and he'd stroll over with Lindy and the children, all of them carrying golf clubs and pockets full of old balls, to play "wilderness golf" (pick a tree and find a way to hit the ball to it). The sandy, scruffy site reminded him of Pine Valley, the renowned golf course in New Jersey to which he'd made many pilgrimages. Geologically, this whole section of the Lake Michigan shore belonged to an unusual dune belt; most of the land was wooded, covered with stands of oak, maple, sassafras, and cottonwood, but there were openings where the family could play full-throttle golf shots. The most remarkable feature of the site was a ridge fifty feet high—a veritable mountain in the flattish lake country—that seemed to cry out for use in a golf course. The more he got to know his sixty acres, the more Mike envisioned golf holes with tees situated on the high ground of the ridge, creating dramatic downhill shots to fairways and greens fitted among the dunes below.

Mike Keiser, a lifelong golfer, was also an armchair golf course architect. For years his bedside book had been a thick volume with pictures and descriptions of the Top 100 courses, and whenever he could steal away for a day or two, he'd visit places on the list, places like Pine Valley and Merion. He knew that he'd never be a scratch golfer, but his score wasn't the measure of his satisfaction in the game. On his own property, he was happy to crisscross the dunes with a golf club in his hand, whacking old balls from one dune to the next as he imagined how golf holes might be fitted into the contours of the land.

Mike couldn't stay away from the dunes. Even when his family couldn't get away for the weekend, even when he might have chosen to play golf, he'd drive out to New Buffalo with his friend Howard McKee, the two of them wearing jeans and work boots and carrying lopping shears and axes. They'd crawl through the wire fence—there was no entry road into the property— and spend hours cutting brush. Their specific mission was to rid the property of the grapevines that grew luxuriantly, slowly smothering the trees to which they attached themselves. Their broader mission was to let certain life questions evolve and percolate as they busied themselves with physical labor.

Mike and Howard had gotten to know one another as fathers of children who happened to be in the same elementary school class, and in some ways they were an odd couple. Mike was a golfer, an athlete, an entrepreneur accustomed to operating independently and swiftly; Howard was professorial in appearance and manner, a trained architect and land planner whose career with the international firm of Skidmore, Owings, and Merrill had involved him in hugely complex undertakings, the kind of projects—like building cities in Saudi Arabia—that required volumes of planning documents and years of patience to bring to fruition. Moreover, while Mike inclined to the right politically, Howard leaned toward the left—but the two found that they both enjoyed their spirited intellectual sparring. The brush-cutting sessions were enlivened by debates about economics, education, and environmental issues, about which they had strong and often opposing opinions.

The personal undercurrent was always there, too. Howard had come to Chicago to take part in the planning for the 1992 World's Fair, conceived as a centennial celebration of the 1893 fair (it actually opened in 1892), generally regarded as the most successful world's fair of all time, the fair that brought together the forces and energies that created the modern city of Chicago. By 1987, it was obvious that the Centennial Fair wasn't going to happen, and Howard was watching three years of work go down the drain. He was thinking of a career change. In certain moods, he was ready to consider radical changes, like returning to Oregon, the place he'd once lived and still regarded as his spiritual home, and spending a few years rereading the Great Books. "I was ready to leave Skidmore, Owings, and Merrill," he says. "I'd gotten to the point where I needed to do something that mattered to me in very direct, immediate ways. I knew that I needed to do what I considered soul work."

Soul work. Mike didn't describe his own restlessness in those terms, but it was clear to Howard that Mike was ruminating about his own future. Mike was forty years old when he purchased the New Buffalo tract, an age often associated with midlife changes. He'd taken part in an Armchair Architect contest sponsored by *Golf Digest,* and he actually believed he had a chance to win it. Moreover, he was close to making a decision to indulge his golf course obsession—and it was becoming an obsession—by building a course on his sixty acres. The property wasn't big enough for eighteen holes, not even for nine holes, but Mike had started looking at adjacent properties that would give him enough land.

Not a golfer himself, Howard didn't entirely understand the hold that the game had on Mike's imagination, and he wasn't quite sure what Mike had in mind when he spoke about more ambitious golf projects that could go well beyond what he was contemplating here in New Buffalo. In the fall of 1987, Mike and Howard went out for one of their regular neighborhood dinners with their wives; the family friendship had actually begun when Lindy and Howard's wife, Kennon, became acquainted. The conversation turned toward the difficulties Mike was having in finding a suitable piece of golf land on the East Coast, and he asked Howard if he could help him find something out west. After all, Howard had spent a lot of time in Oregon and was looking to spend more. By this time Howard knew Mike fairly well, but he couldn't quite gauge the seriousness of his proposal, and he made the request that any architect would make: He asked Mike to put together a "program" that listed his requirements and desires for the property he sought.

A few weeks later, Mike handed Howard a couple of handwritten pages. This was his program, and when Howard read it, he was taken aback. In fact, he was tempted to laugh. He knew that Mike was a successful businessman and a big thinker, but he had no idea that the man who'd been wriggling through the fence on his hands and knees, spending the day lopping grapevines, was formulating a scheme on such an epic scale.

The program called for oceans, waterfalls, and "breath-taking" beauty. It contemplated the appropriation of a small town. It dealt in sums of money that were significant, especially when the money would be coming straight out of Mike's pocket. It seemed almost to have been written in haste, in a telegraphic style with all fluff eliminated, making the scope of the project seem even more stark and audacious.

The program read like this:

* Min. 1000 acres
    Best min 5–10,000 acres   Land budget $10 MM
* Location: initially, California, Oregon, preferably on coast
    or with some coastal access
    Would not exclude Monterey south in 1st pass
* Sandy soil/sand dunes on at least part
* Stand alone water: rivers, streams, lakes, waterfall
    i.e., unusual features a prerequisite
* if parcel is large enough could include a small town
    Regardless proximity (20 miles) to town or larger "with potential"
* parcel cannot be flat; further, it must be breath-taking
* year-round or near year-round outdoor climate
* sympathetic ecosystem
* diversity of environment
GO or NO GO within 6 mos
Staged development thereafter, at a planned expenditure rate of max
    $3MM/year for 10 years
MIN. Amenities
1) 18 hole championship g. c. with extraordinary unique features
    (sand dunes, waterfall etc.)
2) Room for 2 more golf courses
3) Tennis
4) Clubhouse
5) Guest cabins/lodges

6) Natural easy access to National Forest

7) Natural, easy access to canoeing, white water canoeing, mountain and
   rock climbing, wind surfing, fishing (fly), deep sea fishing,
   bicycling, jogging, hiking, etc.

FOR HOWARD MCKEE, a man who'd felt constricted and confined in his work, this program was the wild blue yonder, and—once he overcame his initial surprise—he didn't waste any time coming to a decision. Within a few days, he'd drafted a careful response to Mike's program, outlining a systematic approach to finding a tract of land that would meet the requirements and setting his own fee at $3,000 per month.

By return mail he received a countersigned contract and a check for his first month's fee. Drawn on an account that Mike had set up for his golf expenses, the check didn't have the usual kind of identifying information; Mike's name wasn't on it, nor was there any address or phone number. The title of this account was simply Chivas Irons—the name of the mystical hero of *Golf in the Kingdom,* the legendary golf book by Michael Murphy, a founder of the Esalen Institute. (Mike had misspelled the name; the character in the book is Shivas, with an S, and he used Chivas, with a C, as in the Scotch whisky.)

Here was a powerful coincidence. Howard, though not a golfer, had not only read *Golf in the Kingdom* but had also been a frequent visitor to Esalen. He had been hired to redesign the property in the early 1980s and had become a good friend of Michael Murphy's. Indeed, Howard believed less in coincidence—that is, in the randomness of events—than in synchronicity; he was inclined to see meaning and purpose when events had links and connections. This appearance of "Chivas Irons" at the outset of the project was at the very least a piece of serendipity. It was a good omen.

Howard McKee saves everything, and he placed Mike's handwritten program in a file folder. When he dug it out sixteen years later, he had to laugh, again, at the audacity of the list—even though Bandon Dunes fulfills just about every one of the original requirements. The only thing missing is the waterfall.

2 | The Anti-Tycoon

Mike Keiser spends less on his clothes than Donald Trump
spends on his hair. —JOSH LESNIK

EVEN THOUGH MIKE KEISER has become a significant figure in the golf world, he continues to oversee the operations of Recycled Paper Greetings, along with Phil Friedmann. Mike still chooses all of the "product"—and RPG produces eight thousand items per year, including three thousand new items—and he and Phil still share an office, literally. Their desks are not more than ten feet apart in a large room with beige carpets, fluorescent lights, metal filing cabinets, and piles of stuff everywhere. Phil's desk area resembles that of a stressed-out graduate student with its sprawling trails, mounds, ridges, and cordilleras of clutter; Mike's space, by comparison, is a model of order and tidiness, and his many piles of paper are neatly stacked. Framed pictures of his family hang on the walls, along with a few golf pictures. All in all, this office could be described as comfortably lived-in, and it's clearly the lair of partners who are way past worrying what anyone else might think of their working arrangements.

In articles in golf publications, Mike has been described as a "tycoon" and "the greeting card mogul," terms that are wildly off the mark insofar as they suggest a man who projects wealth and power. He has no interest in the various trappings of corporate structure that would bolster his image or ego. He avoids flash and ostentation. He goes to work in casual, comfortable clothes—khakis or corduroys, usually, and a freshly laundered and pressed Oxford shirt, without tie. His assistant for fifteen years, Karen Thompson, knows that he has an off-site meeting when he shows up in jacket and tie. His title, she says, is flexible: Mike has cards that designate him variously as chairman, president, and vice president, though he prefers to be untitled. ("When Phil and I incorporated, a little lawyer insisted that one of us be president. We told him that we'd like to be known as the baron and the duke, and of course he thought we weren't serious businessmen. We were quite serious, though, about the ability of a title to create a rift when two partners are co-equal, and we've always avoided that.")

When the Chicago streets are wet or slushy, Mike steps out of his shoes and pads around the office in his stocking feet. Even shoeless and tieless, however, he manages to appear slightly overdressed and out of his preferred element; he has the open gaze and deep, permanent sunburn of a man who's spent his best hours out-of-doors. Just a touch under six feet tall, he keeps himself fit and trim, and spends his lunch hour jogging or working out at a nearby gym. He weighs the same 150 pounds as he did when he graduated from college. He likes participatory sports, especially individual sports—skiing, tennis, golf—but has next to no interest in spectator sports. He rarely goes to games unless one of his children is playing

He has large features, a thatch of steel-gray hair, and blue eyes that are remarkably clear and unwavering. Some people feel unsettled and disconcerted by the way Mike fixes his attention on them, as though he is noting their every gesture and taking their precise measure. He seems remarkably free of self-consciousness. He doesn't fill the air with small talk or nervous distractions. He has the gift of authority, for it is clear that he says only what he means to say—not more, not less. He uses words with precision and accuracy, and his working vocabulary includes words like "eleemosynary," "diaphanous," and "monetized." His voice is a baritone and he enunciates with a clarity that would please any speech teacher. The guys who worked for him at Bandon had a field day imitating the deep, measured cadence of his voice. His inflection rarely varies, though he sometimes slips into a different key—dry, droll, and ironic—when he wants to poke fun or make a pun. He is good at puns.

Everyone who's worked with him quickly comes to recognize his habits and style. For starters, he is absolutely not the kind of boss who *makes* work. He hates to waste time. He does not stand on ceremony or insist on protocol. His letters and memos are legendary for their concision and brevity. If he can avoid writing a complete sentence, he will, and his preferred method of written communication is the Post-it. (Lately, his favorite Post-it bears a picture of the American flag, but before that he was partial to a Post-it that carried these words of Dan Quayle's: "What a waste it is to lose one's mind. Or not to have a mind is being very wasteful. How true that is.") He addresses problems the minute they arise. He expects things to begin and end on time, and he is always punctual. He is practically allergic to meetings, at least those with a fixed agenda, but he enjoys free-form brainstorming sessions. He operates entirely in the present, giving his full attention to whatever is in front of him. He has a cell phone but rarely turns it on. Though he bristles with physical energy, so much so that he has a hard time sitting still (in photos Mike's image is often blurry because he is always moving), he rarely appears to be in a hurry. He has time to listen carefully to others. Jim Seeley, a business associate, says, "Mike is a master at eliciting the opinions of others and reconciling different perspectives." As an executive he is emphatically not a micromanager or control freak but, on the contrary, an overseer whose instinct is to grant the greatest possible freedom and latitude to those working for him. He likes the creative, conceptual aspects of business and the energy that flows from successful collaboration. "He doesn't like plans that bind him," Howard McKee says. "He'd much rather keep things open. He likes the razzmatazz."

Yet when the moment comes, he is decisive. He is willing to take risks, and to take responsibility for them. He doesn't make a show of this, but his colleagues always know the buck stops with Mike. He is comfortable with being the boss. His role at RPG, one friend speculates, has reinforced his habits of decision-making; he sees so many ideas for greeting cards, and makes so many decisions every working day, that he can't afford to be ambivalent—and he gets quick feedback about the soundness of decisions. "He's a publisher," says Chris Ogden, a friend who's known Mike for years, "and he has to decide quickly what will work and what won't. Every card has to tell a story in a hurry—there's a setup and a pay-off, and Mike wouldn't be where he is now if he didn't have a gift for recognizing the good stories."

Beyond those everyday decisions lie the large, strategic visions. His business partners and associates are unanimous in praising his steadiness and clarity of vision. He is tenacious. Alfred Hamilton, a longtime friend and for many years a manager at RPG, believes "Mike has a deep reservoir of confidence. He expects things to work." Howard McKee says, "Mike has a unique ability to set a goal, and to make everyone working for him feel that they have an essential part to play in the story. He makes them feel that the goal can't be achieved unless they make it their goal, too." Josh Lesnik was only twenty-nine when he became the first general manager of Bandon Dunes. "I should have been terrified," he says, "but Mike made it seem easy. His whole attitude was, 'We can do this.' I never got any vibe of stress or panic. We talked on the phone every day, and he never seemed worried. He always made me feel that I was doing OK, and I wanted to do better than that—I knew Mike had taken a risk, a big risk, and I really wanted to help him pull it off. He has that effect on people."

MIKE NEVER DOUBTED that he would go into business. His father, a World War II pilot and winner of the Navy Cross, was a stockbroker; his grandfather was a schoolteacher who changed careers and became a prominent banker in Binghamton, New York. Mike, the oldest of four brothers, was born on May 25, 1945, and raised in the town of East Aurora, not far from Buffalo, in a household where business ideas and principles were in the atmosphere, as much a part of his family's heritage as their Presbyterian morality and his father's strong sense of stewardship. ("His idea was the simple, old-fashioned idea of taking care of things, and he wanted to leave everything a little better than he found it. That's the creed I've tried to live by, too.") In addition, the senior Keiser was an avid outdoorsman, not a golfer but a hiker, camper, canoeist, fisherman, and mountain climber who led his brood into the woods on annual summer holidays to the Adirondacks. From him Mike inherited his lifelong passion for the open air, a reverence for nature, and a concern for the environment; from his mother, who grew up in Ridgewood, New Jersey, and played her golf on the famed Ridgewood course designed by A. W. Tillinghast, he inherited his fascination and talent for the game of golf. Together, his parents instilled in him a set of habits and values that have lasted a lifetime; they equipped him with the confidence that is so often the birthright of the eldest child, and they set the needle of his moral compass at true north.

Young Mike was a bright student and good athlete. At an early age, he learned tennis and golf at the East Aurora Country Club, and he has idyllic memories of endless summer days when life was pure and simple, consisting only of blue skies, green grass, golf shots, and delicious hamburgers. The golf course was tight and hilly, a sporty course for a club whose members didn't give themselves airs; for years after their course was built, East Aurora golfers carried buckets and screwdrivers as they played so that they could remove the stones from the greens. By the 1950s, the greens were stone-free, but East Aurora remained an unpretentious sort of place where a young member might play golf one day and the next day pick up a few bucks as a caddy. Mike did both, and took pleasure in both. His childhood impressions of the game had an elemental simplicity, uncluttered by any sense of privilege, and to this day he has a soft spot in his heart for caddies.

He was also fascinated by the challenge of selling things, and his first business venture was in real estate, so to speak: He sold memberships in a tree house club. He was beginning to put together a sense of himself that included many strands—golfer, salesman, steward—but in his own mind he was, perhaps most importantly, a maverick. On Sunday nights throughout the 1950s he parked himself in front of the TV to see *Maverick,* his favorite show, and to follow the adventures of his hero, the cool, decisive, unflappable loner who went his own way but nevertheless adhered to a strict code of honor and justice. When his parents decided to send him to the Nichols School, the leading private school in Buffalo, he felt like an outsider, the kid from the sticks, the one whose father had to drive for an hour to deliver him to any special event. Classmates remember him as a smart, popular, social boy, but inwardly Mike was always on his own, always looking in, always a maverick.

The Class of 1963 was, Mike believes, one of the most successful in the history of the Nichols School, sending many of its graduates to Harvard, Yale, Princeton, and other top colleges. Mike went to Amherst; it was one of the few colleges, he says drily, with a golf team bad enough for him to make. He got off to a rough start when a "green dean" suspended him in the winter of his freshman year. His offense: throwing snowballs. With $100 in his pocket, he set off to Europe, an adventure that paled quickly as he found out how hard it was to scrape together enough money to eat. He was eighteen years old, and he was flat broke when he reached Paris where, thanks to a connection of his mother's, he was able to get a $2 a day job. He stuck it out for a couple of months before using his return ticket, having learned that he didn't much like bumming around. He successfully petitioned Amherst to readmit him and to allow him to graduate with his entering class.

Two summers later, fired up by reports of high-paying jobs, he set out for Alaska with a group of friends. The reports turned out to be exaggerated, and Mike and his pals were reduced to knocking on doors in the wealthy suburbs of Anchorage, looking for yard work. One moment stands out in Mike's memory. "The leader of our little band was a guy named Eddie Lucaire. He was tall, athletic, good-looking, but when the woman opened the first door we knocked on, he froze. He couldn't say a word. He just stood there. So I had to step up, and I think I decided there and then that I didn't want to depend on anyone else. I became the leader. We did pretty well that summer, as it turned out, doing landscape work for $3 an hour. I came home with $1,200, which wasn't bad in 1965."

At Amherst, Mike majored in English for the usual reason—he couldn't figure out what else to major in. By his own account, he was less focused and less driven than many of his classmates, and he hit the books just hard enough to maintain his standing in the dead center of his class. ("I was amazed to do that well—there were smart people at Amherst.") He did play college golf, and kept his handicap down in the single digits; one of his teammates, Tom Sturges, remembers that he and Mike were "also-rans" on a team with one or two strong players.

Politically, he often felt out of step. The years he spent at Amherst, from 1963 to 1967, were tumultuous ones, with political lines sharply drawn. Abroad, the country was committing more and more troops to the war in Vietnam; at home, there were riots and marches. In the fall of his senior year, Mike was one of the few people in his Amherst class who was gravitating toward the military.

That same fall he met a freshman from nearby Smith College. Her name was Rosalind Curme, and she was known to everyone as Lindy. A tall, graceful brunette, she had the looks and bearing of a model, but she was hardly a social butterfly. Her manner was private and reserved. She came from an intellectually distinguished family, counting among her immediate forebears an internationally known grammarian and several prominent chemists. Her mother was one of the original Quiz Kids and had supported herself and her mother, Lindy's grandmother, with her earnings from regular radio appearances. Lindy's parents had met in graduate school, and they moved to Rochester, New York, where they started a family and began their careers. It was unusual for young mothers to hold jobs, but Lindy's mother was unconventional; she was a college teacher with a reputation for brilliance, and she fell in love with one of her colleagues. The divorce that followed was, for Lindy and her brother and sister, momentous; the three children grew up in the care and custody of their father. He made sure that they spent time every summer with their mother, and never spoke unkindly of her, but Lindy always felt that she had grown up in the shadow of a scandal. At Smith College, she had a chance to forge a life of her own, and she saw in Mike Keiser a bright, creative spirit, someone whose energy and gusto she wanted to share—and also someone whose values were clear, traditional, and deeply rooted. She was a sophomore when he proposed to her, and she agreed to marry him, even though it meant interrupting her college career and signing on as the wife of a young naval officer. Given all the circumstances, their decision—both his and hers—might have seemed headstrong, but, young as they were, their friends already saw them as a charmed couple whose marriage was built on attraction and bedrock commitment. They were two young people who knew their own minds.

They were married in 1968. Mike, the son of a decorated pilot, had enlisted in the navy. The Vietnam War was in its most intense, violent phase, and he was prepared to go wherever he was needed. He was trained in Explosive Ordnance Demolition—in layman's language, defusing mines and bombs. As it turned out, he was stationed in Virginia Beach ("the closest I got to Vietnam was Key West"), and his at-sea duty was aboard a carrier in the Mediterranean, where he was in charge of a small detachment of men whose job was to look after the underwater portion of the huge ship.

For most of his tour of duty, however, Mike was stateside; Lindy used her time in Virginia to finish her B.S. in chemistry at the College of William and Mary. Mike's college roommate, Phil Friedmann, occasionally came to visit, and in 1971, immediately after Mike's discharge, Lindy and Mike spent the winter as ski bums in Vail. Phil came out for a five-day visit. It was, in a way, the last hurrah of youth: Phil was scheduled to go to law school in the fall, and Mike planned to attend Harvard Business School, while Lindy had a job lined up in Cambridge. But one thing was becoming absolutely clear: Mike did not want to go back to school. "I was thinking overtime about how to avoid grad school, and so was Phil, and we came up with the idea of selling something that was 100 percent recycled. It was a 'green' idea, but none of us had a clue what went into the making of a Christmas card. At the time we thought of ourselves as ski bums, but we made our decision to go into business on April 10. We decided on Chicago because Phil was from there and had a friend who was a printer. By April 25, we were incorporated and we printed our first card in May. The press loved us, and the first stories stressed the environmental aspect—Christmas cards for the ecologically concerned! Trash turned into greetings! There were lots of stories, but that first year we sold $60,000 worth of cards and barely broke even. We were operating out of a two-room apartment and Lindy had to take a job so that we could pay the rent. We were living on chili. Lindy was one of the founders of the company, but she went to work as a research assistant at Northwestern. The second year RPG took in $300,000, and Phil and I made about $20,000 each. He was traveling and overseeing sales, and I mostly stayed here in Chicago, taking care of operations and selecting cards.

"The company really took off when we met Sandy Boynton. [Artist Sandra Boynton was a young Yale renegade when she submitted her greeting card designs to RPG in 1973. Mike signed her up right away, and over the next two decades she designed roughly five thousand cards, recognizable for their whimsy and their cartoon animals. Her best-known card renders the usual birthday greeting as "Hippo Birdie Two Ewes," and it has remained continuously in print since 1975, with ten million copies sold.] She was the artistic vehicle, engine, motor, call it what you will—we quickly went to $10 million in sales, and by the mid-80s we were approaching $100 million. That made us the third-largest greeting card company, and that's where we are today—but we're far, far behind the top two, Hallmark and American Greetings. RPG has a distinct identity now, thanks mostly to Sandy. We use the work of many other artists, but Sandy set the tone. People recognize our cards as witty and irreverent, not schmaltzy, sometimes slightly off-color but with a kind of edgy humor. We have a special product, a differentiated product, what Hallmark thinks of as an 'alternative' product, and that's all right with us."

The headquarters of RPG is a three-story brick building on a quiet street, two blocks from Wrigley Field. Erected in 1901, the building has a marble façade and many ornamental details—friezes, columns, and cornices—but it was always intended for industrial use. With its squarish banks of frosted, wire-reinforced windows, the place looks like a factory or perhaps a warehouse for a moving company. In fact, it was built for use as a dairy—shades of Mrs. O'Leary's cow!—and Mike likes to show visitors the concrete ramps on which the cows moved to different levels of the building. Obviously, no one has ever undertaken a significant modernization of this building. It is a far, far cry from a glistening downtown office tower. The only outward indication of RPG's presence is an unobtrusive sign over the glass door, showing the stylized, fully crowned tree that has long been the company logo.

Inside, the 150 employees—RPG employs a total of 400 people, but most are at other locations across the country—are comfortably spread out, and the desks, chairs, and tables appear to have been acquired at a fire sale. The priority at RPG is not on fancy furniture. Yet the work spaces have nearly all been individualized, turned into small, personal worlds marked by photos, posters, signs, banners, and all the other possessions that people use to define their space. The employees are a fair cross section of the urban population in their cultural, ethnic, religious, and sexual diversity. The dress code seems to conform to the standard set by chairman/president/baron Keiser, though most employees keep their shoes on. It doesn't take a social scientist to see that the culture of this company is the exact opposite of the high-powered, high-gloss, high-stress corporations in which the individual employee is expected to wear the company outfit, fit the company image, and toe the company line. Here at RPG, the ruling idea seems to be that people like to express themselves, and that they will do their best work if given a chance to do so.

The nerve center of the operation is the Art Room, a windowless space adjacent to the office shared by Mike and Phil. The carpet is beige, the lighting is fluorescent, and a cigar-store Indian stands in the corner. Canvas deck chairs are arranged around a long utility table. The walls have been fitted out with racks to hold several hundred cards, face out. Mike refers to the main wall as the Best Seller Wall, or the Money Wall. It shows, in rank order, the one hundred top-selling birthday cards printed by RPG; a separate rack holds the best sellers for other occasions and purposes. Each card is displayed with precise tracking information about the number of units shipped, the length of time it has been in circulation, its previous rank, and so on. "It mirrors the taste of Americans on a daily basis," Mike says, and the information is of vital importance to the company since it enables RPG to keep its sales racks filled with proven sellers.

The runaway success of RPG did not escape the attention of investment bankers. By the early 1980s, they began to call regularly on Mike and Phil, dangling enormous sums of money in front of them and urging them to venture into new realms of capitalism. Merger-and-acquisition types painted pictures of an empire with RPG at the center, surrounded by a host of satellite companies. "Make a widget that people want to buy—that's the essence of American capitalism, and that's what we knew how to do. It was tempting to think of starting new companies, or building a conglomerate. I like to make things, but I'm not that interested in running them. The bankers were offering me a chance to do something big in business, but I eventually realized that my ambitions don't run along those lines. Companies don't last. Fortunes don't last—but golf courses do. I'd made enough money to do what I wanted, and I wanted to build a golf course. Deep down, I wanted to build a golf course that people would be playing five hundred years from now. In retrospect, I think the best decision I made was to say no to the investment bankers. They wanted me to diversify the company, but instead I decided to diversify myself."

Today, almost two decades later, that diversification is complete, though Mike and Lindy Keiser still live in Lincoln Park, a lively, affluent, close-in neighborhood on Chicago's North Side where they have raised four children: Leigh, Dana, Michael, and Christopher. The girls have begun their careers, Michael has just graduated from college, and Chris—the youngest by several years—is still in high school. The Keisers have been involved in all their children's activities, and now, Mike says, "The centerpiece of our social life is Chris's basketball schedule."

The four children grew up in a huge, rambling, top-floor, lake-view apartment with ceilings high enough to play basketball (yes, Mike did set up a hoop for the boys). The apartment is in a splendid Beaux-Arts building, and contains many features that evoke the style and luxury of the Gilded Age (deeply recessed windows, elegant paneling, stately proportions) and renovations that are completely modern in spirit (a huge kitchen that opens into a recreation and game room). Conspicuously missing from the rec room: a mammoth television. There is a small one, and in a closet somewhere there is a second, still-smaller TV, but Mike and Lindy hate the boob tube. They have offered their children economic inducements not to watch. They are both readers, and there are books all over the apartment. Mike gets, and reads, four daily papers, as well as a number of financial and political newsletters, to satisfy his voracious appetite for news.

The Keisers paid cash for their apartment. Another matter of old-fashioned principle: Neither of them likes debt. Lindy says, "I feel better knowing that we own our home. No matter what happens, it's ours and no one can take it away." This is precisely the attitude that Mike has brought to all of his land purchases, including the purchase of the land at Bandon Dunes and the money for the development of the golf course and resort. He paid cash. He paid cash for everything. Press him on the subject, as I did once, and he admits to having borrowed a few small sums for specific purchases, to help cash flow and to take advantage of low interest rates, but these were exceptions. He is clear about the benefits of paying cash. "Once the money was spent, it was spent. I didn't have to think about it again. There was no one looking over my shoulder, no banker or investor, harping at me to make a profit. Paying cash made it easier to do what I wanted."

On the subject of money, there is one more thing that must be said about Mike and Lindy Keiser: They are extraordinarily generous. Years ago, Mike decided to give away half of his adjusted gross income, and he has tried to do so in ways that don't attract attention. He doesn't like to attend gala functions—he'd just as soon chew off his arm as don a tuxedo and go to a glittery dinner—but he does like to get down to ground level, to visit schools and hospitals and spend time with teachers, healers, and activists. A note of enthusiasm enters Mike's voice when he speaks of the programs that he supports, and he puts aside all reserve when he talks abut people like Mike Koldyke or Marva Collins or other people who are trying to make the world a better place. Now that three of his children are grown up and his golf courses are established, he estimates that his working hours are roughly divided into thirds—a third at RPG, a third on golf projects, and a third in charitable activities. Though he has usually resisted becoming a board member, he has willingly served on the boards of certain favorite institutions, like the Rehabilitation Institute of Chicago.

"I like to give money away," he told me on a day when I tagged along as he visited two Chicago charter schools he supports, and he certainly prefers aiding charities to acquiring possessions. He doesn't seem to own anything that he couldn't bear to part with. He drives a leased, late-model Lincoln sedan whose main virtue, in his opinion, is that it is nondescript. ("I'm not a car guy, never have been. What I want from a car is no trouble. I really don't know what to say when people tell me about their new Beemer, especially people who are my age. Most guys get that out of their system by the time they're thirty.") The one luxury to which he does treat himself, regularly, is a private plane. RPG doesn't own a plane, but Mike is a good client of Net-Jets, a company that offers fractional aircraft ownership. In essence, NetJets is a top-quality charter service, and for years Mike has made his business trips—including hundreds of trips from Chicago to the Oregon coast—in the cabin of a Citation X, the fastest jet in commercial use.

BUT THAT IS GETTING AHEAD of the story. In the mid-1980s, when Mike Keiser first felt the stirrings of an ambition to do something in golf, he didn't know exactly what that something might turn out to be. For years he had been focused on building a family and building a company, and he simply hadn't had much time for golf. He played maybe twenty rounds a year, some of it business golf, some of it vacation golf, most of it on the public courses near Chicago. He actually played more tennis than golf, but for several years, during his lunch hour, he'd go jogging with a golf club in his hand, running from his office to a driving range about a mile away on Diversey Street. The club was always a driver, and he would hit a bucket of balls before jogging back to work. He became such a regular sight that newspaper columnist Mike Royko—who didn't know Mike Keiser from Adam—mentioned him as one of the sights of the city, wondering publicly what kind of nutcase carried a golf club when he jogged.

This young, upwardly mobile, golf-deprived city dweller had a long way to go before he became a golf course developer and a "visionary," a term that to this day makes him squirm. If anyone had told him in 1985 that he was at the beginning of a journey that would lead him to create the American Ballybunion on the Pacific Coast, he would have been startled. Nothing in his experience suggested any such outcome. He'd never been to Oregon and had no plans to go. For that matter, he'd never laid eyes on Ballybunion or any of the other classic links courses of Scotland and Ireland.

As a golf course developer, he was starting out pretty much from scratch. He had never invested in any kind of golf deal, and he wasn't even a member of a golf club. But golf was in his blood, and when he said no to the investment bankers dangling their schemes in front of him, he knew in a general way what direction he wanted to take.

He was headed toward that shining, elusive realm known as the kingdom of golf.

3 | The Lay of the Land

Variety is not only the "spice of life" but it is the very foundation
of golfing architecture. Diversity in nature is universal. Let your golfing
architecture mirror it. An ideal or classical course demands variety,
personality, and above all, the charm of romance.
—CHARLES BLAIR MACDONALD, *SCOTLAND'S GIFT—GOLF,* 1928

AS AN INTELLECTUAL DISCIPLINE, golf architecture generally ranks far
down the list. Only a few universities offer courses in golf architecture, where
the subject is treated as a poor and distant cousin to landscape architecture.
Most of the books on golf course design are handsome volumes, picture
books intended to please the eye and entertain the armchair golfer; the serious, thoughtful books on the subject might fill a shelf or two, not a whole library. Unlike building architects, golf course designers do not have to follow
a course of study, earn a degree, or take an exam in order to hang out their
shingle. And given the nature of the game, in which the golfer is constantly
assessing and evaluating the playing field as he attempts to negotiate its hazards, every golfer readily imagines that he, too, could easily become a golf
course architect. At the very least, he knows he is fully entitled to criticize
the fiend who actually did design the hole he just played.

Fiend, or genius—or both. Golf course architects, as Mike began to learn,
were often provocative and opinionated. He didn't try to educate himself in
any systematic way, but as he made his way back into golf—playing as often as
he could at Cog Hill and Jackson Park, two of Chicago's public courses, and
eventually becoming a member at Butler National, Shoreacres, and Chicago
Golf Club—he started to read about golf architecture, both in books and

magazines. He also started to make regular winter golf trips with old school chums from Buffalo and friends from Chicago, visiting resorts in Florida and South Carolina, where he played courses created by the best contemporary designers. In the spring and summer, when he could steal away for a day or two, he often went to Philadelphia or New York, where he played classic courses like Merion, Pine Valley, and Shinnecock Hills. In 1986, he made a trip to Ireland, the first of many trips to explore the links courses of the British Isles.

In short, Mike was turning into a golf course buff. He loved to play, and on a good day he could still flirt with breaking 80, but his attitude toward the game was undergoing a change. He wanted to understand the whys and wherefores of golf design. What was the difference between a good hole and a bad one? Or, more crucially, between a good hole and a great one? What made one architect able to capture the right proportions and balance, while another just missed? Why did so many old courses have such enduring appeal?

In just a few years in the mid-1980s, Mike saw a huge variety of courses, from local munis to the most exclusive private clubs, from ancient British links to contemporary American stadium courses, from tricked-up resort tracks to the elegant, classic courses that dominated the Top 100 lists. He was gulping down golf course design in large doses, and his interest was more than academic. He was starting to look for property with the idea of building his own course, and he was ready to invest in golf development—and money is an effective intensifier; it gives an edge to any venture. Mike made a few unwise investments before buying property in Oregon, and his investment there was also one that most people in the golf industry would have considered pure folly. But by the time he bought his Oregon property, Mike had done his homework, and he knew what he needed to build a course that would capture the qualities of the great old designs.

PERHAPS THE BEST WAY to convey the evolution of Mike's ambition is to outline the progress, if that is the right word, of golf course design itself. Since the first designer, in the words of Old Tom Morris, was the "Almighty Himself," it can be argued that all subsequent efforts to design a golf course are destined to fall far short of the original.

The linksland, where golf was invented by the Scots, was not designed "by the hand of man." Over eons, as coastal waters receded, the uncovered stretches that linked land and sea were shaped by the erosive forces of wind and tide. This sandy terrain was useful as a place for hardy sheep to graze; their scrapings created further dings and dents in the land (we will pass right over the welcome effect of their dung on the soil). The result of geology and grazing was a rugged, open, topsy-turvy plain of close-cropped grass, a space where it would naturally occur to a fellow—say a shepherd with a crook, and hours of time on his hands—to figure out a cross-country game. That would be gawf!

At Musselburgh, Leith, Prestwick, St. Andrews, Dornoch, and other Scottish towns, the game soon evolved into a form recognizable today, and the only real task for the designer was to figure out where to place the holes. The number of holes varied from town to town (the links of Leith had five holes in a loop, Prestwick had twelve, St. Andrews originally had twenty-two), and there were no generally shared standards of what a golf course "ought" to be. Because the linksland was so endlessly undulating, and because the scale and shape of the undulations differed so widely from one town to the next, and finally because the "designer" lacked the means to alter the terrain in any significant way, the first golf courses were laid out with the idea of locating the holes so that the player had to overcome a set of interesting challenges as he propelled his ball from one hole to the next.

These earliest golf holes were not "built" as much as they were discovered. The architect was usually also the golf "professional," meaning that he made his living from the game; he gave lessons, made clubs and balls, and perhaps, like Old Tom Morris at St. Andrews, was also the keeper of the green, constantly tinkering with the turf, the bunkers, the tees, and the greens, trying to keep the links in good order. If he had a sharp eye and the requisite sense of cunning, he soon had his own ideas about where to place a hole, about what obstacles and situations made for the most interesting play.

The first links courses might have been primitive by our standards, but the close attention of the greenkeepers led to one refinement after another. (As students of St. Andrews know, a fellow like Old Tom was occasionally willing to step in and make significant changes—like doubling the width of the corridors of play, or reversing the order of the holes.) The courses had firm, fast-playing surfaces; and with their treeless seaside locations, they were exposed to the winds that came whistling in. Links golf called for great skill in managing the ball in the winds, and for imagination in rolling it over and around the undulations of the terrain. The very nature of the ground lent itself to a variety of strategic challenges, as the irregularities of hollow and hillock, of bunker and knob, offered the player different paths to follow, according to his skill.

From the beginning, golf was a difficult game—and on links courses, it hasn't become much easier. In fact, many of the great links courses, though they are now more than a century old, have endured with relatively minor changes. They present the same challenge to today's player as they did to the Scotsman armed only with his hickory sticks and his balls stuffed with goose feathers. The wind blows as hard as ever, and the modern golf ball bounds just as crazily over the landscape. It is one of the glories of golf that these old courses are still hale and hearty after all the years.

The last word on links courses belongs to Dr. Alister MacKenzie, the golf course architect most often hailed as a genius. In 1933, in *The Spirit of St. Andrews,* he wrote, "I believe the real reason St. Andrews Old Course is infinitely superior to anything else is owing to the fact that it was constructed when no one knew anything about the subject at all, and since then it has been considered too sacred to be touched. What a pity it is that the natural advantages of many seaside courses have been neutralized by bad designing and construction work."

THE CLASSIC PERIOD of golf architecture extends roughly from 1900 to 1930 and coincides with America's discovery of golf. This country, prosperous and ready for serious leisure, caught the golf bug, and thousands of courses were built in the first three decades of the twentieth century, a building boom that didn't end until the stock market crashed and the hard times of the Great Depression stanched the flow of money. In Great Britain, too, these years marked a period of expansion and creativity as homegrown architects cleverly adapted the principles of links golf to suit different kinds of terrain.

Indeed, that was the great issue of the classic period: How could a golf architect preserve the character of the game on sites that did not have the inherent advantages found on linksland? On moors and heathlands in England, on forests and farms in the United States, course designers sought to create holes that would present some of the same challenge and fascination as those on the links, and they came up with an astounding array of solutions to the problem. Most golf historians, and most golfers who've been fortunate enough to play the classic courses, believe that the architects at work during this period were especially gifted, and that their collective legacy is an array of golf holes unmatched for their originality, beauty, and variety. The classic era ended with a flourish of brilliance in the 1920s, a decade that is often called golf's Golden Age.

Charles Blair Macdonald, a wealthy Chicagoan who had studied at St. Andrews, was the first American—perhaps the first person anywhere—to call himself a golf course architect. A big, blustery fellow with an ego the size of the Ritz, he was a skilled player, winner of the first official U.S. Amateur title in 1895, and the designer of the first 18-hole course in the country, the Chicago Golf Club. Yet he aspired to build another, more splendid course, an "ideal course" that would not only equal but surpass those of Great Britain, and he searched for years for a piece of ground that could serve his purpose. Finally, on Long Island, on the shore of Sebonac Bay, he found the place he was looking for and built the National Golf Links. When the course opened in 1912, the best golfers of the day, both British and American, agreed that the National fulfilled Macdonald's lofty ambitions.

Macdonald had very deliberately copied several famous holes from the great links courses. The National had a Redan, patterned after the original

Redan at North Berwick; it had an Eden, modeled after the hole at St. Andrews; it had an Alps, a Sahara, and a Road Hole, all with precedents across the Atlantic. On his trips to Great Britain, Macdonald had gathered surveyors' drawings of these holes. While he didn't slavishly reproduce them, he rejoiced in the discovery of a "natural" Redan, a "natural" Alps.

Macdonald assumed that the character and quality of the land determined the character and quality of the golf holes that could be built upon it. He fretted mightily about the difficulties of remaining true to the spirit of the original Scottish holes, and his book *Scotland's Gift—Golf,* contains a vigorous defense of his architectural principles. Always he insists on variety and diversity and the need to respect natural forms. He is appalled by the "monstrosities created on many modern golf courses which are a travesty on Nature . . . No golfer can but shudder for the soul of golf."

The prime importance of the site, the re-creation of great holes from links courses, the emphasis on nature, the disdain for artificial features—these beliefs were, for Macdonald, the foundation of sound golf design. The success of the National Golf Links undoubtedly "served as incentive to the elevation of the game in America," just as Macdonald hoped it would, and many architects followed his lead. Yet they didn't always share his view that the pedigree for a good golf hole had to be traced back to Scotland. On the contrary, the most talented architects of the classic era gave themselves great latitude to create, and this imaginative freedom resulted in the flowering of many different styles of design.

The only limit to creativity was, always, the land itself. The classic designers had to work with the natural terrain for the very good reason that they couldn't transform it. The modern golf architect can call in the bulldozers whenever he wishes, but the architect of the 1920s had to depend on men with shovels, and on horses or mules dragging heavy pans to smooth or shape the earth. To be sure, some courses were built at fabulous expense on sites that required transformation. (Macdonald himself built a course called The Lido that was an engineering marvel; this seaside site on the south shore of Long Island was transformed by two million cubic yards of sand acquired by dredging the bottom of a channel, and the cost was $1,430,000, or about $40 million in today's dollars.) But the best architects still believed that good land—undulating land, not steep but with pronounced topographical features, and with porous soils, not a heavy clay—was a sine qua non for a good golf course.

Today, the best courses of the classic era are landmarks, and they seem to express perfectly the landscape from which they were conjured. At Pinehurst, Donald Ross—the prolific transplanted Scotsman who supervised the design and construction of some four hundred courses around the United States—labored for decades over his masterpiece, Pinehurst No. 2, a layout that captures the essence of the Carolina sandhills. On Long Island, A. W. Tillinghast, in his last hurrah, poured every ounce of his creativity and daring into Bethpage Black, and made the forested site reveal its grandeur. In New Jersey, George Crump—and his many advisers—translated scrubby wastes into Pine Valley. In California, Jack Neville draped several golf holes on the cliffs above the surf, and Pebble Beach was born. A few miles away, Alister MacKenzie went him one better, at least in terms of sheer daring and ethereal beauty, at Cypress Point.

The boldness of these designers, and their willingness to try something different, something grand and memorable, can hardly be overstated. The best architects of the era did indeed possess the classic design virtues of balance, harmony, and proportion, but they were not always restrained. Far from it. Many of the holes we admire today were boldly, even radically, innovative, and when built they were the subject of intense controversy. When C. B. Macdonald wrote *Scotland's Gift—Golf,* he was clearly still smarting from some of the criticisms that had been leveled at him, and he wrote, "Sometimes it takes years to discover and appreciate hidden qualities which only time discloses . . . No real lover of golf with artistic understanding would undertake to measure the quality or fascination of golf by a yardstick, any more than a critic of poetry would attempt to measure the supreme sentiment expressed in a poem by the same method. One can understand the meter, but one cannot measure the soul expressed."

In such passages Macdonald lets us know that he does not regard golf as merely a game, nor golf architecture as merely the making of a game board. He saw golf design as an art, an attempt to speak to the highest aspirations and deepest emotions. Many other architects of the classic period, like Tillinghast and MacKenzie, also have a great deal to say about the importance of beauty and the appeal of golf to the senses and the spirit.

In 1927, in *Golf Architecture in America: Its Strategy and Construction,* George Thomas summed up the requirements for the profession. Thomas, the architect of Riviera, Bel-Air, and many other California courses of the Golden Age, did not speak of technical skills, but of deeply human qualities: "To learn golf architecture one must know golf itself, its companionships, its joys, its sorrows, its battles—one must play golf and love it."

THE MODERN PERIOD of golf architecture begins after World War II, and it might as well be called the Age of Jones. Although his career began earlier, Robert Trent Jones was from 1950 to 1980 the most influential, most imitated, and most innovative architect on the golf scene. He was also, and by a wide margin, the most famous. To this day, his name is practically synonymous with the practice of golf course design in much the same way that Xerox is synonymous with the copying machine; Jones was the first architect who turned his name into a powerful brand, and his initials, RTJ, are recognized by golfers everywhere.

A pivotal event in Jones's career, and in modern golf course design, was the 1951 U.S. Open, played at Oakland Hills. The course had been originally designed by Donald Ross, but the last time the Open had been played there, in 1937, the pros had had a field day. Even though the course had been lengthened from its original Rossian dimensions, players like Sam Snead, armed with steel-shafted clubs (the course had been built in the days of hickory shafts), could just blow it over the fairway bunkers and attack every hole. The United States Golf Association asked RTJ to "doctor" the course and make it tougher. They didn't want the U.S. Open to turn into a birdie binge.

Jones's response was not to lengthen the course—he actually made it play slightly shorter than it had in the 1937 Open—but to tighten it. He got rid of the old fairway bunkers and replaced them with deep new bunkers that were placed at precisely the distance where a strong player's drive would finish. Short of the bunkers, the landing area was more generous, but the golfer who wanted to hit his driver was going to have to be dead accurate. The space between the bunkers was only a little more than twenty yards. From the tee, as one writer said, the fairway looked just about wide enough for a group of Indians to pass through walking carefully and in single file. One of the top contenders, Ben Hogan, complained that the changes had eliminated whatever strategic advantage a superior player might have had; there wasn't any room out there, nowhere to hit the ball to get a better angle into the green. There was only one place to position a drive, and that was the place dictated by the architect. A golf writer dubbed the course "The Monster."

On the last day of the tournament—a Saturday, the day of the double round—Hogan played thirty-six holes of superb golf, capping off his victorious performance with a 67. At the award ceremony, he announced, "I'm glad I brought this course, this monster, to its knees." He is also reported to have said to Mrs. Jones that if her husband had to play the courses he designed, he would be in the bread line.

In the story of the 1951 U.S. Open, three of the major themes of modern golf architecture are present. First, there is the recognition by the powers that be, in this case the USGA and RTJ, that older courses would have to be retooled to defend them against the improvements in golf equipment. Second, the players no longer felt that they were matched against nature, as had previously been the case; they felt that they were pitted against the architect. Third, the architect had no compunction about dictating to the players exactly how the golf course should be played.

This was a momentous shift, one that seemed necessary and inevitable, and it was years before all the ramifications of modern design became apparent. Most courses were nowhere near as demanding as Oakland Hills, obviously, and RTJ didn't approach every new commission with the idea of throwing down the gauntlet. At some of his most highly regarded courses,

like Peachtree, he built enormous tees and greens, allowing for many variations of tee-marker and pin placement, thus creating a course of great strategic interest. Perhaps his best-known holes were his "heroic" holes—holes
that were also described as "no-guts-no-glory," and pushed the risk-reward
formula to its thrilling extreme. These heroic holes usually called for a long,
dangerous carry over water; the golfer who took the risk and pulled off the
shot had a decided advantage over the golfer who pursued a safer, more plod-
ding route. RTJ was by no means the first to design such holes, but he designed more of them than any of his predecessors, and they became one of
the hallmarks of his courses.

Jones was a graduate of Cornell, where he had put together his own major
in golf course architecture, and he had traveled extensively to study classic
courses. He wrote thoughtfully and persuasively about the principles of design, declaring that golf holes were either heroic, strategic, or penal in nature, and that a good architect mixed these three types of holes according to
his site, blending them into one harmonious composition. He also offered a
formula for the degree of fairness that he sought to create: "hard par, easy
bogey." The average golfer who is trying to break 90 might object that there
is no such thing as an "easy bogey," not on most golf courses and certainly
not on RTJ's layouts. On most of his courses, Jones made liberal use of water
hazards (while classic courses had few water hazards, modern courses have
water, water everywhere); he also created large, elevated, multitiered greens,
and deep greenside bunkers that gnawed into the putting surface—in short,
he employed an array of features that made for exciting, exacting golf for
better players but were daunting to the less skilled.

A tipping point had been reached. Given the technological advances in
equipment and in course maintenance—golfers were now playing from
sleek, groomed fairways to perfect greens—golf architects felt that they had
to strengthen their courses' defenses. RTJ and his contemporaries were also
designing long, strong courses that were plentifully supplied with formidable hazards. A short list of exemplary courses of the modern era—Bay Hill
and Laurel Valley, by Dick Wilson; The Dunes Club and Bellerive, by RTJ;

Stanwich, by David Gordon; the "Monster" at the Concord Hotel, by Joe Finger—is a roll call of layouts that put a premium on power and daring if the golfer intends to rise to the challenge presented by the architect. Most holes on these courses reveal exactly what is required to play them successfully, what hazards must be avoided and what hazards must be carried, and they don't always offer (if I may speak from personal experience) the aforementioned "easy bogey."

Nor did the architects place a premium on trying to make the courses appear natural. To be sure, some of RTJ's most memorable holes—like the 13th at the Dunes Club, a horseshoe-shaped par 5 built around a lagoon—were brilliantly crafted into an existing landscape, and Joe Finger's "Monster" is handsomely framed by the dark evergreens of the Catskill forests. But the old formula was now turned upside down: Golf holes were built, not discovered. Golf architects of the modern era weren't constrained by the site, and they were willing to transform topography to suit their eye and their ideas—how could they not be when they had the machines to create any kind of golf hole they could imagine? There is something intoxicating about the power of the big machines, the scrapers and excavators and bulldozers (in the golf course construction business, those who go overboard in their use of machines are said to have caught "yellow fever").

Architects of the classic era tended to use certain features from one course to the next, but their courses were site-specific and so their overall styles are hard to pin down. They were chameleon-like, taking on the coloration of their surroundings. By contrast, an architect of the modern era, with machines at his command, could achieve the same look wherever he chose. Moreover, it was easier to build courses that had certain kinds of uniformity than to fuss with all the quirks and irregularities of a site; instead of building a series of tee boxes, for instance, a long runway tee could be quickly laid out, and even an inexperienced bulldozer operator could build the thing. Beyond that, it was commercially advantageous to have a distinctive, recognizable style; RTJ was not the only architect to realize that golf was turning into a business and that it was valuable to developers to have a "name" attached to their project. To have a golf course by Robert Trent Jones as the centerpiece of a golf course community was a seal of approval, a guarantee of quality, a brand that could sell a lot of houses.

Collectively, the architects of the modern era were creating a new kind of golf course, and their innovations gave a new twist to the questions of fairness that had always been woven into the discussion of golf course architecture. On a links course, designed by the Almighty, there was no way to complain about fairness unless a golfer felt like embarking upon a theological argument. If a shot down the fairway hits a natural mound and kicks sideways toward a bunker, well, the Scots were of the opinion that a golfer should accept his punishment as part of the Almighty's possibly capricious plan. But if the golf architect was a fellow named RTJ or Dick Wilson, and he had moved mountains of earth in order to create a lake, and he then tucked the green on a peninsula jutting out into that lake—in that case a golfer might be entitled to mutter a word or two about fairness.

All in all, the modern era was a period of profound changes in the way that golf architects went about their business, and in the way that the game was played. The greatest symbol of these changes, and of the new era in golf, wasn't any one golf course, or any single innovation in golf equipment, or even the bulldozer; no, the object that revealed the shifts in the game had to be the golf cart. Introduced in the 1950s, it caught on immediately in the United States, though not in Great Britain. Now a golfer could ride, not walk, and golf architects could—and did—design courses where the holes were not contiguous but strung out over miles of terrain, with long rides between holes. For those who otherwise might not have been able to make their way around a golf course, the cart was a blessing—but the spirit and rhythm of the walking game was altered. Advances in technology were evident everywhere you looked, from the clubs in a golfer's bag to the shape of the golf holes themselves. Modern golf offered plenty of speed, excitement, and risk—but some of the wild, natural, gamy flavor of the links was inevitably lost as the game moved into the last half of the twentieth century.

• • •

THE POSTMODERN ERA in golf course design dates roughly from 1980, or from the emergence of Pete Dye as the leading figure in the field. A contrarian by nature, Dye was unquestionably the most brilliant, provocative, and original designer of his generation. Early in his career, he seemed to be able to toss off effortlessly one stunning new course after another. His string of triumphs ran unbroken, from courses like Caso de Campo, The Golf Club, Crooked Stick, and Harbour Town, to the stadium course at Sawgrass, opened in 1981, a course designed to host the Tournament Players Championship, the tournament billed sometimes as the "fifth major" and sometimes as the "anti-Masters." Winds of controversy swirled around both the tournament and the golf course, and Pete Dye became the man of the moment in golf course architecture, supplanting—at least in terms of the attention that his projects attracted—the old lion of the profession, Robert Trent Jones.

Dye's ideas about golf courses blew like a fresh breeze into the realm of golf design. In reality, as Ron Whitten noted in *The Architects of Golf,* "few features of a Pete Dye layout were truly revolutionary," but they often seemed to be so, "probably because they were so opposite to the style ushered in by Robert Trent Jones in the 1950s and adopted and modified by nearly all contemporary American and British architects." RTJ's best courses were known for the size and scale of their features, for their heroic holes, and for their flowing, sinuous lines. Pete Dye usually worked on a smaller, more intimate scale; he preferred abrupt, jolting changes to the more gradual transitions of a Jones design, and he liked to mark these changes—around bunkers, or tees, or water hazards—with railroad ties (the standing joke was that Pete Dye would be the first man to build a golf course that burned down). At the TPC at Sawgrass, he built pot bunkers, enormous waste areas, and grassy mounds—not to mention a forbidding island green that became, almost overnight, one of the most notorious and most familiar golf holes in the world.

The island green was the kind of hole that his critics called "dye-a-bolical," and the TPC at Sawgrass was the first of the PGA Tour's "stadium courses"— courses that were explicitly built as tournament courses, with massive mounding designed to give spectators a clear view of the action. Built in a reclaimed swamp, with water hazards on seventeen holes, TPC Sawgrass is a quintessentially American course in the sense that it is artificial through and through. The site had been flat as a pancake and soggy as oatmeal. Everything on the course was manufactured; not one single feature—well, maybe a couple of trees—had been there before the golf course. If there was anyone who reveled in the power of the bulldozer, who just loved to turn a landscape inside out, it was Pete Dye.

Dye's courses seemed as far removed as they could possibly be from links courses, yet he had made an extended tour of Scotland early in his career and had returned to the United States fired up with all kinds of design ideas inspired by what he'd seen in Great Britain. He was wickedly inventive in adapting links features to his own designs, and some of his best holes—like the par-5 11th at Sawgrass, or the beautiful par-5 2nd at the Ocean Course at Kiawah—are brilliant examples of strategic design. When his hard-edged courses were criticized for their artificiality, Dye answered that transitions in nature were often abrupt, so why shouldn't his be the same? Dye wasn't trying to conform to anyone else's ideas about golf architecture, and it was clear that he had a passion for the task; he was never happier than when he was out there in the dirt, rearranging nature to suit his own eye. With their pronounced features, his courses raised the "fairness" question over and over again, and invited golfers to focus on his methods and concepts. Pete Dye stuck his neck out, and if a golfer had a complaint, he knew where to direct it.

So what made these courses postmodern rather than modern? In some ways, obviously, Dye's design work was simply a continuation and extension of certain modern principles. Just as the architect of postmodern buildings finds ways to combine the elements of different eras and styles, so Dye had discovered fresh ways to unite the old and the new. Dye was familiar with the long history of golf design, and he had a flair for using traditional features in new and imaginative ways. He wasn't afraid to plant a pot bunker in a lush American fairway or to give a new look to the grass mounds, the "chocolate drops" that had been around forever. Even his use of railroad ties had Scottish precedents; the Scots had used "sleepers" to shore up many a large bunker.

Other designers of this era, Dye's contemporaries, showed the same willingness to draw on an extensive repertory of features and forms even when their style was totally different. Tom Fazio, for instance, integrated links-style holes with marsh holes at Wild Dunes, a course that helped make his reputation; he went on to become perhaps best known as the architect of opulent courses like Shadow Creek, a course that puts its own twist on the idea of the postmodern.

Shadow Creek, in Las Vegas, was bankrolled by casino mogul Steve Wynn, a lover of illusions who was actively involved in designing the course with Tom Fazio. Since he wanted to impress the high rollers, and since one way to do that was to spend money, Wynn decided to open his wallet. Shadow Creek was reported to have cost $41 million dollars to build, making it the most expensive golf course in the history of the planet (a claim that was soon disputed by another casino mogul, Donald Trump, who said that his course in Florida cost $45 million). How do you spend $41 million on a golf course? By building a forest in a desert, that's how. Thousands of trees were planted at Shadow Creek, and millions of dollars were spent to create waterfalls and sparkling streams that looked, as countless visitors testified, absolutely natural. Out there in the Nevada desert, you could easily imagine that you were in the North Carolina highlands. Amazing! Shadow Creek was a marvel, but of course this was what they did in Vegas. In a place where the hotels re-created the splendors of Paris and Venice, why shouldn't a golf course re-create a whispering forest? As a fantastic display of the theme-park mentality, Shadow Creek was a sensation and, appropriately, it commanded the highest green fee on record, $500 a round.

At a course like Shadow Creek, it wasn't just that the creators had served up various novelties for the golfer; the whole course was a novelty. The customer paid not merely for the golf but to see the place, to marvel at its extravagance. No one claimed that Shadow Creek was going to offer the golfer what Macdonald wanted to deliver, the experience of nature that leads to contemplation, a "sense of eternity," and "the full exaltation of playing the game of golf." At Shadow Creek, the golfer was invited to contemplate the immense sleight of hand that had gone into producing the golf course, as well as the price tag it carried.

IN THE POSTMODERN ERA, golf moved ever more deeply into the realm of commerce, for the 1980s marked the beginning of a building boom. The most fundamental statistics—number of golfers, number of rounds played, number of courses being built—were all on the rise, and the rise was steep enough to inspire feelings of what seemed like completely rational exuberance. Golf was catching on in a big way.

According to the National Golf Foundation, the number of American golfers had risen from eleven million in 1970 to fifteen million in 1980, and by 1990 it would make another quantum leap to twenty-three million (where it has remained, more or less, despite all the excitement surrounding the emergence of Tiger Woods as the most recognizable athlete in the world). All across America—all around the globe—people were taking up golf in record numbers, playing on brand-new, high-profile courses with brand-new, high-tech equipment. In Japan and South Africa, even in Russia and China, courses sprang up. In the United States, the number of 18-hole courses grew from just over 7,400 in 1970 to more than 11,000 in 1990. The pace of construction didn't peak until the year 2000, when new courses opened at the rate of one per day. By then, the number of courses had risen to 14,000, almost twice as many as there'd been only thirty years earlier.

The average cost of a golf course had also risen sharply. From a business point of view, the 1980s was the decade when golf exploded, and the price of everything—from a sleeve of balls to a club membership—rose to heights that made old-timers gasp. But the old-timers did a lot of gasping during the 1980s, for golf was undergoing a sea change. Metal spikes were out, soft spikes were in. Persimmon was out, metal woods were in. Steel shafts made way for graphite. Golf balls were being made of "space-age" materials, which seemed to mean that nobody really knew what they were made of, only that they went farther. Armed with the new equipment, young players on the PGA Tour—and on the local munis—were hitting the balls prodigious distances and playing an altogether different game, making some older courses look quaint and antiquated and, well, just plain old. New courses had to be longer, obviously, and they differed in many other ways; they bore about as much resemblance to traditional courses as a Big Bertha to a brassie.

Golf was still about getting the ball into the hole in as few strokes as possible, and traditions of fair play and sportsmanship remained firmly in place, but the other changes kept coming, and they weren't merely superficial. The idea that golf was the pastime of a privileged few, played only behind the gates of exclusive clubs, had never been very accurate and was now clearly outdated; the 1970s and 1980s brought a dramatic growth in public golf. In 1970, there were 3,500 private courses and 3,900 courses that were accessible to the public, either daily fee or municipal courses. The building boom completely changed that balance: In 2002, the number of private courses had risen modestly, to 4,300, while the number of public courses jumped to 10,400.

Along with these numbers, the very image of golf changed, an image that had long been dominated by scenes from sedate, stately country clubs—or stuffy, silly country clubs, if you took the *Caddyshack* point of view. The game that had once seemed to belong to white-haired guys who wore plaid pants and bucket hats was attracting a new generation of movers and shakers, of flat-bellied players and show-me-the-money agents, of entrepreneurs who developed new companies, of well-heeled developers and corporate strategists looking to carve out roles for themselves in what was shaping up as the golf "industry." As the marketing types proclaimed, golf was no longer your grandfather's game.

Was golf entering a new Golden Age? A lot of golf writers seemed to think so, but there were a few who didn't share in the euphoria, who didn't like the artificiality of contemporary design or the price tag it carried. One critic was a young man who had studied golf architecture at Cornell, spent a year abroad, and then worked for Pete Dye before striking out on his own as a golf course architect. He was also the architecture editor for *Golf Magazine,* and his articles were mostly restrained and civil, but he was known for his strong, irreverent opinions about contemporary golf design. In 1992, he published a book, *The Anatomy of a Golf Course,* that amounted to a manifesto, a call for a return to the original values of the game.

His name was Tom Doak, and he was one of the writers whom Mike Keiser read avidly as he forged his own opinions about golf course design. In his many files—Mike is a clipper of articles—Mike stowed away several articles by young Doak, along with articles about the golf boom and the kinds of business opportunities it was creating.

He was getting ready to make his move.

4 | Out with the New, In with the Old

I wasn't interested in commercial golf. I was interested in dream golf.
—MIKE KEISER

MIKE WAS NOW a keenly interested observer of golf trends, and he had direct experience of one of the most important, the growth of the upscale daily fee course. During his first years in Chicago, lacking money and connections, he was in no position to join a private club. His "home course" was Dubsdread, one of four public courses at the Cog Hill complex in the town of Lemont, Illinois, about thirty miles from his apartment in Lincoln Park. Mike would rise early on a weekend morning to join other young dads in the dew-sweeping brigade. They got the first tee times, played fast, and hustled home to spend the rest of the day with their families.

At Cog Hill, Mike shelled out his money to play a round, and he became aware for the first time that golf was a business. Having grown up in the environment of private clubs, he'd never thought much about the economics of the game, but Cog Hill was owned by Joe Jemsek, a pioneer in the golf industry, and the facility was operated in order to turn a profit. At a time when public golf generally meant inferior golf, Jemsek had decided that the standards at Cog Hill would rival those of any private club. The courses at Cog Hill were in tip-top condition and the service was impeccable. Jemsek was famous for pampering his clients—he was often seen in the high-ceilinged, heavy-beamed clubhouse, greeting people like guests as he passed around the cheese platter—and his pride and joy was Cog Hill No. 4, a.k.a. "Dubsdread," a Dick Wilson layout that was unquestionably one of the best-designed, best-maintained, and most demanding public courses in America. Jemsek's mission to put Cog Hill on a footing with top private clubs was accomplished when Dubsdread was selected to host several USGA championships, including the U.S. Amateur and the Publinx Championship. The course now has its annual moment in the national spotlight as host of one of the PGA Tour's longest-running events, the Western Open.

For Mike, Cog Hill was an eye-opener. It gave him his first glimpse into public golf, and he liked it. A natural entrepreneur, he made careful note of the way that Jemsek ran his business, and the kind of quality that distinguished Cog Hill from other public courses. Joe Jemsek had found a way to add special value to an ordinary product, and people were willing to pay for it.

The lessons for the visionary-in-the-making weren't immediately clear, but he'd had a glimpse of the way that golf and entrepreneurship could be united. When the time came to build his dream course at Bandon Dunes, Mike knew that he wanted it to be a public course, open to all golfers. And on the opening day, Mike Keiser—like his model Joe Jemsek—would be standing on the first tee to welcome every single one of them.

MIKE'S FIRST EXPOSURE to the work of top contemporary golf architects came on his winter trips with a gang of friends from Nichols School. Many of them still lived in Buffalo, a city notorious for its harsh winters, and these golf trips were an escape to the latitude of palm trees and subtropical breezes. For Mike the trips were a chance to reconnect with old pals like Warren Gelman, a Buffalo lawyer who was the group's organizer and "commissioner," and before long the original Buffalo group was augmented with friends from other eras in Mike's life—Chicago friends, Amherst friends. Mike is not a hail-fellow-well-met, but he relished these trips and looked forward to them. He liked, and still likes, the comfort and security of a group of golf buddies, the friendly competition, the needling, the byplay, the story-swapping, and the hoisting of glasses at the 19th hole. He was never the last guy at the bar—on the contrary, Mike was usually one of the first to retire—

but camaraderie and good fellowship were integral to his idea of the game. These friends would become the "retail golfers," his informal brain trust of counselors and advisers when he built Bandon Dunes.

On those early trips the group went to resorts in Florida and South Carolina, and played courses built by Pete Dye, Jack Nicklaus, Tom Fazio, and other architects who were at the forefront of their generation. Mike went to Hilton Head several times, and he was one of several members of the group to invest in the Melrose Club, where Jack Nicklaus was designing a golf course. Why not? The Melrose Club seemed to have everything going for it—an oceanside site, a top architect, and a location on Daufuskie Island, near Hilton Head, a thriving golf destination. The developer was looking for a national membership for the Melrose Club. Even before the course was built, it was being hailed as the next Augusta, and Mike signed on the dotted line.

Jack Nicklaus had declared the site to be an "uncut jewel" and he routed the golf course so that its finishing hole, a par 5, flanked the Atlantic Ocean and led players to a green that seemed to jut out into the waves. The course had pot bunkers and other "links" features, though it also had holes that were Carolina marsh holes, with lagoons and bulkheading. The Melrose Club was conceived as an ultraprivate "lifestyle community," and the developer, the Club Corporation, owned and managed some of the most prestigious properties in golf—yet this project never did as well as expected, either commercially or aesthetically. Before long there were changes in ownership, and Mike's membership morphed into an interest in the Daufuskie Island Club and, ultimately, into the purchase of a lot at Bloody Point, a development at the southernmost tip of the island.

Bloody Point, named for a battle between colonists and outgunned Indians, was also envisioned as a high-end, ultraprivate development. The place was peaceful and remote, and the course, designed by the acclaimed team of Tom Weiskopf and Jay Morrish, was planned as a walking course, with tees close to the greens (eventually carts were allowed, but the cart paths are carefully hidden). Bloody Point was a parkland course, but it was remote and rugged; the rough was shaggy, the bunker sand was coarse, and areas had been left for wildlife habitat, including nesting sites for bald eagles and ospreys. The holes were crafted into coastal marshes and dark water lagoons, out of sight of the building lots.

Mike never built on his lot. After a couple of rounds of golf, truth be told, he'd had his fill of Bloody Point. The same thing had happened at the Melrose Club. He'd been caught up in the glamour and excitement of a new venture, and those big names—Jack Nicklaus! Tom Weiskopf!—had been a part of the attraction, but the courses just didn't hold up for him. Furthermore, the developers at Bloody Point had made the decision that golf developers almost always make: They saved the choice beachfront property for building lots in order to maximize their profit. The golf course had been shoved inland, where the only water views were of the slow-moving Mungen River.

Mike had to hold onto his lot for years before finally selling it, and he learned a few expensive lessons. The first was that there were no guarantees in the golf business, not even when a project came packaged with names like Nicklaus and Weiskopf. The second was that he wasn't much interested in any development where real estate came before golf. The third and most important was that he just didn't like contemporary courses very much.

When pressed to elaborate on his aversion to contemporary design, Mike can tick off several pet peeves. One is that the courses aren't designed for players like him—that is, for average golfers. "Most golfers are average golfers, but the new courses are being designed for the pros, or for the 1 percent of the golfing population that can hit a drive three hundred yards. For the rest of us, these courses are just too hard. There's nothing fun about being asked hole after hole to do things that you can't do." Another complaint is that golf course designers are carried away with the power of the bulldozer. "In the old days, when golf courses were built by hand, architects had to use the features of the land to create interesting golf holes. Now, with machines, golf course designers can do anything, and they seem to feel that they *have* to do something spectacular—they can't just leave well enough alone."

Mike's preference for natural holes, as opposed to holes that proclaimed their artificiality, was the bedrock of his attitude toward golf design, and he had no interest whatsoever in courses that were a showcase of a particular "style." On his golf trips, he made it a point to check out the new, must-play courses, but he was usually disappointed. "When I played highly ranked courses by Nicklaus, or Pete Dye, or other contemporary architects, I usually felt that I was checking something off my list. I didn't want to go right out and play another eighteen—and for me that's what makes a course great. You come off and you want to go right back out and play it again. I just didn't feel that way about Sawgrass or Melrose. The trouble with contemporary American architects is that they all want to do their own thing. The classic architects didn't mind doing things that had already been done. Macdonald and [Seth] Raynor weren't trying to invent new holes. They were frankly imitating holes they had seen in Great Britain. But most modern architects want to put their own stamp on their courses, and I think that's usually a mistake."

AS A MEMBER of the Amherst College golf team, Mike had played matches on several historic courses. The Amherst home course, The Orchards, was a Donald Ross design with a distinguished past (and future—in 2004 it hosted the U.S. Women's Open). In away matches, Mike had teed it up at other traditional courses, but at the time he was far more concerned with getting the ball into the hole than he was with the fine points of golf course architecture.

Now, when Mike was invited to play at Merion Golf Club as the guest of Tom Sturges, his former Amherst teammate, he leapt at the chance. Very few courses have as rich a championship history as Merion, located outside Philadelphia. It was the place where Bobby Jones had completed the Grand Slam, and it was where, during the 1950 U.S. Open Ben Hogan marched into legend on a pair of unsteady legs, winning the national championship only a year after a near-fatal head-on crash with a bus.

Mike had a blissful day there. He loved the artful, complex routing, the mixture of long and short holes, the cunning use of natural features like the small brook and the old quarry, the flashed bunkers known as "the white faces of Merion." He felt almost as though he'd never looked—never *really* looked—at a golf course before. He was charmed, intrigued, and fascinated by Merion, and he resolved to learn more about it. He knew that he wanted to play it again, and often. He made a promise to himself to play other courses of that vintage.

Then Tom Sturges set up a game at Pine Valley.

Mike was utterly, completely, hopelessly dazzled. In an unpromising, scruffy, sandy landscape in New Jersey, not far from Philadephia, he'd found a course that seemed to capture the magical possibilities of golf course design. The look of the place was different from anything he'd ever seen, with its vast, natural bunkers in which scrub pines flourished. The fairways and greens seemed to be perched precariously in the midst of this wild, threatening landscape, requiring the golfer to play to a distinct target. Mike wasn't the first golfer to recognize the difficulty and the allure of Pine Valley, but he knew that he had encountered something exceptional and original. "I'd been playing golf for many years, but I'd never been so enraptured by a golf course as I was at Pine Valley. It was head and shoulders above any course I'd ever played, and I was awed. I just loved playing it. Before then I hadn't paid much attention to the ratings, but after Pine Valley I put a new entry on my To Do list: Play the Top 20 golf courses. I suppose my lit crit background kicked in, too, because I started reading about the top courses, trying to understand how they were analyzed and evaluated. Books on golf courses became my bedside reading, and I pored over them as though I was reading the Bible."

Pine Valley had been a revelation, and it touched off a new, voracious curiosity about the game, and, in particular, about design. His invaluable friend, Tom Sturges, arranged visits to other shrines, including Shinnecock Hills, National Golf Links, and Maidstone, the group of Long Island courses known as the Holy Trinity. All these classic courses stirred something within Mike, something more than just admiration for an accomplished piece of work. Somehow or other the architects of Pine Valley and Merion and National Golf Links had perfectly expressed the feeling that he had about what a round of golf ought to be, the feeling of expectation and adventure. They'd captured the flow and rhythm of the game, presenting a sequence of surprising, stirring holes, each one different from its predecessors but all of them forming a single, harmonious whole.

In plain terms, these courses were the work of artists.

When Mike read about these artists, the architects of Merion and National Golf Links and Pine Valley, he learned that they were men with whom he could easily identify. They were all well-to-do businessmen who slipped away from their careers in order to build golf courses. Hugh Wilson was a young insurance man when he went to Great Britain to study the classic links courses; he obviously absorbed what he needed, and incorporated what he'd learned in the design of Merion. Charles Blair Macdonald was a stockbroker who seemed to believe that his mission in life was to introduce golf to the United States; he brashly announced that the National Golf Links would rival the great British courses, and he made good on his boasts. But the man whom Mike admired most was George Crump, the founder and designer of Pine Valley, a Philadelphia hotel owner who bought the land for the course, lived on the property for years while designing it, and marked every inch of the place with the stamp of his personality. To this day, George Crump's full-length portrait hangs in the place of honor in the clubhouse, and his spirit presides over Pine Valley. His story is woven into the fabric of the club's lore.

George Crump was a generous man who loved golf, hunting, and his friends, not necessarily in that order. He didn't marry until he was in his forties, and he suffered a tragic loss when his young wife died after a year of marriage. He was bereft, and in an effort to leave his grief behind, he went on an extended trip to Europe. There he played golf, and he began to study the British links courses. When he returned to the United States, the idea of building a golf course intrigued him, and he bought a piece of land that he had noticed from a train window as he traveled to Atlantic City on a golf outing with friends. To anyone else, the sandy property might have seemed unappealing, but Crump had learned in Great Britain of the importance of sandy turf to great golf. Once Crump acquired the land, he raised money for construction by getting his golfing friends to subscribe to the club, and he devoted himself completely to the project. He lived in a bungalow on the property, by himself, surrounded by his beloved dogs—even though he had given up hunting and fed hundreds of ducks every evening.

He was increasingly detached from the hotel, The Colonnades, that had made him a wealthy man. The golf course was his home, his job, and his life. Crump poured all of his money into the golf course, his own and the money invested by more than a hundred friends. During the process of design and construction, Crump had a steady stream of visits from his investors, a group that included Hugh Wilson, George Thomas, and A. W. Tillinghast, all of whom were or would become golf course architects, and they were invited to make their comments and add their ideas, many of which Crump incorporated. For a time he entertained the idea of having each of Pine Valley's eighteen holes designed by a different person. As it turned out, Crump hired H. S. Colt, the Englishman who had designed Sunningdale, to assist him in the routing of the course, and then he personally supervised the construction, which began with the removal of more than twenty-two thousand trees. Crump fretted over every detail of the golf course, which was explicitly intended to be a challenge to highly skilled players. Nearly every hole required a forced carry over hazards of sand and brush, and Crump, who seemingly neglected his own health, died before Pine Valley was completed. By this time he had spent at least $250,000 of his own money on the golf course—more than $12 million in today's dollars—and his fortune was depleted. Friends had to contribute funds to complete the last four holes, and the club's board of directors adopted a resolution proclaiming that "Pine Valley remains his enduring monument."

Mike Keiser would agree with that. "George Crump is my hero," Mike once said when we were talking about Pine Valley. No one grasped more fully than a prospective developer like Mike the full extent of what Crump had achieved in building a golf course that was so pure, original, and uncompromising in its design. He understood, too, that George Crump would be long forgotten had he devoted himself to the hotel business. As he moved closer to creating his own first golf course, Mike took Pine Valley as his model and his inspiration.

MIKE HAD COME to a fork in his road. He was a late-twentieth-century developer who happened to be in love with early-twentieth-century courses, and his individual models weren't the corporate honchos or the megabucks hotshots who were building glitzy new courses; he was drawn to the old-fashioned model of the Crumps and Macdonalds, the amateurs who weren't simply developers but designers as well. His tastes and instincts drew him to courses of a kind that were light-years removed from what was being built in the 1980s. His road seemed to be leading him back in time to a project that would echo the classic period.

And he was definitely in the market for a significant project. In 1985 and 1986—about the same time that he joined the Melrose Club and made his discovery of the classic courses—he began to search actively for a chunk of land where he could build his own golf course. He had real-estate agents up and down the East Coast looking for a suitable property, and they sent him videotapes. ("I spent a lot of weekends watching those videotapes, and Lindy must have thought that her husband had developed a strange hobby.") He was also looking at land in North Carolina and Virginia, where Lindy's brother-in-law, John Willey, was chasing down properties. In 1986, Mike came close to buying a parcel of land in Virginia that was earmarked for home development and two courses designed by Robert Trent Jones. He decided to take a pass since, in Willey's assessment, "Jones's involvement means that you will have less control."

In Loudon County, Virginia, he was tempted to buy a 350-acre farm that stood in the path of development in one of the fastest-growing regions in the country. The conditions were perfect for an upscale daily fee course, but Mike again decided to take a pass—though not for business reasons. The place just didn't fire his imagination. He was still running RPG, and his aim wasn't simply to launch another successful business. Years later, standing on the ridge at Bandon Dunes, he would explain his decision this way: "I wasn't interested in commercial golf. Of course, I wanted every course I had anything to do with to make money—the bottom line is a kind of scorecard. But I was interested in dream golf."

And what dream golf meant, very specifically, was a course that could hold its head up in the company of places like Pine Valley and Merion and the National Golf Links, courses that had a powerful hold on the imagination of golfers, at least those influential golfers who ranked and rated the courses.

The impulse to rank golf courses dates all the way back to the beginning of the game, presumably back to the moment when a couple of besotted shepherds were shaking their crooks at each other and disputing the relative merits of the links of Leith and those of Dornoch, but it began to be formalized in 1962 when *Golf Digest* decided to publish its first comparative rankings. That initial list was called America's "200 Toughest Courses," and it didn't attempt to judge courses for their beauty, memorability, or playability, to name just a few of the qualitative factors that soon entered into the system of judging. Over the years, the number of criteria grew, as did the size of the panels; the lists became ever more closely scrutinized, almost talismanic in their importance, and spawned arguments as though it might really be possible to establish beyond a shadow of a doubt whether the course ranked 77th in the country was better than the course ranked 78th. The lists acquired a life of their own, and specialized lists kept proliferating (best resorts, best since 1960, best in the whole wide world), but on the master list the courses of the classic period seemed as fixed as stars in their constellations. Toward the bottom of the Top 100 lists, where newer courses were found, there was plenty of churning and turnover, but up in the stratosphere of the Top 20, the names remained the same. Just about every golfer alive could recite the list: Pine Valley. Augusta National. Pebble Beach. Pinehurst. Oakmont. Oakland Hills. Cypress Point. Shinnecock Hills. Merion. These courses were the classics, the landmarks, the standards. They were like the quartz-crystal clocks in the Naval Observatory, the clocks that keep perfect time, the clocks by which every watch everywhere in the world is set.

Mike thought that the rankings, while perhaps skewed somewhat in favor of historic courses, gave a fair idea of what average golfers preferred and valued. His own methods weren't scientific, but he liked to know what his playing partners were thinking, and to see if his opinions lined up with theirs. On Long Island, for instance, he found that he preferred National Golf Links to its more famous neighbor, Shinnecock Hills. Shinnecock Hills has always been more highly ranked than National, and Mike—professionally curious about the tastes of consumers—liked to pose a hypothetical question: Given ten rounds to divide between Shinnecock and National, how often would you play each course? "You'd be surprised," he reports, "how many people say they'd play one round at Shinnecock and nine at National." The sample was highly selective, but the answers were confirmation that his own instincts might be just as trustworthy as the elaborate systems used by the national magazines. "I was trying to learn what I liked and what I didn't like, and why I liked it and why I didn't. I wanted to see if my ideas would match up with those of the subjective 'experts' who rank these things. And I was realizing that what we did at RPG wasn't all that different from what happened out in the golf world. We selected a unique product, an artistic product, and put it out on the market. There's an exact ranking system for greeting cards—it's called sales—and you can tell in a hurry whether people like it or not, whether your own taste matches up with theirs. A golf course is a much different kind of product, but the rankings are about how much people like different courses, and about all the complicated reasons why they like them."

IN JUNE OF 1986, Mike decided it was time to fill another gap in his golfing education. He and Lindy were making a trip to London to visit the Ogdens, former neighbors in Lincoln Park, and Mike and Chris Ogden decided to take the opportunity to schedule several rounds of links golf. Chris, at the time the London bureau chief for *Time* magazine, made the arrangements himself, and he did it the old-fashioned way, by writing to the secretaries of the clubs where he wanted to make tee times. This was in the days before tour operators made all the arrangements and shuttled vanloads of visiting golfers around Scotland and Ireland. The Scottish clubs were slow to reply to Ogden, and very fussy in their requirements. The Irish clubs were far more welcoming: Basically, they said come whenever you like. And so, after a few days in London, Mike and Chris caught a plane to Northern Ireland and began their golf adventure at Royal County Down. On this leg of the journey, they were a twosome; later they would be joined by Chris's father, Mike, and his son, another Mike. The foursome would be recorded in memory as Three Mikes and a Chris.

At Royal County Down, Mike and Chris got their first taste of the conditions that would prevail throughout the trip. Irish golf hadn't yet been discovered, and the green fees were modest—usually about 10 punts, or Irish pounds, as best Chris can recall. The courses were mostly empty until the late afternoon, when locals stole out for a round after work. Most of the courses Chris had arranged to play were seaside courses, and they had a wild, rugged look; they weren't petted and groomed and manicured like American courses. Chris had arranged for caddies, who usually turned out to be craggy-faced, tweed-clad, weather-beaten, and hawk-eyed. These Irishmen knew their golf and quickly got on a first-name basis with their American clients. On the first day, after playing thirty-six holes and finally coming off the course in the long Irish twilight, Chris and Mike sank happily into deep chairs in the clubhouse at Royal County Down, wet their whistles, and dined on pork roast and cracklin' that was served up by an ancient barman.

Mike was in heaven. He loved the simplicity and grandeur of the golf courses and the complete lack of pretension in all the other arrangements. The clubhouses were modest, the food was plain, the hotels were drafty, the weather was the usual Irish mix of rain and mist with occasional peeks of sunshine, but the golf was splendid. The Irish were informal and welcoming and the whole environment of the game was new, strange, and invigorating. One measure of how much Mike and Chris had come under the spell of the links was that they didn't much care for Killarney, in the Republic of Ireland, finding that the Killarney golf courses, set in the romantic scenery of lake and mountain, felt too much like American parkland courses.

The first hole built at Bandon Dunes, the par-3 12th,
is a microcosm of David Kidd's bold, dramatic design.
Photo by Wood Sabold.

Mike Keiser, founder of Bandon Dunes.
Photo by Wood Sabold.

Not yet thirty years old when
he came to Bandon, Scotsman
David Kidd sometimes wondered
if Mike expected his father, Jimmy
Kidd, to design the golf course.
Photo courtesy of Bandon Dunes Resort.

Howard McKee, Mike's partner from the beginning, was a nongolfer who approached the project as "soul work."
Photo by Wood Sabold.

Shorty Dow, the longtime caretaker of the Bandon property, became the project's unofficial guide, host, and storyteller.
Photo courtesy of Bandon Dunes Resort.

Key members of the Bandon Dunes construction team, from left to right: Roger Sheffield, bunker builder; Pete Sinnott, construction supervisor; David Kidd; Jim Haley, lead shaper; Mike Keiser.　Photo by Wood Sabold.

Josh Lesnik, the first general manager of Bandon Dunes, plays construction golf.
Photo courtesy of Bandon Dunes Resort.

A few months later, the landscape had been transformed.   Photo by Wood Sabold.

Opening day at Bandon Dunes, May 2, 1999. The rain wasn't enough to dampen the spirits of Josh Lesnik, left; Steve Lesnik, the CEO of KemperSports, center; and Mike Keiser, right, who stood at the first tee and watched every foursome tee off.
Photo by Wood Sabold.

Simple and unfussy, the original shingled Lodge was located only paces away from the putting green and the final hole of the Bandon Dunes course.
Photo by Wood Sabold.

The 5th hole, with tufted mounds in the fairway, is a one-of-a-kind hole that didn't even show up on the original routing plan.   Photo by Wood Sabold.

Another stunning par 3, the 15th hole at Bandon Dunes shows the golfer the flag on the horizon.   Photo by Wood Sabold.

The 16th hole at Bandon Dunes is located at the highest point of the cliffs, a site once considered for the clubhouse.

Photo by Wood Sabold.

By this point in the trip, the other two Mikes had joined them, and the foursome set off for Ballybunion. There they found a Quonset hut in use as a clubhouse, and the accommodations in the village (which now boasts a statue of President William Jefferson Clinton) were a far cry from what they are today. But the New Course designed by Robert Trent Jones had recently opened, and the Old Course had won the seal of approval from eminent golf writer Herbert Warren Wind—he declared that Ballybunion was "nothing less than the finest seaside links I have ever seen"—and Tom Watson, who endorsed it by making Ballybunion the course where he practiced for the British Open. The three Mikes and Chris were aware that they were in for something special when they stepped up to the first tee and found that the local cemetery juts into the right side of the fairway. It is simply the first signal that Ballybunion is a thing absolutely unto itself, and by the time they reached the 7th hole, a par 4 on a cliff edge high above the Atlantic, they were giddy with pleasure.

They played both courses that day. They'd been warned that the New Course, now called the Cashen Course, was extremely difficult, and it was; they lost so many balls that they had to send a caddy back to the clubhouse to purchase more ammo so that they could complete the round. The rain was coming down, hard at times, but they were having a blast as they tried to play across the towering dunes. The following day they played the Old Course again, and Mike Ogden, Chris's father, announced when they finished the round that his golf career had ended. "I've just played the best course in the world," he said, "and that's it. I'm going to retire now."

He meant it. He continued the trip, and walked the courses as the others played, but he gave his clubs to his son, Chris. He never played another round of golf.

For Mike Keiser, that Irish trip had been inspirational. "Our golf was absolutely horrendous, but it didn't matter. It was still a wonderful trip. I'll never forget how I felt when we got to Ballybunion and I saw those unbelievable dunes, and those holes perched on the cliffs over the ocean, and I thought, Wow! This wasn't just a different kind of golf. It was a different kind of experience."

The whole trip had been mind-expanding. It had given Mike a new perspective on the game, and it had completed the first phase of his education in golf architecture, taking him all the way back to the beginning. He'd worked backward, from the postmodern and modern period, through the classic, and now he'd made the first of what would soon be many trips to the linksland of the British Isles. Somehow, though the bunkers were different, the grass was different, and the style of play was different, Mike felt at home on these courses. On the treeless, seaside courses, the wind was always blowing, and a golfer had to invent shots to advance the ball over the shaggy dunes and the wild, heaving fairways. Mike liked the challenge of these shots. He liked the companionship of the caddies and the fact that the game was always played on foot (the Irish and the Scots speak derisively of golf carts, which they call buggies, pronounced *boogies*). He liked the fact that the game was played swiftly, the pace Mike prefers. "I felt as though I was discovering a different game, even though it's a very old game. Links golf is where it all started. They've been playing golf in Ireland and Scotland for hundreds of years—and I asked myself, what makes those courses hold up today? They're not just museum pieces. They're still fun and exciting to play, a lot more fun and exciting than most modern courses."

Mike Keiser isn't one to back away from big ideas, and that first Irish trip planted the seed of an audacious dream. He wasn't prepared to announce that he was going to build the American Ballybunion, but the thought of links golf began to fuse with his preference for classic American courses—courses that were built by hand, courses whose individuality held up over time, courses that had the gamy, wild flavor of their natural surroundings.

Mike Keiser was out of step with the spirit of the 1980s, and he knew it. He wanted to build a "throwback" course, and he wanted to build it in the same involved, hands-on fashion as his hero, George Crump.

Which is how the Dunes Club, in New Buffalo, Michigan, came into being.

5 | The Dunes Club

You can call this the best nine-hole golf course in the country
and not have to wear a disguise when you say it.

—DAN JENKINS, IN SPORTS ILLUSTRATED

EARLY ON A PERFECT June morning, I settled into the passenger seat of Mike Keiser's leased Lincoln for the drive out to the Dunes Club, and we beat the rush hour onto Lake Shore Drive, heading south with the blue expanse of Lake Michigan on our left and the ranked, sparkling towers of Chicago on our right. The city of big shoulders seemed radiant in the sunrise, and as we tooled past the green swath of Grant Park, with the Magnificent Mile visible just beyond the lawns and the crowns of the trees, Mike chatted about Howard McKee and the Centennial World's Fair—the fair that had brought Howard to Chicago and, in the end, frustrated him. Ahead of us were the Field Museum of Natural History and the Adler Planetarium, both standing in the landscaped grounds of a promontory that juts out into the lake. This area, the Museum Campus, is a popular destination for tourists and families. Lake Shore Drive made a sweeping curve as it approached the campus, and Mike gave Howard and his fellow planners credit for rerouting this major artery. With a certain civic pride, he noted other changes on the South Side of Chicago: the McCormick Convention Center, the new Comiskey Park, the recently enlarged Soldier Field.

As we passed the ragged edge of the city, we also crossed the state line and entered Gary, Indiana, where the vast, empty hulks of the steel mills dominated the landscape, and Mike started to speculate on just how and when this desolate Rust Belt city would recover. That it would recover he had no doubt; with a friend he'd been thinking of buying up property and perhaps building some form of housing. This kind of speculation comes easily to him, and led naturally into one of his favorite topics, the caddy program at the Dunes Club. "There's a lot of unemployment in this area, as you can see. When I was building the Dunes Club, I knew I wanted it to be a walking course, and I knew I wanted caddies—but Al [Kissman, a local real-estate agent] told me that the caddy program would never work. He wanted to see golf carts. Most of the locals wanted golf carts—they seemed to think walking was what happened on a muni, not on a classy golf course, and they told me that I'd never find caddies. Well, I hired Dave Hettinga as the pro, and Dave knew everybody around New Buffalo. He was a state trooper whose dream had always been to be a golf pro, and he didn't have any problem finding the caddies we need. Now we have about forty regular caddies, and they make out pretty well."

The drive to New Buffalo takes just over an hour and a half from Lincoln Park. As we passed the smokestacks and steel mills and power grids of Gary, we were skirting the southern tip of Lake Michigan. Mike kept the Lincoln moving along at a good, steady clip, and we soon turned off the lightly traveled interstate onto a smaller road, one that headed north along the eastern shore of the lake. The road shrank down to two lanes, and trees began to crowd in on either side. The houses had the inviting look of summer houses everywhere, places built not for show but for comfort and enjoyment. Mike drove me past his place, a low, lakefront house in the shade of tall oaks and maples. Mike and Lindy were among the first to locate a summer house in this subdivision just south of New Buffalo; even though there are now about thirty other houses in the subdivision, they all have their privacy.

"I wasn't happy when I heard that someone was going to buy the land across the street," Mike told me, "but I had no thought of buying it myself. Al Kissman told me that they had an offer from someone who wanted to build condos, and I didn't want to see a wall of condos over there. Al knew that I was concerned, and he came back to me to tell me that the contract was held up with all kinds of contingencies. He also mentioned that the sale price was low. How low? I asked him. Three hundred and five thousand dollars, Al said. I was dumbfounded. I had no idea that the price was so low, and I must have reacted when I heard it because Al knew he had his hook in me. I called my lawyer that weekend, and by Monday we presented an all-cash offer—which they accepted. I've found that people usually take the cash."

And thus Mike became the owner of sixty wooded acres. He had no particular plans for the property beyond holding it. New Buffalo was gradually being "discovered," changing from a down-at-the-heels, mostly forgotten little lake town into an active summer resort, and Mike was confident that he wouldn't lose money on his investment. After the sale went through, he would occasionally steal over to his property, golf club in hand, accompanied by Lindy and the kids, to play wilderness golf in the areas that were open enough. Beneath the ground cover the soil was light and sandy—and the lightbulb went on in Mike's head. This was exactly what the land at Pine Valley must have looked like before the golf course was built. Wooded dunes! George Crump had started with the same thing. Here on the shore of Lake Michigan he had stumbled upon property that happened to be the midwestern counterpart of Clementon, New Jersey, and he saw the potential for a golf course.

In the spring of 1987, not long after acquiring the property, Mike entered an Armchair Architect contest sponsored by *Golf Digest,* and that helped to get his creative juices flowing. ("I actually believed I had a chance to win that contest until I found out that there were twenty-two thousand entries. And one of them, I later learned, was submitted by a youngster named Eldrick Woods.") When he played wilderness golf with his family, or when he came with Howard McKee to do their Saturday lopping and clearing, Mike kept imagining fantasy golf holes, many of them deployed around the high ridge that crossed the property.

He didn't really expect to build these golf holes. In his search for a golf course site, Mike had been looking at tracts that comprised hundreds of acres. A few venerable courses, like Merion and the Old Course at St. Andrews, are snugly fit into sites of just over 100 acres, but for the construction of a modern golf course, 150 acres is regarded as a minimum, and most golf course designers breathe more comfortably when they have 200-plus acres to work with.

His sixty-acre piece of dunesland was nowhere near large enough to accommodate a full-size golf course, and Mike knew it. The property didn't figure in his golf plans until Al Kissman approached him about buying another piece of land, this one a parcel of forty acres with some frontage on the lake. Al had correctly gauged Mike as a man who likes everything connected with the purchase of land—he likes to see it, to walk it, to evaluate, to imagine its potential. This lakefront property, Al argued, would be an excellent investment. The asking price was $1 million, and whoever bought it stood to make a sweet profit by selling it off as building lots. Mike's interest in a real-estate speculation, however, was zero. His goal was to build a golf course, and he didn't want his money tied up in any long-term investment on the shores of Lake Michigan. His only interest in the property was whether it would yield golf holes, and he reluctantly decided that the forty acres didn't fit together with the land he already owned.

Yet the idea of adding to his original sixty acres and building a golf course right here, right in his front yard, had been planted. He'd been looking up and down the East Coast for a site, but why not here? Gradually the fantasy began to slip across the line toward reality. As he worked on the property with Howard McKee, as he walked it with his golf club in his hand and his kids along for the romp, he couldn't stop thinking about the land's potential. Yes, it was too small for a regulation course, and it was thousands of miles away from the places where Mike had his scouts looking for golf course property, plus it was far from a market that would support a daily fee course. But when a contiguous piece of land—not lakefront, but a parcel of thirty wooded acres—came on the market, he decided to buy it. He wanted to go ahead and build a 9-hole course.

To be precise, he decided to build a 9-hole course that would have the look and playing qualities of Pine Valley.

Talk about audacity! It is always daring and usually foolhardy to imitate a landmark, since the result will inevitably be compared to the original—and will almost surely be found to be nowhere near as good. In this case, Mike wasn't even going to build a regulation golf course, but a scaled-down version on a tight budget. Any golfer who has played a copycat course (they exist in all corners of the country, these novelty courses with disappointing imitations of famous golf holes) knows how hard it is to reproduce the appeal of a great hole, let alone an entire great course.

Mike wasn't operating according to the dictates of prudence and he certainly wasn't guided by any market studies. His desire to build a course that paid tribute to Pine Valley was, like any passion, irrational and irresistible. It had been growing for years, and if he was about to embark on a complete folly—well, at least a 9-hole golf course in New Buffalo, Michigan, would be a relatively small and private folly.

Not that he ever envisioned the Dunes Club as his own personal playground—"That would have been unacceptable," he said—but he didn't give much thought to how he'd go about establishing a club and attracting members. Correction: He didn't give *any* thought to establishing a club, according to Dick Nugent, the golf course architect whom Mike brought in to work on the design and routing of the course.

DICK NUGENT WAS AT the peak of his career, though he didn't seem at first glance to be someone who could design a course in the style of Pine Valley. A Chicago-based architect, he was best known for his work at Kemper Lakes, where he collaborated with Ken Killian to build a course that had been conceived as a test for the pros and was selected to host the 1989 PGA Championship. Long and tough, with numerous water hazards, Kemper Lakes was a thoroughly modern course, and it had risen as high as the 38th spot on *Golf Digest*'s Top 100 list.

Mike was looking to build a completely different kind of course, and he "interviewed" Dick Nugent by playing golf with him at several of Chicago's older courses. It turned out that Nugent, Chicago born and bred, had caddied at some of these courses, and he had both affection and affinity for their more traditional layouts. His design portfolio included restoration work at Medinah, Butler National, Glenview, and several other venerable layouts. As he and Mike discussed the project at New Buffalo, they were feeling their way toward a partnership in which ideas could be freely exchanged. Nugent remembers that as they toured Shoreacres, a course regarded by architecture buffs as one of the finest examples of Seth Raynor's design work, Mike asked, "Why do I like this course so much?"

"Because it breaks all the rules," Nugent replied.

Dick Nugent had recognized that his client did not like the conventional and predictable. They were coming, by degrees, to understand and respect each other's point of view. This informal, feeling-out process would be the way that Mike chose all the architects involved at Bandon Dunes; he never set up a formal interview procedure, and he wasn't at all interested in trying to pin down every detail of the relationship in a contract. On the contrary, he wanted to keep things as open and flexible as possible, and his agreement with Nugent simply kept evolving. They shook hands on a "deal" that Nugent would draw up a routing plan, and they made several visits to Pine Valley, where they toured the course with the superintendent and entered into detailed discussion not merely of how to achieve a "look," but how to build and maintain such a golf course.

Mike wanted to be sure that he and Nugent were in complete accord about the appearance and strategy of the golf course before starting on any work, and he also wanted real involvement in the design process—not the token involvement that is customary in most client-architect relationships. In fact, Mike had labored over his own routing plan for a 9-hole golf course. He told his friend Tom Sturges that he wanted to see if he could come up with a better routing plan than the professional.

"I like doglegs," Mike said, "and I tried to design a course with several doglegs. Some of them were great holes, I thought, but when I got to the end, the only way I could finish the course was with a par 5 shaped like three sides of a square. It went out 220 yards, turned right for another 200 yards, and took another right turn to get to the green. Dick told me in a diplomatic way that my routing was a disaster, and we used his—which has six parallel holes. Parallel holes are usually to be avoided, but the way the course is arranged, with the different lengths and features of each hole, and with trees separating the holes, you don't really notice that they're parallel."

MIKE MADE HIS POINT about parallel holes as we walked down the fourth fairway of the Dunes Club. In truth, I hadn't noticed that this fairway ran parallel to the third hole, for they are separated by a stand of trees. Though thousands of trees were removed, the property is still heavily wooded, and nearly every hole at the Dunes Club feels entirely private, a world unto itself.

The whole course has an air of privacy, almost of secrecy. The entry, for instance, is not marked by gates or signs. It is not marked by anything at all. You could drive past it a hundred times without ever noticing the paved turnoff that runs through the trees. But for those who know where they are going, there is just enough room to navigate a car past the trees that grow in the pavement; then, beyond a wire fence—a construction-type fence— the visitor catches a glimpse of groomed turf, a putting green, a net and an Astroturf mat (this is the driving range), a terrace, and a tiny, charming, white-shingled clubhouse. On that June morning, the terrace was alive with birds—orioles, sparrows, and downy woodpeckers—flitting back and forth among the many feeders.

Pete Sinnott was waiting for us, along with our three caddies, and he was the third member of our threesome that morning. Pete's company, Serviscapes, along with Wadsworth Construction, built the Dunes Club, and Serviscapes still does the maintenance work on the golf course. During the building of the Dunes Club, Pete went along on the visits to Pine Valley, and he became not just a trusted adviser but a good friend of Mike's; they have made many a golf trip together, and Mike hired Pete to manage the construction at Bandon Dunes. Pete is a veteran of the golf business, having served as both pro and superintendent for courses owned by Bethlehem Steel before striking out on his own. Lean, tanned, and wiry, Pete looks like a smaller version of Mike, and he has a quiet intensity that manifested itself, once we set off on our round, in a couple of snap hooks.

We were all spraying the ball that morning, and the Dunes Club is not the place for a wild hitter. The course is not particularly long—3,465 yards from the tips—and the fairways are not especially narrow. But they are lined with thick fescue which, in June, simply swallowed golf balls. My caddy, Harvey Pallas, a veteran looper who had another life as a professional bowler, said severely, "This is position golf at its finest," and tried not to look disapproving when I knocked another ball into the fescue.

Even Mike was having difficulty that morning keeping the ball in play, though no one would ever know from his demeanor whether he is playing well or poorly. He has a crisp, athletic swing with his long clubs, a swing with a fluid rhythm and tempo. His natural ball flight is a low draw, and when he gets quick—look out for the snapper! With his irons he acknowledges that his swing has been affected—"ruined," he laments—by his experience on links courses and his effort to play low, punch shots. It was clear at the Dunes that he liked to bump the ball whenever he could, as opposed to playing a higher, more lofted shot, and he frequently used his long putter when he was within fifteen or twenty feet of the green. The long putter is a relatively new addition to his arsenal, and he wasn't having any trouble rolling the ball close. In his faded stand-up bag, he was carrying new clubs that his son Michael had finally persuaded him to buy; for years he'd been playing with "yard sale" clubs. (He'd had the new clubs for a couple of months, and the sticker with the price and the bar code was still affixed to the shaft of his driver; he hadn't noticed it until that morning.) But he had left one old favorite in the bag, a Cobra Baffler, a railed utility club that dates back to the original generation of metal woods and bears all the nicks and dings of long, honorable use. This is Mike's go-to club, and he uses it to shape all kinds of shots within a range of 140 to 200 yards. He belongs to the "miss 'em quick" school of thought, and plays without any fuss or folderol. On the tee he doesn't take any practice swings, and on the fairway he does not mutter about trying to determine the exact yardage. On the green he steps up to his putt at the exact moment that the previous putt rolls to a stop. His memories of favorite rounds invariably include a mention that the pace was brisk.

His game was somewhat ragged on this particular morning since he, along with Pete, was acting as my host, making sure I took in the features of the Dunes Club. There was a lot to notice, starting with the tees that aren't boxes but large, multitiered areas of closely mown turf, some of them fantastically contoured. On some holes these tee complexes provide as many as six or seven distinct platforms, each offering a different distance, elevation, and angle of attack. There are no tee markers. The local rule is that the player with the honor has the privilege of selecting the place where everyone will peg it up, in much the same way that the player in H-O-R-S-E gets to choose the next shot.

At the second hole, a par 3 over a sandy waste, the choice of tees can make a difference of 60 yards. Furthermore, the tees here are in two separate locations and they open up the green from completely different angles, so that the hole can be played with a 7-iron into the fat of the green—or it can require a faded long iron to skinny green. That minidesert, by the way, is marked with clumps of fountain grass and scrub pines, and the green is fringed with more gnarly stuff. All in all, this is a hole where you *seriously* want to stay on the short grass, though the same could be said for every hole. The groomed areas of the course are beautifully conditioned, but they are closely bordered by thick fescue and unruly scrub, or by sandy waste areas, and scrub gives way quickly to dense stands of tall trees, mostly oaks and maples.

My dour caddy kept indicating the exact portion of the fairway where I should be hitting my ball, the place that would give me the best angle into the small, undulating greens, and I could see that this was a supremely tactical course. Both par 5s, for instance, require a second shot over cross hazards that are frankly reminiscent of Hell's Half Acre at Pine Valley, but the par-5 8th hole has a wicked quality all its own.

This hole, 513 yards long, starts with a drive from an elevated tee to a wide fairway. Easy enough. But the second shot then has to carry what we'll call Hell's Quarter Acre to the far right side of the fairway. Otherwise, the approach with a wedge or 9-iron will be stymied by the overhanging branch of a monster oak that owner Keiser left hanging there for precisely that reason. (And it was Mike's decision to keep the tree, not Nugent's. They had several arguments about trees during the construction, and Mike was always in favor of sparing them. Nugent came to think of him as an "unabashed tree hugger.") As if branches weren't trouble enough, the green on this zigazag hole sits in a bowl up at the top of a slope and is half-hidden by a big-shouldered dune on the right.

I was beginning to understand how thoroughly this 9-hole layout tested a fellow's golf.

LUNCH IN THE CLUBHOUSE was an unfussy affair. Burgers and bratwurst are the staples of the menu, and various snacks—chips, crackers, cheese—are put out for the taking. Members sign for their sodas or drinks. The pro shop, one of the world's smallest, is about the size of a respectable closet. The locker room is an alcove with a shoe rack and two changing rooms which, though small, provide voluminous showers. When Mike asked his friend, architect Larry Booth, to design a clubhouse, the instructions were to keep it simple. Booth came up with a design that is both elegant and homey, and the Dunes Club—with a membership that now numbers about ninety— has the feeling of an escape, a refuge or sanctuary. For high-profile Chicago golfers (think Michael Jordan, or Mike Ditka, or Mayor Daley) who want to repair to a place where they can be absolutely guaranteed that their golf will be private, the Dunes Club is the ticket.

Pete Sinnott explained how the Dunes was built. He'd been brought to the project by Dick Nugent, and he recalled a day in February 1988 when he, Mike, Nugent, and John Cotter of Wadsworth Construction walked the property and shook hands on a deal to build the course. "Mike just said, let's go. It was a very efficient operation even though everything evolved in the field. Dick Nugent had done some drawings and a routing plan, but we worked from the stick routings [little flags stuck into the ground to indicate the general placement of tees, greens, and other features]. I don't know what arrangements Mike had with Dick Nugent or Wadsworth, but he and I have never had a written contract about anything. Mike was on the site at least once a week, and the whole process was very fluid, with everyone equally involved. I'd say Dick Nugent was there every couple of weeks. Mike would look hard at what was happening, and he'd ask questions and make requests. The site lent itself to having Pine Valley as a model, so we always knew what kind of look and aesthetics we were going for. The whole project was done for less than a million dollars. It was just a thrill to work like that."

By the spring of 1989, the 9-hole layout was ready to play, and the place had a name and a logo. It didn't have a clubhouse—the only building on the property was a maintenance building—and the only access to the property was by way of a maintenance road. There were no members, and no membership director, and only a few sketchy plans about how memberships would work and what they'd cost. But one day during construction, a pair of curious neighbors turned up to take a look at what was going on behind the fence. They were golfers, Chicagoans who had summer places in New Buffalo, and they liked what they saw. They wanted to know how much it cost to join, and *voila!* They plunked down the money. The Dunes Club, out of the blue, had its first members, Brian Jerome and Steve Thompson, two of Mike's best friends today.

For Mike, this was affirmation. Indeed, the whole project had been an affirmation of the course that he was charting for himself. One of the most important things he had learned was that he *liked* building a golf course. He liked being out-of-doors, liked the smoke and noise and sand, liked the camaraderie of the field, liked the whole experience of making something so real and tangible, of bringing something new into being. He also liked the loose, collaborative style of working with men he trusted. Moreover, he had found the role that suited him—and it was not that of golf course architect, the man who came up with the original plans and drawings and had to worry about the technical details of drainage and irrigation. What Mike liked was the role of impresario, the man who put the whole deal together—who found the land, hired the team, articulated the concept, obtained the permits, interviewed the members, set the fees, worked with the designer of the clubhouse and logo, hired the pro, and had a say in just about every decision from the items on the menu to the tiles in the ample showers. He was like a producer of a Broadway show, the one who had to make sure that all the moving parts worked together to create a single, harmonious whole. The others had key contributions to make, but when all was said and done, the Dunes Club was Mike's baby.

IT DIDN'T TAKE LONG for word about the Dunes Club to leak out. Golf aficionados keep a watchful eye out for new tracks, and the few who had seen the place started a lively buzz. The raters from the Chicago District Golf Association were among the first to spread the word about the Dunes, and writers from local and regional publications showed up to review it. They recognized the layout as exceptional, and Dick Nugent asked Ron Whitten, the architectural editor at *Golf Digest,* to come by for a look.

"As far as I was concerned," Mike says, "Ron Whitten was God." Whitten was the most prolific, most informed, and most respected golf course critic in the country, a man whose opinions carried enormous weight. He was the editor of a book on golf courses that Mike kept on his bedside table, and he, more than anyone else, was the authority on whom Mike based his own ideas about golf course design.

Whitten didn't meet Mike on his first visit to the Dunes Club, but he can still recall everything about his first impression, from climbing the fence to get into the place to his growing excitement as he played the course. Before long, in the *Golf World* of September 6, 1991 (*Golf World* is the weekly news publication of *Golf Digest*), Whitten published his first review of the Dunes Club. He described it as "a throwback to an earlier era," and recognized the Pine Valley influence. He also found similarities to Garden City, a classic course on Long Island noted for its sandy turf, and he singled out the 8th hole as the best on the course.

Whitten is not one to rave, but the Dunes Club had won him over. He would visit the Dunes Club again, with Mike, and he would write about it at greater length. He mentioned it often in interviews, pronouncing it the best 9-hole course in the country—a judgment made more or less official by *Sports Illustrated*, which devoted several pages, including a two-page center spread photo, to 9-hole courses in October 1997. The article was entitled "Small Wonder," and the Dunes Club, like its model Pine Valley, had secured its own No. 1 ranking and begun to create its own mystique.

The accolades have continued to roll in. In the February 2000 *Golf Digest*, Dan Jenkins included the 8th hole on his Dream 18, opining that the course would easily make the Top 100 lists if it were an 18-hole course. Its size, however, was not a fatal defect to the raters at *Golf Magazine;* on their 2003 list of the Top 100 courses in the United States, the Dunes Club was ranked 77th. It was the only 9-hole course on the list.

For Mike, who hadn't really set out to prove anything, the results were more than gratifying. By following his own instincts, by building a small course close to home, by going completely counter to the prevailing trends, he had created what amounted to a sensation—a throwback course in the middle of nowhere, a 9-holer with a national ranking. Not bad for a first-time developer.

6 | Eureka!

We were flying around like Masters of the Universe, but that's not how
we found Bandon. It was the plumber who guided us to the site.

—MIKE KEISER

HOWARD MCKEE HADN'T WASTED any time getting started on a search for property on the West Coast. While Mike was building the Dunes Club and keeping his feelers out for golf course sites on the East Coast, Howard was traveling back and forth to California and Oregon, contacting real-estate agents from Portland to San Francisco to let them know that he was looking for a large piece of land of "breath-taking beauty." In his letters to agents and potential sellers, he used those exact words, quoting Mike, and asking to be shown properties that could compare with Yosemite. This was asking a lot—it was asking the moon!—but Howard knew that hype is the language of real estate, and he didn't want to waste his time looking at inferior sites. He had cut his ties with Skidmore, Owings, and Merrill, and he approached this task as the commencement of a new era of his professional life. He looked upon the assignment that Mike had given him as an opportunity to launch a large, lasting project. He approached it as "soul work."

The whole state of Oregon, as he quickly discovered, seemed to have a For Sale sign on it. The economy was in free fall (except in Portland, where an urban renaissance was under way), and many large landholders were trying to unload property. The Oregon Parks and Recreation Department owned more property than it could manage, and it was quietly trying to sell off some of its raw land. The Catholic Archdiocese of Oregon was also looking to get rid of several large tracts of undeveloped property. The most eager sellers, however, were the companies that had ruled the state's once-mighty timber industry. Oregon timber had been a signature product, not just a source of wealth but a part of the state's lore and heritage, like Iowa corn or Texas oil. By the late 1980s, timber operations in the Sunbelt states had won a lion's share of the market, and companies like Weyerhaeuser and Georgia-Pacific were shutting down their mills in the Pacific Northwest. They still owned thousands of acres—some of it clear-cut, some of it still pristine, all of it taxable—and they would have been overjoyed to sell. As a prospective buyer, Howard was given VIP treatment, and he saw a lot of Oregon through the windows of a small plane provided by Georgia-Pacific.

He was happy to be back in Oregon, the place he regarded as his spiritual home. For most of the 1970s, he had been the head of the SOM Environmental Studies office in Portland, and he had bought and still owned an old farmhouse at Cascade Head, the spectacular headland in northwest Oregon that had once been where Indians from the coastal tribes went on their vision quests. The environment of Cascade Head was exceptionally rich and diversified, a haven for rare plants and creatures, particularly valued for its stands of native grasslands and its abundance of wildflowers. With twelve thousand acres of federally protected lands and estuaries, Cascade Head had been designated a National Scenic Research Area, and the entire headland—its thriving forests, salmon-rich streams, and blankets of wildflowers—was standing testimony to the virtues of sound, sustained environmental management.

Howard, a staunch environmentalist who was on a vision quest of his own, was completely in sympathy with the ethos of Cascade Head. He is an unusual mixture of principles and passions: an intellectual who has a deep respect for nature and the supernatural, a man of science who puts a premium on the work of the imagination, a rationalist who never forgets the mysteries of the psyche. He is a high-minded thinker who loves to putter around on his property and to work with his hands, a philosopher who likes to sweat. He is a serious man who laughs easily and uproariously. He sometimes comes across as a hard-nosed realist, at other times as a New Age dreamer and a bit of a woo-woo. Those who worked with him weren't always able to pin him down philosophically, but they were in agreement on two of Howard's most conspicuous traits. One, his intellectual curiosity was voracious, and whenever a subject interested him, he learned it inside out and upside down. Two, he was brilliant; he could think and talk circles around most people, but he did so in a way that made them feel flattered to be in a conversation with him. "His approach," one associate said, "was always that we're in agreement on this issue, but you just don't realize it yet. He was always one step, or ten steps, ahead of you, and he was confident that he could bring you around to his point of view." Grant Rogers, the director of golf instruction at Bandon Dunes and a close observer of his fellow man, simply declares, "Howard is one of those people who *knows*." (Grant can be enigmatic, and when I asked him to expand on his statement, to explain what Howard knows, Grant seemed to be embarrassed for me. He looked away and said, "Everything.")

Howard had been the first in his family to go to college. Born in 1939, he grew up in Charleston, West Virginia, in a respectable, hardworking family—his father was a painting contractor—and he did so well in high school that a local graduate of Columbia University persuaded him to apply to Columbia, in New York City. Howard was accepted, and he spent the next decade soaking up knowledge. He was a star student, and he left Columbia with three degrees: a B.A. in economics, an M.A. in architecture, and an M.A. in urban design. When he was hired by SOM, he became a protégé of Nat Owings, one of the firm's founders and an architect with an unusual breadth of vision; Owings was a champion of multidisciplinary thinking, and SOM architects were taught to consider their buildings not simply in terms of design but, more broadly, in terms of all the different purposes and functions that a building had to serve. The team approach was valued at SOM, and it was one of the reasons that SOM attracted so many prominent corporate and commercial clients; the Sears Tower in Chicago and the Lever House in New York were among SOM's major commissions. In the realm of public design, SOM was also a leader, and one of Howard's first jobs was in Washington, where SOM played a key role in the redesign of Pennsylvania Avenue. As a young architect, Howard learned to ask the question, Does this building serve the common good? The answer to that question went beyond aesthetics, and it posed the challenge that Howard would face over and over in his professional career. "It is interesting," he wrote in a handwritten comment on a project for Mike, "how difficult it is to marry philosophy and reality."

Early in his career, he worked on huge projects that brought together professionals from many disciplines in an attempt to come up with solutions to intricate, complex, and sometime mind-boggling social problems. In Saudi Arabia, for instance, the city of Yanbu was being created virtually from scratch, and SOM had to factor in the security issues that surround oil pipelines while also addressing the sensitive matter of relocating the nomadic bedouins: What kind of arrangements would help them to settle down peacefully? How could they be made willing to say farewell to their tents and camels and live in fixed abodes? How could they be integrated into a modern, technological society? These weren't problems that an architect or urban planner could solve at the design table, and Howard, grappling with global issues, was seeing just how many informed points of view were needed to create a complete picture.

He went to Portland in 1971 when the SOM office was engaged in the task of finding solutions to the city's transportation needs. Portland was trying to bring one of the last sections of the interstate highway system into the downtown area, into a cityscape defined by handsome, historic cast-iron buildings. Instead of jamming high-speed, heavily traveled roads into the city center, the planners and politicians in Portland worked for years to develop an integrated transportation system that would preserve the character of the city and revitalize its downtown; with Howard at the helm, Skidmore, Owings and Merrill was in the thick of the effort. The result was the creation of the Portland light rail system and Transit Mall, innovations in urban transportation that are studied and emulated by city planners from other parts of the country.

Now that he was back in Oregon as Mike's facilitator and forward observer, Howard was renewing his ties with friends and associates from those days. He felt a little like Br'er Rabbit in the briar patch. He was at home.

WITHIN A FEW MONTHS, Howard had found a piece of land that seemed to meet most of Mike's criteria. The Cascade Ranch, near Medford, Oregon, had the size, and it had the breathtaking beauty. This working ranch was a 12,000-acre spread ringed by the snow-covered peaks of the Cascade Mountains. The high reaches of the property were dotted with sparkling lakes, and the property included a tiny town called Lake Creek. In the summer of 1988, after hearing Howard's glowing reports, Mike made a visit with Lindy.

They all spent a day driving and tramping around the place, led by Bob Johnson, a local real-estate agent, trying to avoid the cow chips, the flies, and the snakes. Mike damn near stepped on a timber rattler as he climbed a barbed-wire fence, and he executed one of those astounding straight-back snake leaps, covering approximately the same distance going backward as a world-class broad jumper covers going forward. It was clear that Lindy didn't much care for the place, and Bob Johnson, who'd had the ranch listed for over a year, could feel the chances of a sale slipping away. At dinner that night, Mike plied him with specific, pointed questions about the property, which was in bankruptcy. "He approached it as a business proposition," says Johnson, who has been involved in many subsequent real-estate transactions with Mike. "He was trying to determine exactly what would be required to make a deal, but I honestly didn't expect him to make an offer. I was completely surprised the next morning—it was a Friday—when he said he was going to buy it. He told me I'd hear from his lawyer on Monday, and on Monday morning, first thing, I got the call."

Mike bought the Cascade Ranch for $2.8 million, cash. Just like that, he had planted his flag in Oregon. Even now, years later, he can't fully account for his purchase of the ranch, since it was nowhere near the sea and obviously wasn't a site for a links course. But he liked the land and he thought that a property of that size, near Medford, one of the fastest-growing areas on the West Coast, had to be a solid investment. The trendy resort town of Ashland was nearby, and the area didn't have much golf. Over the next several years Mike would collect articles about golf ventures in the area, and he would even lay out a golf course of his own at the Cascade Ranch.

For the moment, however, the ranch was a piece of earth in need of healing. The previous owner had logged off all of the valuable timber, drained some of the lakes, abused the irrigation system, overgrazed the pastures, and generally left the ranch in rough shape. Howard's original mission had been to locate property, but now he took over as a kind of caretaker, hiring a ranch manager, Chuck Bruce, a wiry, redheaded cowboy who had grown up just down the road, to help him nurture the place back to a condition of economic viability and ecological good health.

Seamlessly, Howard had stepped into a new role. He was no longer just a scout for Mike but a steward of the property. It marked a turning point in their relationship, for Mike had a chance to see not only Howard's practical skills—he redesigned lakes, roads, the ranch house, and the irrigation system—but also his planning and political skills as he initiated discussions with county officials to see just what constraints applied to golf and resort development at Cascade Ranch (strict constraints, as it turned out). Mike would come to rely on Howard's political savvy and environmental integrity, and he was still in an acquisitive mode. He was just discovering Oregon, and the prices there were almost too good to be true. He'd bought a vast ranch, a little kingdom, for about the same price that he would have paid for a prime beach lot back east. Was there any coastal property for sale?

He wanted Howard to keep looking.

There was. In the spring of 1990, Mike was standing on a cliff near the town of Pistol River, looking at a view of the Pacific Coast that could have been a postcard, a place where the land fell off dramatically into the sea and the sea itself was strewn with immense black rocks, formations that had been fantastically shaped and sculpted by the waves. He had just bought five hundred acres here on the cliff top for $1 million.

Pistol River is on Oregon's South Coast, a designation that covers the area from Coos Bay at the mouth of Coquille River to Brookings at the southernmost edge of the state. It is perhaps the least settled stretch of coastline in the Lower 48. The small towns are few and far between, and they are situated at the mouths of the many rivers—Pistol River, Sixes River, the formidable

Rogue River—that lattice the wild, rugged, topsy-turvy countryside. The rivers are famous for their runs of salmon and steelhead, and Highway 101 is a two-lane road as it twists and curves through dense stands of spruce and fir and redwoods. Every now and then the land flattens out, and the road runs past sheep pastures or cranberry bogs, but this is mostly a landscape of mountain, ocean, and dark forest. It is Paul Bunyan country, and down near the California border, where the supremely beautiful Smith River runs through a stand of majestic redwoods, the scenery still looks as awe-inspiring as it must have to the earliest settlers.

Mike was completely smitten with this part of the country, though the land he'd acquired was too steep for golf. He'd become the owner of what had been the vacation property of a prosperous Philadelphia mortician who must have loved his profession: The U-shaped house was decorated with ma-terials—heavy drapes, satin tassels, shiny pillows, and an overall feeling of velvety plushness—that were eerily reminiscent of a funeral home. Mike and Lindy didn't spend much time there, and Howard detested what he called its "McDonald's arches." Working with a local plumber and handyman, Warren Felton, Howard set about making changes to the main house and converting the small outbuildings—chicken coops, once upon a time—into small rental units for vacationing fishermen, hikers, and kite-surfers.

The plan at Pistol River was to acquire another tract of oceanside land. Since 1989, when Mike took a Rogue River fishing trip with his father and his eight-year-old son Michael, he'd had his eye on a piece of property known as Crook's Point, a small peninsula that had been owned for five generations by the Crook family and used to graze sheep. To Mike's eye, the 90-acre peninsula had the potential to become the site of the next Pebble Beach, and he had begun to negotiate for its purchase even before he bought the house at Pistol River. The Crooks weren't interested in selling the land, but Mike persisted. "Each time I see it," he wrote to them, "I'm reconvinced that a golf course would be the only natural addition to what Mother Nature has wrought; anything else would detract from the site." Because of their reluctance to sell, Mike asked the Crooks to entertain a long-term strategy, possibly a long-term lease or option to buy, in return for which he would initiate the "long, tedious, and expensive process of building a golf course." He anticipated major challenges in obtaining approvals, but he pointed out to the Crooks that if he should succeed, their remaining holdings "will have been vastly increased in value."

He had turned a corner in thinking about his own future as a builder of golf courses. For one thing, he was now committed to building his dream course here on the Oregon coast. For another, that course was going to be a links course.

In Gold Beach, Oregon, on a chilly December morning, a real-estate agent named Annie Huntamer had a problem with her kitchen sink, and she called her plumber to fix it. His name was Warren Felton, and he happened to be the same man who was doing the work at Pistol River. While he fixed the sink, Annie heard all about Mike Keiser and Howard McKee and their search for golf property. Annie happened to know of a piece of property farther up the coast, at Bandon, that seemed to fit the description of what Mike wanted. Did Warren think that Mike was serious? Yes, absolutely. This was a big piece of land, twelve hundred acres, and it was going to be expensive. The sellers were asking almost $5 million. Was Mike capable? Warren thought so.

Annie Huntamer had never handled a sale like the one she was about to make. The property wasn't listed by her agency, but it had been on the market for a long time, and the owners—a group from Seattle—were eager to sell, either in whole or part. In fact, they'd had the land surveyed and drawn into eight different parcels, thinking that these smaller pieces might be easier to sell. They were glad to give Annie permission to show the property. She was so excited that she couldn't wait to set the transaction in motion, and she placed a phone call to Mike Keiser—to his home in Chicago—on a Saturday afternoon in early December of 1990.

Talk about a call coming out of the blue. Mike was taken aback, but he was also intrigued. He told Annie he'd get in touch with Howard.

Howard happened to be in Oregon. He was at Sunriver when he got Mike's call, but that afternoon he was able to hitch a ride from an airstrip at Sunriver to Coos Bay. He was on a tight schedule. Annie Huntamer met him at the Coos Bay airport and drove him down to the Bandon site, where she had arranged for him to meet Shorty Dow, the vocal, peppery caretaker of the place. Shorty had been looking after this property since 1964, and he introduced himself to Howard as he always introduced himself, as "the mayor, the governor, and the sheriff" of the place. He offered—this, too, is a part of his standard greeting—to show Howard where the bodies were buried. One of his main jobs as caretaker was chasing off the trespassers, the hunters and off-road-vehicle types who used the place, locally known as the Circus, for noisy recreation. Shorty had a reputation for carrying a gun and being ready to use it; he didn't actually wear a pistol, but he kept one handy, under the seat of his Jeep Cherokee. A retired mechanic who'd put in his time at Weyerhaeuser, Shorty lived in a single-wide trailer with his wife, Charlotte, and he looked a little like Popeye, though his expression was mischievous, and he always wore glasses and a baseball cap perched at an angle. He owned hundreds of caps and preferred the big, boxy ones—the kind with mesh backs and high fronts—emblazoned with the names of heavy-equipment manufacturers. The last bit of his ritual greeting was the exchange of business cards, and when he got Howard's he offered his in return:

GUITARS * FIDDLES * TOE TAPPING

Bull Shit * Master of Ceremonies * I Don't Get It Jokes

Shorty Dow

RETIRED

Coons Killed	Golf Balls Lost
Wind Broken	No Shit Stories
Guitars Picked	Sand Dunes Leveled
Brush Cut	Dogs Pet
Pick-Ups Fixed	Pot Lucks Eaten
Guns Fired	Finger Given

Shorty was ready and willing to show Howard around on the trails he'd cleared, but Howard warned him that he didn't have much time. Shorty asked, "Are you a smoker? Because if you are, you might as well sit down and smoke a cigarette. You're not going to see this place in twenty minutes. Don't even bother."

Howard did spend part of that afternoon with Shorty, and he wasn't particularly impressed by what he was able to see. The most accessible part of the property was the area called the Circus, a semiopen meadow where the sandy slopes were rutted and eroded by the heavy use of the ATVs. To the south and west, where the parcel adjoined Bullards Beach State Park, there were large, rolling dunes, but Howard wasn't tempted to explore them; a fierce wind was blowing that day and the sand was flying. Shorty showed him a couple of small lakes and drove him out a narrow trail to see the high cliffs above the ocean, but the trail was hacked through a dense stand of one of the most obnoxious plants Howard had ever seen, a thorny, prickly, impenetrable shrub called gorse. Most of the site was choked with this gorse.

All in all, as Howard reported to Mike, the Bandon property wasn't promising. It was a big piece of property, and it did have ocean frontage, but the gorse was a serious negative. Furthermore, the place was exposed to heavy, raking winds.

Wind and gorse. Howard wasn't a golfer, but Mike felt a definite quickening of interest when he heard those words. Wind and gorse are as essential to links golf as powder snow and moguls are to big-mountain skiing.

Early in 1991, Mike flew out to Oregon, accompanied by Pete Sinnott. They met Annie Huntamer in Bandon, where they were joined by Bob Johnson and, of course, Shorty Dow. Mike had a golf club in his hand and a few golf balls in his pocket. There was as much gorse as Howard had warned him about, but there was also Scots broom, and fern, and scrub pine, and rhododendron. There were stands of spruce and fir and Port Orford cedar. When the party explored Chrome Lake, Bob Johnson could see that Mike was taking a shine to the place. This piece of land was roughly rectangular in shape, with its northern end slightly misaligned and its southern boundary sliced off at a diagonal. It contained several distinct landscapes: the high, gorse-covered cliffs overlooking the Pacific; active, Sahara-like dunes; grassy wetlands; quicksands; forests of spruce, pine, and cedar, with a dense understory of rhododendron; a "meadow" with its own flora and fauna; a creek, Cut Creek, that ran swiftly for half a mile before vanishing into the sands of the beach; and, roughly at its center, in a notch between two high ridges, a set of lakes that fit together like pieces of an ancient puzzle. Those ridges formed the spine of the property, rising in some places more than two hundred feet above the surrounding landscape, providing views that stretched all the way to the horizon.

At lunchtime, they ate sandwiches not far from Chrome Lake. They'd had a glimpse of the many different environments, and Shorty, who had led the expedition and regaled everyone with his varmint tales, decided that it was time to climb the trail to the crest of Back Ridge, the highest place on the property.

There Mike had the moment that has been described by every golf course visionary from Tom Morris to Donald Ross to Bobby Jones to Jack Nicklaus. "The Almighty intended this place for gawf," Old Tom declared when he first laid eyes on the dunes of Machrihanish. "It seemed that this land had been lying here for years waiting for someone to lay a golf course upon it," Bobby Jones wrote after his first sight of the valley that now forms the amphitheater at Augusta National.

"Holy shit," Mike Keiser thought when he came over the top of Back Ridge and got his first elevated view of the land that would become Bandon Dunes. Since then he has come up with words more eloquent, but when he saw the whole sweep of the land, the miles of dunes rolling off to the south and the miles of surf rolling in to the broad beach, he was reduced to speechlessness. This place had the kind of grandeur and the breathtaking beauty that Mike had asked Howard to find. He might not have known exactly what form that beauty would take when he gave Howard his wish list, but on that cloudy day in January 1991, he knew that he'd found it.

There was something of Jay Gatsby in Mike Keiser. He wasn't as romantic as F. Scott Fitzgerald's timeless American hero, but he certainly resembled

Gatsby in his willingness to move heaven and earth in pursuit of his dream. "For a transitory enchanted moment," Fitzgerald wrote at the end of *The Great Gatsby,* "man must have held his breath ... face to face ... with something commensurate to his capacity for wonder."

Here at the edge of the continent, on a day when the sky and the sea were the color of pewter, Mike had discovered the place that matched his capacity for wonder.

THE BANDON PROPERTY had been offered for sale at $4.8 million. The owners were a group of Seattle businessmen, led by one Duke Watson, who had been frustrated in their attempts to develop the land as a resort. Over the years they had developed a number of plans calling for the construction of vacation homes, golf courses, and other recreational amenities, but every request was denied. Oregon's land-use laws are among the most stringent in the country, and the Seattle group—having invested a substantial amount in various efforts to develop plans that would meet with approval, not to mention the carrying costs of the land—was ready to throw in the towel.

Mike and Howard, of course, quickly became aware of the various development plans that had been rejected. The outlook for the kind of development that Mike envisioned was, to put it mildly, discouraging. Mike decided to use this as a bargaining point in his favor. He also decided not to work through agents but to negotiate directly with Duke Watson and his partners, and he flew to Seattle to present an offer in person. He lunched with Duke Watson and offered an amount that would have seemed absurdly low if it hadn't been, like all of Mike's offers, all cash. He didn't ask for an option, or a study period, or any other contingencies. He was prepared to sign a contract that same day to buy the land for $2.4 million.

Duke Watson and his partners left the room to confer. In half an hour, they had agreed to the sale.

Two-point-four million dollars for 1,215 acres. That came to slightly less than $2,000 an acre. In hindsight, it had to be the one of the best land deals since that Dutchman, Peter Minuit, purchased the island of Manhattan from the Indians for $26 and a bottle of booze.

Part Two

BANDON DUNES

7 | Bandon-by-the-Sea

Just think of the millions of people in New York City right
now—they can't imagine there's a place in the world like this.
—Shorty Dow, commenting on a pile of coyote scat

Bandon's luck was about to change.

The little town (pop. 2,500) at the mouth of the Coquille River, in the southeastern corner of Coos County, was in a fitful struggle to reinvent itself as a resort town. For more than a century, Bandon's economic fortunes had been dependent on logging, fishing, and dairy farming, and its harbor was home to a small fleet of steamers that made regular voyages to San Francisco laden with cargoes of lumber, salmon, milk, and cheese. By 1991, however, most of the sawmills had closed down, the fishing fleet had all but vanished, and the number of dairy farms in Coos County had declined from more than five hundred to fewer than twenty. This whole part of Oregon—with its weedy log yards, rusted mills, abandoned farms, and ports where the only activity was the wheeling of the seabirds—had the look and feel of a place that the world had passed by.

Bandon-by-the-Sea, as the town sometimes called itself, did have an array of shops and restaurants, and the town had always attracted a certain number of visitors to view the fantastically shaped rock formations that lined its beaches. Some of them, called seastacks, rise like giant, twisted chimneys; others contain hidden caves; and the most famous of the Bandon formations, Face Rock, does indeed resemble a face—a face about the size of an aircraft carrier. Here at the mouth of the Coquille, these formations seem all the more strange and inexplicable since the land does not rise sharply into mountains, as it does at Pistol River and other places along Oregon's South Coast; the river created a broad, level valley, and the land north of the Coquille—Mike's land—lies just below the southern tip of the Oregon Dunes.

Officially, the Oregon Dunes occupy a 56-mile stretch from Heceta Head, near the town of Reedsport, to Cape Arago, about 20 miles north of Bandon. These impressive dunes have been in formation for the last twelve million years. The sand in the dunes comes from sedimentary rock in the coastal mountains; as the rock was moved downstream by rivers, it tumbled and abraded itself into sand. Near the sea, the sand piled up on itself, and the effect of wind, tides, and ocean currents formed it into dunes, which in some places reach two miles inland and rise to heights of five hundred feet. This section of the coast has been designated a National Recreation area, and it is popular with vacationers who like to race across the dunes on their ATVs.

The land that Mike purchased at Bandon had many of the same features as the Oregon Dunes; it had sandy soils, foredunes, hummocks, deflation plains, and European beach grass. But the Oregon Dunes roll inward at sea level, and Mike's property had steep headlands—a significant difference to geologists, but not to a man who was looking for a place to build a golf course. Mike had already built one course on an unlikely piece of dunesland, and now he had taken possession of a larger, grander, and even more remote stretch of dunes.

The place hadn't always been unlucky. Indeed, the Oregon Gold Rush began in 1852 at Whiskey Run Beach, just north of Mike's property. For centuries before that, this part of the Oregon coast had been the domain of the peaceable Indians of the Coos and Coquille tribes. They lived from the bounty of the land, catching salmon and steelhead in the rivers, gathering the abundant shellfish, and harvesting camas—a lily-like plant whose root, ground up, provided the starch in their diet—from prairies that sparkled with blue flowers when the camas was in bloom. On the broad beach at Whiskey Run, members of various branches of both tribes used to gather for an extended summer encampment, a kind of reunion at which men were able to hunt and fish with their friends, and women renewed ties with family members.

This annual congregation ended abruptly when gold was discovered there in 1852, reportedly by Indians who saw glittering flecks in the heavy black sands that had accumulated along the beach. It didn't take long for word to spread, and by the summer of 1853, the "Bostons," as the Indians called the white men, had erected a shanty town named Randolph, complete with restaurants, stores, cabins, boardinghouses, saloons, and brothels. As many as a thousand miners converged on the spot, and, inevitably, there were conflicts with the Indians, culminating in an attack on a camp of Coquilles. Sixteen Indians were killed, twenty more were captured, and the attackers burned their lodges. The U.S. government overseer in the region was outraged when he arrived a few days later to assess the conflict, and he filed a damning report: "I regard the murder of those Indians as one of the most barbarous acts ever perpetrated by civilized men." When the residents of Randolph got wind of the report, this agent had to flee to save his own skin.

The miners were a rough crowd, but the ocean storms were rougher. The region was pounded by severe storms—some accounts of these storms include tsunami-like waves—that washed away the gold-laden black sands, and in 1857 a writer from *Harper's New Monthly Magazine* described the town as a scene of waste and desolation, where the last "disconsolate families" were slowly tearing down the abandoned houses and using the wood as their heating fuel.

Most of the miners drifted off to seek their fortunes elsewhere, but a few settlers did remain at the mouth of the Coquille River, and they established a small community. In 1873, when George Bennett arrived from Ireland, he found farms, stores, a church, and other rudiments of civilization. With degrees from Trinity College, Dublin, Bennett had left his home in the town of Bandon, near Cork, reportedly to escape from an unhappy marriage. His neighbors knew him as Lord Bennett, a title that might well have contained a sly dig at his pomposity. As a justice of the peace, Bennett settled local disputes and officiated at weddings, bringing a high solemnity to the smallest occasions. He was a farmer, a timberman, a writer, and when the moment came to name the town, he prevailed: Like the village he had left in Ireland, this new place was called Bandon.

Bennett did much to advance the progress of the town, but perhaps his greatest gift to this part of the world went unrecognized—was lamented, in fact—for years.

Lord Bennett introduced gorse to Oregon.

The gorse plant (*Ulex europaeus*) is native to the British Isles. In Ireland it is often called "furze," and in Scotland patches of gorse are known as "the whins." Golfers regard the whins, which line many a hole on British courses, as a punishment. Gorse does have some value as winter fuel, and in the springtime, when the deep-green foliage is covered with canary-yellow blossoms, gorse lights up the landscape and emits a sweet, almond-like fragrance. It is deceptively picturesque, for gorse is a thorny, prickly demon of a plant that will tear the clothes right off a man's back.

In Oregon, the gorse flourished. Irish gorse rarely grows much higher than six or seven feet, but here the plants grew to a height of twenty feet, and they were wildly invasive, spreading rapidly in the sandy soils and covering acres of dunes with growth that was literally impenetrable. The good news was that the gorse stabilized the dunes; the bad news, as the citizens of Bandon were to find out in 1936, was that gorse is highly flammable.

Summers are dry in this part of Oregon, and when *Ulex europaeus* dries out, it is little more than tinder. Like some kinds of pine, it contains a pitch that burns with a bright, crackling intensity.

On September 26, 1936, a couple of fires got started near Bandon, one several miles to the east of the town, the other north of town in the Whiskey Run area. Both roared through the gorse, and the fire was so furious that anything combustible quickly added to the blaze. Pines, fir trees, cedar trees, and wooden buildings seemed to explode into flame. Throughout the day, a strong east wind was blowing and the sky was filled with smoke, but many citizens of Bandon went obliviously about their ordinary Saturday routines. With its two pumpers and a chemical truck, the Bandon Volunteer Fire Department was able to extinguish the small brush fires that came close to the town.

The true magnitude of the danger wasn't felt until that evening when the men who'd been unsuccessfully fighting the outlying fires began to straggle into town. They spread the warning that a conflagration was advancing, and soon the night sky was streaked with fantastic bursts of flame. Houses, stores, and churches ignited, one survivor wrote, "like matches being struck." Hundreds of residents, trapped by the walls of flame, crowded down to the dock, where every available boat—the lighthouse tender, Coast Guard boats, even rowboats—ferried people to safety. Hundreds more sought out the ocean beaches, where they waded into the surf or dug themselves into the wet sand to escape scalding heat.

Even so, twenty-one people died in the fire, and the town was almost completely destroyed. The tragedy was reported in newspapers all over the world. For many of the townspeople, and even for those in succeeding generations, the blame for this fire was fixed on the gorse. Thereafter the plant was regarded as a noxious weed to be eliminated, if possible—which it wasn't—or at least to be controlled.

It would be more than fifty years before Mike Keiser came along and found a virtue in the gorse.

MIKE WASN'T THE FIRST one to see the potential for golf in the property he had acquired. The ownership group led by Duke Watson had wanted to build a golf course, and the owners before that, the Gant family, had been visionary in their golf schemes, as well. According to Shorty Dow, who worked for them, "All three Gants were golfers. They had the idea of building seventy-two holes clear down to Bandon, three and a half miles of golf, with a helicopter at each end to carry you back. And Duke would have built a golf course if they hadn't passed the land law on him."

The formidable Oregon land-use law, hailed by environmentalists and hated by developers, was passed in 1975. Shorty Dow was against it; Howard McKee had helped draft it. Mike Keiser was well aware of its strict provisions when he bought the land. "I thought the odds were probably 3-to-1 against getting the permits we needed to build a golf course," he said. "I didn't want to have anything to do with that process. I left it in Howard's hands. I had complete faith in him."

"Blind faith," Howard said, who had gone into overdrive even before the sale of the property was recorded. He had done a thorough review of the efforts, and failures, of the previous owners to obtain permits to develop the property. When the land-use laws were being debated, Howard was living in Portland and had played an active, back-room role, helping to craft language that would satisfy the environmentalists as well as the practical politicians who had to get the laws passed. Now, as he prepared to seek approval for development at Bandon, he had a solid idea of how to proceed.

The first step was to get to know the land. For Howard, this meant hiring consultants and gathering scientific data. Down on the beach, he set up a small weather station, a wee structure that looked like a doghouse with a windmill, but that gathered precise information about rainfall, wind velocity, and wind direction. He also hired the best environmental consultants; the botanical consultant presented him with a vegetation survey containing fourteen "major mapping units" (mixed conifer forest, Sitka spruce wetland, shore pine forest, willow/alder wetlands, gorse-dominated lands, gorse-affected lands, shrub land, emergent freshwater wetlands, emergent estuarine march, stable sand dune, active sand dunes, disturbed areas, and domestic grassland). The consultant also raised a red flag: He identified a plant, the silver phacelia, that was potentially endangered. (Shorty: "Silver phacelia? Sounds like a venereal disease. If I'd known how much trouble it was going to be, I would've gone out and dug the stuff up.")

Shorty and Howard were not natural allies, but after their initial stand-off, they warmed to each other. Having been caretaker of the property since 1964, Shorty had his own knowledge of the place, and had even typed out his own inventory of plants and animals. Less systematic than those of the consultants, Shorty's list included "bear grass, numerous kinds of fern, roses (small), old apple trees, pear trees, new apple trees, old plum trees, manzanita, thimbleberry, wild currant, scotch broom, gorse, Indian paint brush, lupine, wild iris, lots of wild flowers (unknown), 1 lilac, 1 flowering quince, 1 monkey puzzle," and several other species, as well as various animals, notably, "1 bear (seen), still there." Shorty, whose father was a trapper, took a keen interest in all the wildlife that flourished on the property. When Howard and Shorty were out walking the property, Shorty always led the way, and he liked to dart into the brush if Howard lagged behind. "Howard was brilliant," Shorty said, "but he was from the city. All I had to do to lose him was step off the trail and he'd start calling, 'Shorty? Shorty? Where'd you go?' Mike would say he knew we'd get the permits because I had the horse sense and Howard had the other brains."

Howard definitely had his own way of looking at this property, and that way went well beyond an inventory of natural resources. The more he saw of it, the more he was intrigued by its complexity. This particular piece of earth didn't reveal itself at once; it had a multidimensional, mysterious character, encompassing everything from the booming grandeur of the Pacific Ocean to the hidden, intimate serenity of Round Lake. Before drawing up any fixed plans, or even preliminary plans, Howard wanted to get to the essence of the property, its spirit. He wanted to grasp what a poet might have called the "genius" of the place. "I wanted more than a mechanistic understanding. I would have liked to live on the land for a while the way the Indians did, to experience it in different seasons and different weathers. They believed, and I do, too, that the way you get to know a place is to listen to it, to try to hear what it has to tell you. That doesn't happen in a day."

Though he didn't camp on the property, Howard gradually came to a couple of decisions that became enshrined as first principles in the planning process. One was that the natural complexity would be preserved. No matter what improvements were made, no matter where the golf courses were located or what buildings would eventually be needed, Howard was determined to preserve for future visitors the same sense of adventure and discovery that he was experiencing.

The second principle was that a "village" would grow up around the lakes.

Give Howard a map, and he will patiently explain—with his long-fingered hands fluttering and hovering over the contour lines—how the topography dictates a natural location for a village. About half a mile inland, a steep ridge, Back Ridge, runs roughly parallel to the ocean, and it rises sharply about 150 feet above the rest of the land. "Back Ridge is the spine of this property. It's like a small mountain range, dividing the forest from the meadow. On the ocean side, you're in an open environment of grasses and dunes. On the inland side, you're in a rain forest. You can see that there's a low place where the ridge disappears and the lakes occur. They form a natural gathering place, almost a crossroads. The environment is benign here, not harsh. There's an abundance of fresh water, and there's plenty of nearby shelter in case a storm rolls in. We know the Indians used this place, and I wanted this area to be our center, too—our village, if you will."

The concept of a village, a central place for people to come together, is familiar to land planners. In most societies and cultures, human beings gravitate toward a center and take care to preserve it from encroachment. Howard's vision of Bandon began with the conviction that an essential human need—at least as important as golf!—was a place for people to gather in safety, harmony, and companionship.

MIKE'S GOAL AT BANDON was to provide "dream golf," and he and Howard didn't always see eye to eye. Sometimes, when Howard spoke of a village, Mike would say that all he wanted was a golf course and a simple clubhouse—and a double-wide trailer would do just fine. He was joking about the double-wide trailer, but he was completely serious about preserving the simplicity and wildness of the land, and he could trace his ideas about nature—and about golf—to William Wordsworth, one of the English Romantic poets he had studied at Amherst.

Mike doesn't often quote poetry, but when asked to contribute an essay to a book entitled *Golf Architecture: A Worldwide Perspective,* he began by quoting several famous lines from Wordsworth's "Tintern Abbey." He then made his own claim for the particular beauty of a golf course:

Let us be serious about the poetry of a well-wrought golf course. Like a heart-stopping Wordsworth poem, it will be with us for all time, and his verse inspires us to look through his eyes at golf courses when the beauty of nature is crafted by human intervention. A great golf course is "nature perfected." It is neither wholly natural nor can it be wholly unnatural or manufactured. . . . A walk in the vast and barren sand hills of Nebraska is not nearly as compelling as a round of golf at Sand Hills Golf Club, and that conclusion will likely be shared by a non-golfer as well. As visually appealing as the purely natural can be, the sublime splendour of a carefully wrought string of fairways at daybreak is even more visually compelling.

With those words, Mike wasn't just venturing into aesthetics but into theology. He was writing about golf courses as holy places, as indeed they are for many, perhaps most, golfers. Religious images are a part of the language of golf, and no one blinks when Augusta National is described as "the cathedral in the pines," or Cypress Point is called the "Sistine Chapel" of golf. Popular destinations are "meccas," and golfers flock to them in the spirit of pilgrims to a shrine.

Such images are familiar, and they capture a truth about golf that is otherwise impossible to express. There is something about the game that does stir the soul, even the soul of a hacker—and most golfers, as Mike often points out, are hackers. A golfer can botch shot after shot, he can hit skanks and slices all day long, and he still can't wait to get out on the course the next day. Why? Because the joys of the game do not depend upon mastering physical skills. They depend upon—well, upon a sense of the sublime, a sense of something far grander than the simple matter of advancing a small ball across the countryside.

Which is the whole reason for Mike's extended quotation from Wordsworth. The poet was a Deist who sensed in natural beauty the handiwork of the Almighty. When Wordsworth wrote "Tintern Abbey," he was giving voice to the feelings that are so intrinsic to a golfer's experience but so difficult to articulate:

... And I have felt
A presence that disturbs me with the joy
Of elevated thoughts; a sense sublime
Of something far more deeply interfused,
Whose dwelling is the light of setting suns,
And the round ocean and the living air,
And the blue sky, and in the mind of man ...

So spake Wordsworth. The Mike Keiser corollary was that the dwelling of the Almighty could also be found—sometimes even more vividly and powerfully—in a golf course.

At Bandon, Mike had a landscape that provided everything that the poet had named. The light of setting suns, the round ocean, the living air, the blue sky—it was all there.

Now he had to build a golf course that measured up to the majestic setting.

8 | The Best-Laid Plans

If you think people are coming here to play golf,
you're out of your fucking mind.

—STEVE LESNIK TO MIKE KEISER, MARCH 1992

MIKE WAS FLYING OUT to Oregon more and more often, sometimes with groups of friends to whom he wanted to show the property, his "retail golfers"—and sometimes with his associates in the golf business. Pete Sinnott had become a regular companion, and Dick Nugent also came out for a look. Mike wanted Nugent's impressions of both the Bandon site and the Cascade Ranch, but he quietly determined that he wasn't going to offer Nugent the job of designing a course at Bandon. Dick Nugent was getting on in years, and Mike's instinct was to look for a younger man, someone who could bring a bold, fresh vision to the project.

Before choosing an architect, though, he decided to seek the general advice of Steve Lesnik, the CEO of Kemper Sports Management. The two men had already become business partners and occasional dinner companions after being introduced by Allan Reich, a lawyer who'd done work for both KSM and Recycled Paper Greetings. It was obvious that they had a lot in common. Beyond golf, they were both stimulated by discussion of economics and public affairs. Yet they didn't hit it off at all at their first meeting. Steve saw Mike as a man who'd achieved business success in another sphere and viewed golf through the lens of a hobbyist, and Mike felt that Steve probably saw him as an "easy pocket." And while Mike was an astute, appreciative student of golf course design, Steve was indifferent to design unless it enhanced the bottom line. (In a meeting about one of KSM's properties, Steve listened to a glowing account of a young architect's design talent and said flatly, "For all I know, this guy may be the Michelangelo of golf course design. Good for him. But I've never heard of him, and we're not going to use him.")

In short, Steve Lesnik embodied the corporate approach to golf, and he had built KSM into a national company with a thick portfolio of courses that were owned, managed, and leased. KSM had a particularly high profile in the Chicago area; the company headquarters was in Northbrook, Illinois, and KSM's flagship course, Kemper Lakes, was located in Long Grove, Illinois. Kemper Lakes was nationally ranked, and in 1989 it had become the first public course ever selected to host the PGA Championship.

By the early 1990s, when Mike was just emerging as a figure on the golf scene, Steve Lesnik was an acknowledged leader in the golf industry. Mike began to see that Steve, with his unwavering focus on the business and marketing of golf, was driven to make a superior product, and Steve began to realize that Mike wasn't just a dilettante who'd gotten lucky at Dunes Club but a man who was serious about making his mark in golf—serious enough to invest in several KSM properties, sometimes without even going to visit them. "Investing in golf was more interesting than putting money in bonds," Mike felt, but he also wanted a chance to learn firsthand how golf courses performed as businesses. By 1991, the two men had overcome their mutual wariness, and they had established a habit of dining together several times a year, usually at the Four Seasons in downtown Chicago. Mike knew that he could rely on Steve for blunt advice, and in March 1992 he flew Steve out to Oregon to get his opinion of the potential of the properties he had acquired—Cascade Ranch, Pistol River, and Bandon.

The wind was howling on the day they visited Pistol River. At Crook's Point, the exposed and rocky peninsula that Mike had been coveting, the surf churned furiously around the huge formations of black rock. When Steve opened the door of the car, the wind nearly twisted it off its hinges, and Steve had to yell to make himself understood over the roar of the weather. "If you think people are coming here to play golf," he screamed, "you're out of your fucking mind."

THAT WAS THE FIRST time that anyone had suggested that Mike was delusional about bringing golf to the Oregon coast, but it certainly wasn't the last. Steve had carved out for himself a role as one of Mike's closest advisers, a sort of personal bad cop, the one who wouldn't mince words or kowtow, the one who wasn't going to paint a rosy picture when all he could see was booming surf and black rocks. This role was completely in keeping with the reputation that he had established as a tough, prickly, no-nonsense CEO who ran a top-down organization and liked—in fact, insisted on—having the last word. He was a no-holds-barred competitor. Even his son, Josh, now an officer of KSM, says, "My dad could have been a lawyer—I would have hired him. He's the kind of guy you want as a lawyer, because you are *not* going to beat him. He's just not going to let it happen."

In the golf industry, Steve Lesnik was an outrider, a guy who didn't swing a golf club until he was in his thirties and didn't have any sentimental feelings about the game to clog or clutter his business perspective. His path to golf was both circuitous and fortuitous; he was very much a product of the urban East Coast. He grew up in Connecticut, went to college at Brown, and took his first job as a cub reporter for the *Stamford Advocate,* where he covered local news and politics—everything but sports. His salary was $85 a week. He was soon married and in search of a job that paid better. He landed at the Insurance Information Institute, where one of his duties was to handle public relations, and he soon transferred—cautiously—to Chicago, though he held on to the house in Connecticut. Neither he nor his wife, Mady—short for Madeleine—had ever been west of the Hudson River, and they both felt entirely at home in the Jewish milieu of the New York metropolitan area. Before long, Steve was a candidate for a job at Kemper Insurance, which was about to start its own in-house PR operation, and Steve was interviewed by the head of the company, Jim Kemper.

Steve Lesnik was twenty-eight years old, and Mr. Kemper was pushing sixty, but the two men bonded instantly. From that moment forward, Steve Lesnik's career—his life—was shaped by his close association with Mr. Kemper, an innovative businessman, a leading spokesman for the insurance industry, and a passionate golfer. Kemper was one of the first insurance companies to become "consumer oriented" (the emphasis on consumer protection and consumer rights was just beginning to be articulated in the late 1960s and early 1970s), and Steve became Mr. Kemper's executive assistant, a job that carried considerable heft within the company. He had plenty of successes, including a major role in developing the ad campaign, the Kemper Charge, that made the company instantly recognizable; he also incurred the resentment of other, older executives. He was clearly the boss's favorite, and he and Mr. Kemper were all but inseparable.

The corporate golf course—think Firestone, or U.S. Steel, or IBM—has long had a place in the American game, and Mr. Kemper decided to build Kemper Lakes near his corporate headquarters on the outskirts of Chicago. He hired Dick Nugent and Ken Killian to design the course, and they gave him what he asked for—a course that could host a major championship. Kemper Lakes attracted the accolades that Jim Kemper had hoped for, but like almost every other corporate course, it turned out to be a financial albatross. It was treated, says Steve Lesnik, as a "company toy," a perk for employees, not as a business venture in its own right. When Mr. Kemper looked at the balance sheets for his golf course and saw how much money it was costing him, he invited his young protégé to step into this entrepreneurial niche. Was there a way to change the golf course from an economic liability to an asset?

Steve accepted the challenge, and he made a couple of significant decisions. First, he decided that the golf course would be separated out from the other company business so that the perception of it would change. It would no longer be a company toy. Second, he decided to operate it so that it would make a statement about Kemper; he wanted it to be nothing less than the best public course in the Midwest. He gave instructions that the place was to be perfectly groomed, that service was to be tip-top, that everyone on the staff was to be dressed in spiffy outfits. Last but not least, he decreed that Kemper Lakes would charge more than anyone else. If it was going to be the best, it was going to have a price tag to match.

The strategy worked. Kemper Lakes might not have been the nation's first "upscale daily fee course"—Joe Jemsek's course at Cog Hill could lay claim to that title—but the golf course turned a profit every year and made its way onto the Top 100 lists. Long before that 1989 PGA Championship, the success of the course had spawned Kemper Sports Management.

Golf course owners and operators, aware of the success of Kemper Lakes, had started to call Steve Lesnik for advice. In 1979, when Mr. Kemper stepped down as CEO of the insurance company, Steve also resigned. He started his own PR firm, and he agreed to run Kemper Sports Management for a year—a year that turned into five, then ten, then twenty. Golf, it seemed, was a growth industry, and in 1983 Mr. Kemper, sixty-eight years old at the time, decided that he wanted to make something more of KSM. With Jim Kemper as the power behind the throne, and Steve Lesnik as the CEO, KSM went into a growth mode, gradually extending its reach and eventually becoming a full-scale golf course management company with its fingers in many different pies, from municipal courses to daily fees to high-end private clubs. With the clout to develop its own courses and an annual PGA Tour event in the Washington, D.C., area on its resume, KSM was a force to be reckoned with. The name of Steve Lesnik began to appear regularly on the annual lists of Most Powerful Men in Golf.

WHEN HE RETURNED from his Oregon visit in 1992, Steve Lesnik and the staff at KSM put together an evaluation of the three sites: Pistol River, Cascade Ranch, and Bandon Dunes. The twenty-page booklet, simply printed and bound, was customized for a single reader: Mike. The title was "Keiser Oregon Golf Initiatives" and the mission was to "develop outstanding golf properties on Keiser owned land in Southern Oregon by the year 2000 that provide an ROI [return on investment] at least equal to prime rate based on allocated net cost of land, holding costs and investment in golf assets." The booklet included a few charts and bar graphs, but the style was clear, clean, and uncluttered. KSM laid out concepts and strategies in the bulleted, shorthand fashion that Mike preferred, with no punches pulled.

About Pistol River, KSM had nothing good to say. "Owned property too rugged for golf course . . . Promontory inhospitable to golf . . . Weather negative."

Prospects for the Cascade Ranch were much more favorable, and KSM summed up initial impressions in glowing terms: "Views spectacular . . . Vastness a plus . . . Natural setting and beauty . . . A+ layout preserves ranch aesthetic . . . Provides marketing hook . . . In the immediate competitive area, only three public courses exist." More than half of the twenty-page report was devoted to the Cascade Ranch, with voluminous information, relatively speaking, about the rates of tourism and demographic trends of the area. The primary recommendations for the Cascade Ranch included a "go-for-it" option: "Build an outstanding course at Cascade Ranch . . . Initiate mini-Pinehurst of the Northwest."

As for the Bandon property, KSM was far more pessimistic. In the review of "key facts, suppositions, and premises," KSM made the following observations:

- No permanent base of golfers.
- Insufficient destination tourism to provide enough golfers.
- Without huge, successful marketing effort, neither likely to increase sufficiently.
- Dunes property would make spectacular courses which would draw play.
- Course in woods probably would not constitute "draw."
- Perception of weather a negative.
- Huge population base but at driving distance of eight to ten hours.
- No air facility to expedite tourist travel by air.
- Area not well known nationally.
- Re golf, Bandon is "start from scratch" situation.

The fundamental question, in the view of KSM, was whether or not it was possible to create a "tourist/golfer destination with appropriate lodging." This destination could take several forms, as spelled out in the next questions:

QUESTION 3: Can we create next Pebble Beach?

High end	celebrity/select draw	lodging
Caliber of courses	tournaments	use of dunes
Proximity to ocean	wetlands	transportation/air

QUESTION 4: Can we create Pinehurst of the West?

| White collar/corporate | multiple courses | draw course |
| Tourist lodging | residential housing | transportation/auto |

QUESTION 5: Can we create Myrtle Beach of the West?

Blue collar	Canadian large draw
Beach	arcades
Miniature golf	chain lodging
Second homes	marketing arm

And when it came to conclusions about Bandon, KSM recommended:

- Retain planner to design master plan for Bandon.
- Plan for multiple courses eventually, but initiate one on agreed dunes site.
- Create initial tourist accommodations.
- Build roads to site.
- Use "name" architect.
- Market/promote well in advance.
- Identify target golfer:

  | Blue/white collar | No. California |
  | RV user | Retirees |

- Create new golf destination—"Myrtle Beach of Northwest."

MYRTLE BEACH IS THE South Carolina resort area with a vast conglomeration of golf courses and motels, a place where everything is a bargain; today, the very idea that Bandon could have turned into such a place seems as laughable as the idea that Tiffany's could just as easily have become Wal-Mart. In 1992, however, KSM's recommendations seemed perfectly logical.

Their vision of Bandon was based on discernible fact: Many of the tourists on Oregon's South Coast *did* come from northern California, and they *were* RV users and/or retirees. This part of the world just wasn't a draw for affluent travelers, and no one could dispute KSM's premise that "Re golf, Bandon is a 'start from scratch' situation."

Mike Keiser tucked the booklet away in his file cabinet. He wasn't interested in becoming the Grand Pooh-Bah of a second Myrtle Beach.

MIKE WAS JUST GETTING to know someone else who was starting a golf course from scratch, a gruff, frugal, outspoken, and revolutionary golf developer, Dick Youngscap. In the Nebraska sandhills, an area at least as remote as Bandon, Youngscap was trying to put together the money and the design team to build a golf course. Trained as a building architect, he had made his reputation in golf with the Firethorn Golf Club in Lincoln, Nebraska, a much-lauded Pete Dye design that opened in 1985. Firethorn was a "links-style" course, and the experience of building it set in motion the quixotic dream of building an "authentic" links in the heartland of America—specifically, in the sandhills of Nebraska.

I put quotation marks around "authentic" because, for golf purists, one of the first qualifications of a links course is that it must be seaside. The other two indispensable conditions for a links course, as set down by golf writer Jim Finegan, are that it must be sea level and sand based. The sandhills site acquired by Dick Youngscap was not at sea level, and it was a thousand miles from the sea, but it was definitely sand based, and it just *looked* like classic linksland. There were big "blow-outs" everywhere, places where the wind had eaten away at the naturally growing grasses, exposing large, irregular patches of sand—bunkers! And the land rolled and rippled in all directions, with just the right kind of topographical variation for golf. Here on this treeless, windswept site in the middle of the Great Plains, Dick Youngscap could practically see the golf course he wanted, and he hired the architectural team of Bill Coore and Ben Crenshaw to design the course.

The contract negotiations between Youngscap, who has a personality as strong as horseradish, and the famously polite duo of Coore and Crenshaw, were a bit of a mismatch. Ben has earned the moniker Gentle Ben, and Bill could easily be called Courtly Coore; they are men of many talents, and they are unfailingly gracious, but they are not hard-nosed businessmen. Dick Youngscap told them how much he admired their work, but he was having trouble raising the money for a remote course on the Great Plains, and, well, their fee was just too steep at $400,000. Ben said he loved the site and wanted to do the project and he was willing to forego his half of the fee. That was generous, said Youngscap, but he was just going to have to find a few more investors before he could offer them a contract—at which point Ben decided to become an investor.

So Dick Youngscap had his architects, but he kept looking for investors. Through Ron Whitten, he'd heard about Mike Keiser; Whitten had recognized that Dick and Mike were cut from the same cloth. Youngscap hadn't actually met Mike, but he sent him the prospectus for Sand Hills, inviting him to invest as a founding member. "I sent the paperwork off, and I expected to hear back from Mike. I thought he'd have a few questions, but he never called. He just sent the check. He became a founding member without ever talking to me."

During the construction of Sand Hills, Mike did fly to Nebraska to check out the construction, and he and Dick Youngscap bonded as fellow mavericks. "I got the impression," Dick says, "that Mike was drawing his own conclusions from what was going on. He was thinking that if Sand Hills, located where it was, could be successful, then anything could be successful. He had already bought Bandon, and the way we approached our projects was somewhat similar. Our idea was to find good ground and build a good golf course and bring people to it. What we were doing wasn't unique. It was just that people hadn't done it this way for eighty years. Go back to Pine Valley or the National and you go back to a time when the golf course got its character from the site. Then golf became market driven, and people started building courses in places that were completely inhospitable, like Arizona. In the whole state of Arizona, there's not one natural site for a golf course, but there's plenty of sun, and a big population of retirees, and good year-round weather—in other words, there's a market, so there are hundreds of golf courses. Mike and I turned that around. We said, OK, we don't have markets, but we have great ground."

Dick Youngscap took a huge risk at Sand Hills; he'd done something that no one else had dared to do, and the golf course was instantly praised as one of the treasures of the game. The remote location hadn't prevented the opinion makers in golf from finding their way to milepost 55 on Highway 97. Sand Hills is now ranked No. 1 on all the lists of modern courses. Dick Youngscap had been warned that he was embarking on a folly, but he had put everything on the line to build the golf course he wanted to build, not the golf course that everyone else thought would succeed. For Mike, the lesson was crystal clear: If you wanted to create something exceptional, something extraordinary, you had to be fearless. You had to be prepared to follow your dream.

Still another benefit of being involved with Sand Hills was an introduction to the work of Coore and Crenshaw, with their take-what-the-land-gives-you design philosophy. Mike loved the course—and it didn't hurt that on a glorious, sunstruck day, in a special preopening round with the architects and other founders, he shot one of the best rounds of his life, a 73. If Bill and Ben hadn't just done Sand Hills, Mike would have tried to sign them up to design the course at Bandon—but he didn't want to seem to be copying what Dick Youngscap had just done. He would have to wait ten years before he was able to act on the wish to have a Coore-Crenshaw track in Oregon.

And the final lesson: A golf course doesn't have to cost a fortune. Youngscap was able to get Sand Hills built for a fraction of what other developers were spending. He was the kind of developer who just didn't believe in throwing money around, and at a time when the average cost of golf course construction was about $5 million, the price tag for construction at Sand Hills was only $1 million.

MIKE DID NOT ASPIRE to create a second Myrtle Beach, and while he would have been happy to build a golf course as good as Sand Hills, he didn't want to build a private club. Youngscap felt that he had no choice but to operate Sand Hills as a private club; he couldn't imagine how he'd ever draw enough public golfers to make Sand Hills viable. But Mike wanted his Oregon course to be public, and he asked himself this question: How could he get golfers to pay attention to a place as remote as Bandon?

Answer: Run a contest.

Golf Digest's Armchair Architect contest had been such a popular feature that Ron Whitten had devised a second, more elaborate contest in which participants were asked to design three golf holes. Thanks to the Dunes Club, Mike had gotten to know Whitten, and he felt comfortable enough to make a proposal. What about another Armchair Architect contest? Ron had done a 1-hole contest, and a 3-hole contest, but this one would be the ultimate, the supreme, the Mother Goose of all Armchair Architect contests—an 18-holer.

And it wouldn't be just an academic exercise, either. Mike would turn the site over to amateur architects, each of whom would design one hole. And then Mike would build the holes.

"I told him he was nuts," Ron says. "I told him that amateur architects could only ruin it. He had a special place at Bandon, and he needed a special architect."

Ron had spent several days walking the site, accompanied by Shorty Dow ("Never saw a man walk as much as he did," Shorty remembers), and he'd been awed by the site, especially by the shape and scale of the dunes. Known for his encyclopedic knowledge of the history of golf course design, Whitten relished the opportunity to get out into the field and look at raw land. Though educated as a lawyer—he was assistant district attorney and later assistant city attorney in charge of prosecution in his hometown of Topeka, Kansas—his lifelong passion had always been golf course design, and, after becoming a contributing editor on architecture for *Golf Digest* in 1985, he had become one of the most influential critics in American golf. When he dared, as he often did, to write a derogatory word, club members grieved for their course as if a family member had fallen ill. Whitten knew that he had to be bluntly honest in order to be trusted as a golf course critic, and to distinguish his columns from the endless stream of hype and puffery that usually passes for architectural criticism. Most writing about golf course design, he has often said testily, is pure crap. His own opinions were based on an unassailable breadth of knowledge, for he had compiled, with architect Geoffrey Cornish, the most comprehensive reference book on the subject, *The Architects of Golf*. He was in charge of all of *Golf Digest*'s features relating to architecture, including the annual survey of "Best New Courses" and, of course, the ranking of "America's 100 Greatest Golf Courses."

Mike doesn't give up easily on his ideas. Though Whitten had emphatically rejected his suggestion for an 18-hole contest, he came back at him with another proposal: What if Whitten not only supervised the contest itself, arranging the conditions and selecting the winners, but also stayed on as a kind of facilitator for the whole project, making sure that the amateur designs weren't in conflict with one another? In other words, he would be more than the editor and administrator; he would be responsible for making sure that the contest produced a single, unified, coherent design.

Not a chance, said Whitten.

Mike still wouldn't take no for an answer. His third proposal was the most tempting and flattering of all: Would Whitten consider designing the course himself?

This offer didn't come with a contract attached; that wasn't Mike's style. It was more an invitation to begin discussion about the design process, and Whitten, the critic, had to let it simmer. He was a writer and scholar, not an architect, but he had fantasized about someday getting into the arena and getting his hands dirty, designing a course of his own. Now he was being offered a chance to do exactly that, on a site that he had immediately recognized as holding the potential for a spectacular golf course. This was a rare opportunity, and Whitten knew it. But he had just taken on new responsibilities as a writer, and he'd just remarried. He lived in Kansas and he had children to look after. He couldn't know how long the permitting process would take or how often he'd have to be in Oregon if he accepted the job.

And so, reluctantly, he turned it down. "If I'd known it was going to take them five years to get the permits, I would have taken it," he says now. "By the time they were ready to get started, in 1997, I could have gone out there and designed the course. Mike obviously wanted an amateur architect to build that golf course, and that's basically what he got in David Kidd."

9 | Meet the Family

My dad and Mike had a mutual admiration society.
Sometimes I thought that Mike expected my dad to design
the golf course, not me. —DAVID KIDD

MIKE KEISER IS A CLEAR, logical, and orderly thinker who often responds to questions by enumerating the major elements of his answer. The first time I asked him why he hired David McLay Kidd to build Bandon Dunes, he replied, "I hired him for three reasons. One, he was Scottish, and I thought he must know something about links golf. Two, he was young and he'd listen to me. Three, I could fire him anytime I wanted."

That answer is pure Mike, for it is both romantically optimistic ("he was Scottish and must know something about links golf") and utterly pragmatic ("I could fire him anytime I wanted"). It is also pure Mike in the sense that it was the short, succinct version of a decision that was reached only after several months, many journeys, long deliberation, and a sequence of highly improbable and serendipitous events.

After being turned down by Ron Whitten, after crossing Dick Nugent off his list, after deciding that he wouldn't use the team of Coore-Crenshaw while they were working for Dick Youngscap, Mike really didn't have many places to turn. With Pete Sinnott, and without any fanfare, he did make several trips to look at contemporary courses that were described as "links-like," but he didn't see anything that impressed him. He'd already decided against using any of the leading American architects; he didn't think any of them could build an authentic links course, and, as he said bluntly, "They don't listen to people like me. They want to do their thing, and I wanted to be involved."

There was one young golf course architect, Tom Doak, whose name kept popping up. Dick Youngscap had recommended him, as had Mike's friend, Bill Shean, the man whom Mike sometimes describes as "Mr. Chicago Golf." Shean had won many titles, including the U.S. Senior Amateur and the British Senior Amateur, and he happened to be in Mike's foursome on that banner day at Sand Hills. He was also a longtime admirer of Tom Doak, and he put Tom and Mike in touch; Tom made a visit to the Bandon site and wrote a long letter to Mike, laying out the reasons why he should be considered for the commission. Mike admired the "scandalous honesty" of Doak's golf course reviews, and he was completely sympathetic to Tom's approach to golf course architecture, but he was hesitant. The Bandon site was remote, and Mike—as his proposals to Whitten had made clear—was interested in having the course designed in a way that would attract favorable, widespread attention. "I wanted America to buy into the story of how it got built," he said, and Tom Doak was simply "too controversial."

Then, in February 1994, on a clubhouse terrace in Palm Beach, Florida, Mike described Bandon to Rick Summers, an entrepreneur who had friends and business associates throughout the golf world, one of whom was Jack Nicklaus. As it happened, Rick was in Florida for a gathering hosted by the Golden Bear, and Mike was his guest. "At first I thought, OK, here's another guy who wants his own golf course, and I asked Mike how much land he had," Summers recalls. "He said, 'twelve hundred acres.' So I knew he was serious. He didn't have zoning yet, but he didn't seem too worried about that. He was talking about creating farmland if he couldn't build golf holes, and putting sheep out to keep the grass down, and getting his course built that way. I already knew that Mike was somebody who thought outside the box, but when he told me the property was five hours from Portland, I said, 'Mike, are you crazy?' He wanted to talk about the dunes and the gorse and the ocean, and I could see that he was going to do this. He was prepared to take a risk. I told him that if he wanted to talk to Jack about building the course, I could team him up. But Mike wasn't interested. He'd been to Scotland and Ireland and he was looking for somebody who could build a real links course. So I thought of Jimmy Kidd, David's father. Jimmy was at Gleneagles, and I was working with Gleneagles Golf Developments, and I made the introduction."

Mike was obviously intrigued by the prospect of working with a Scottish firm, and Rick Summers bowed out as soon as he set the wheels in motion. Like Steve Lesnik, Rick had made the conventional recommendation: On a site as remote as Bandon, the obvious strategy was to bring in a big name to build the course, and there was no bigger name than Jack Nicklaus.

Mike, however, was far more interested in meeting the Kidds.

First, though, he would meet with Ian Ferrier, the head of the Gleneagles Golf Developmentss (GGD). The company had been launched with the grand vision of creating several properties around the world that would be modeled after Gleneagles, the luxurious resort in the Scottish Highlands. The timing could hardly have been worse; the early 1990s saw a worldwide recession, and in 1994 GGD was a fledgling company, still looking to build its first golf course. When he flew from Scotland to meet with Mike, Ian Ferrier could offer only verbal assurances that the company had the know-how to design and build a links course.

From Chicago, Ian made the trip to Oregon. He flew to Portland and then took the puddle jumper to the little airport in Coos Bay, where he was met by "a figure straight out of the Wild West"—Shorty Dow. Shorty packed him into his truck, drove him to Bandon, and walked him till he was ready to drop. "I'd been to some rough and exotic sites around the world," Ian says, "but I'd never visited one that was harder to get around than Bandon. The gorse would tear the trousers right off you. At the end of the second day, Shorty strapped his pistol on and asked me if I wanted to go bear hunting with him, and I declined. I said, 'Shorty, bear hunting is not part of the remit.'"

Still, as forbidding as the gorse was, Ian Ferrier recognized the potential of the site, and he wanted it for Gleneagles. He made arrangements for two of the principals of GGD, the father-son team of Jimmy and David Kidd, to visit Oregon.

JIMMY KIDD WAS a force in British golf. Tall, white-haired, blue-eyed, ruddy-cheeked, and high-spirited, he had one of the plum jobs in Scotland, a job with a lofty title: Director of Agronomy at Gleneagles. He was in charge of maintaining all three of the Gleneagles golf courses—the King's Course, the Queen's Course, and the PGA Centenary Course (originally known as the Monarch's Course, and often called the Nicklaus course, for it is a Nicklaus design). Gregarious and hugely likable, Jimmy was a founder of the Scottish and International Golf Greenkeepers Association, he was in demand as a public speaker, and he was widely recognized as an expert in turf management. At Gleneagles, which hosted the Scottish Open for several years—and the Scottish Open was second only to the British in terms of prestige and popularity—Jimmy had proven his ability to bring a course up to the most exacting championship standards. Indeed, Jimmy was responsible for restoring the King's Course, a task he had approached as meticulously as an archivist, using old drawings and photographs to bring back the original luster of the quirky James Braid design. From his neat-as-a-pin office just off the first tee of the King's Course, Jimmy Kidd supervised a workforce of nearly a hundred, and he never forgot that his own career had begun with a shovel and rake. He'd been raised on a farm, one of seven children, and he was the first to own a car. To have risen to a place of prominence, to have charge of the grounds of one of Scotland's most celebrated properties, was to have succeeded in life, and Jimmy savored his success—and he didn't let it go to his head. He had the unusual combination of charisma and a common touch. He drove fast cars and liked to wear stylish clothes, but he was also a man who'd give you the shirt off his back. More than once, when I asked people to describe Jimmy, I heard that old-fashioned phrase, "He's just a prince."

David was a Kidd off the old block. He had his father's presence, wit, and gusto, though at age twenty-seven—the age at which he first looked at the Bandon property—he lacked his father's social grace. He could be a bit "stroppy," as he says. (Cocky is the more familiar American word.) Not that he'd been pampered as a youngster; he, too, had cut his teeth around golf courses, and if there was one skill he had mastered by sheer dint of putting in long hours, it was the art of raking a bunker. He had worked summers on the crew at Gleneagles, and there was never really any doubt in his mind that he'd follow his father into a career in golf—though he hadn't been all that keen on playing golf as a youngster. The Kidds owned a caravan at Machrihanish, the town in the far west of Scotland with a legendary course laid out by Old Tom Morris, and David spent many a long summer day on that course carrying a fishing rod instead of a bag of clubs. There are trout in the burn that crosses the second fairway, and young David was more interested in catching them than he was in hitting balls over them. For him, growing up in a household where the whole atmosphere was suffused with golf, the actual playing of the game must have seemed like a case of coals-to-Newcastle. Nevertheless, when the time came for him to choose a career path, he attended Writtle College in Essex, a college devoted to the study of "land sciences" and surrounded by a farm, estate, and gardens that served as an open-air laboratory. Though Writtle didn't offer courses in golf course design (David has since returned to Writtle to lecture on the subject), it did offer a full array of courses in landscape design, land planning, and the other subjects that tie directly into golf course architecture. While still a student at Writtle, David took an internship with Southern Golf, an international golf construction and contracting firm, and he was assigned to a project that was nominally under the control of someone he describes only as a "jet-set architect."

For David, that term amounts to an oxymoron, for he had inherited not only an irresistible fascination with golf but a set of attitudes that came straight from his father. Superintendents, and the members of their crews, are the unsung and usually unseen stalwarts of golf, the ones who get their hands dirty, the ones who do all the nasty jobs, who get up before daybreak to make sure that the course is pristine, and the ones on whose efforts the whole structure of the game depends. To the superintendent, golf is about turf, drainage, fertilizers, seeds, fungicides, pesticides, herbicides, machines, pipes, pumps, hoses, shovels, saws, mowers, and assorted other machines. From the superintendent's point of view, the golfer who complains about divots on a teeing ground is like the spoiled princess who complains about the pea under her mattress, and a jet-set architect is, likewise, a spoiled, pampered creature who hasn't a clue about the way that golf courses actually get built, about the sheer amount of grunt work that goes into every single detail. The jet-set architect is even worse than the princess, since he, of all people, should understand what it takes to create a good golf course.

David's boss would fly in every four weeks or so to see how the project was going. In fact, it was going just as one might expect—the people on the ground kept coming upon situations that didn't work, making decisions of their own, changing the plans, and pressing ahead. "We'd find property lines drawn in the wrong place, or slopes too steep to be playable, or mounds that blocked the sight lines—little stuff, and we'd go ahead and fix it ourselves. The boss would show up weeks later and never notice. He'd say, 'Yes, great, this is exactly what I had in mind, exactly.'"

David had confirmation that golf begins in the dirt, not that he really needed confirmation. Living down in England, he was married to his college sweetheart, Lyn, and he was beginning to develop a taste for the good life, for fast cars and fine wines, but he was also a natural dirtball, a guy who liked to wear jeans and muddy boots and go screaming around a work site in a stinky, noisy four-wheeler. When he graduated from Writtle and left Southern Golf, he went to work, briefly, as an associate in a regional golf course design firm, and in 1991, at the age of twenty-four, he assumed the title of director of design for Gleneagles Golf Developments. His father, obviously, had something to do with the appointment; Jimmy was in charge of agronomy for GGD, and in the company's organizational scheme, Jimmy and David were coequal, both under the supervision of Ian Ferrier. David continued to live in England, and he traveled around the globe, looking at properties for potential development as golf course sites. He designed plenty of master plans that never came into being and golf holes that didn't get built. One lesson that was seared into him is that most golf course projects never get off the drawing boards. "They're just smoke and mirrors until you're actually moving ground," he says.

Another was that despite his upbringing, he had a lot to learn about golf courses. "I was raised around golf. The family friends were the superintendents at Turnberry and St. Andrews and Wentworth, but those years at GGD were an education. They were my postgraduate work. Every time I went to look at a site, I went to look at all the golf courses round about, and between that and the design work I was doing, my learning curve was pushed near vertical. Frankly, I was underemployed, but I was designing and reading—I have the same books in my library as Tom Doak. I've often thought that if I'd been given the chance to do Bandon a year earlier, I simply wouldn't have been ready. At the time it came, though, I was prepared."

WHEN THEY WENT to Oregon in October, David and Jimmy Kidd were a long, long way from the luxuries of Gleneagles. They were staying at the Sea Star, a motel in Bandon where a twin-bed room cost $29 a night, and they were spending their days trying to clear paths through the gorse so that they could have a look at the property. Shorty and Charlotte Dow had opened up a few trails, but most of the land was simply impenetrable. (Years later, standing on the 4th tee at Bandon, David wanted to make a point, and he turned to face the wall of dense, ten-foot-high gorse that was about as inviting as a thicket of razor blades. "This is what this whole site was like. Suppose I were to say, 'There it is. I want you to get in there and find me a golf course.' Not so easy, is it? But that's what Mike was asking us to do.")

Nevertheless, the Kidds were over the moon with excitement about what they were able to see. The ocean was plain enough, and the cliffs, and dunes. Jimmy kept after Shorty to clear as much as he could, to open the sight lines, but he and David were reveling in the remote, rugged beauty of the place. They couldn't always contain their glee. One of Shorty's indelible memories of the Kidds is seeing the two of them, father and son, take a plunge over the edge of a cliff. There was a sand dune below to soften the landing, and when they saw the drop, they didn't hesitate, not for one second. "They yelled 'Geronimo!' and over they went," Shorty says, "like a pair of kids on vacation."

Shorty was their indispensable guide, and Charlotte Dow baked her delicious pies for them. The Dow home became what it would remain for years, the hospitality center for visiting golf operatives. In a Bandon coincidence, it turned out that Shorty had been born on the day that the Gleneagles hotel was opened: June 7, 1924. Calling on his musical friends, Shorty the fiddler arranged for many an evening's entertainment and provided the background music for the building of Bandon Dunes.

Jimmy and David were eager to get the land cleared—completely cleared—but on that initial visit they had to get around as best they could. They could only guess at the configuration of the land under the gorse, for the topographical maps are created from aerial photos, and the camera lens couldn't penetrate the gorse. The result was that the maps didn't show the true elevation changes—and these, of course, are vital to a golf course designer. The maps didn't show accurate property lines, either, and the Kidds had to make other guesses about environmental restrictions, soil types, setback regulations, and many other factors that were crucial to even a preliminary design. Almost the only thing that they did know for sure was that the first course—they were thinking that GGD would eventually design two courses at Bandon—would be on the northernmost part of the property, north of Cut Creek, with several holes running along the high cliffs overlooking the Pacific. Some of the dunesland south of the creek was more open and inviting, but this was the habitat of the endangered silver phacelia, and Mike and Howard were doubtful that it could be used for golf. As near as the Kidds could calculate, the proposed site to the north of the creek contained sufficient land for a golf course, about 180 acres.

"Then Mike calls," said Jimmy, "and says he's coming out with his entourage, and he wants us to make a presentation. He wants to videotape it! We didn't have a single drawing at the time, and he was arriving in three days to make a video."

Somehow or other, the Kidds pulled it off. In the small, sparse meeting room of the Sea Star, they were able to present Mike and his "entourage"—a group that consisted of Pete Sinnott, a delegation from Kemper Sports, and a few friends—with a first, rough pass at a design for the Upper Links at Bandon Coastal Dunes Property.

David had done his best to site the tees and greens accurately, and he'd come up with a routing for a course designed in two 9-hole loops, measuring 7,100 yards and playing to a par of 72. He'd worked furiously to complete a schematic drawing, and he'd even hand-colored the original copy, using green to indicate the fairways, blue to mark the lakes and the ocean, and tan to show the bunkers. The contour lines are, to say the least, sketchy. The routing has three holes along the ocean, all of them set about 100 yards back from the cliff edge, inside the low ridge of foredunes.

Only one hole on that initial routing, the 17th, bears even a faint resemblance to the golf holes that were actually built.

Nevertheless, Mike Keiser liked what he saw. He and Jimmy, exactly the same age, hit it off like a pair of bandits. When they talked golf, they were speaking the same language, and Jimmy confirmed the ideas that had been simmering in Mike. Others had doubted his vision, but Jimmy—a Scotsman, a man steeped in the lore and history of the game—practically shivered with excitement at the prospect of building a links course here on the Pacific. He was ready to clear the whole site to open up the glorious views of the ocean. Life offers two kinds of high moments, he told Mike: "There are rocking chair moments, sweet moments that you know you'll remember when you're sitting in your rocker and looking back on them. And then there are the pee-down-your-pants moments when you're so excited you don't think you're going to be able to hold it back. That's how I felt at Bandon—every time there was an opening in the gorse and I caught a glimpse of what the golf course could look like, I had no doubt that we could build a fantastic golf course, none whatever."

Jimmy and Mike did most of the talking over the next few days, but David listened carefully. When he returned to England, David sat down and drew a more refined version of the schematic routing plan. He also drafted a letter, dated November 11, 1994, that articulated several of the key concepts that had been discussed and that would define the golf course development at Bandon. They were the working assumptions of his design:

- Single clubhouse providing atmosphere for 19th hole as well as logistical solutions.
- Clubhouse emanating from a central village, also set back from coast line to provide the draw and anticipation of the beach.
- Course should make its way promptly yet without undue haste to the cliff tops . . .
- A holistic approach would be the ideal; a golf experience uncluttered or suppressed by housing, roads, car parking, unnecessary structures and the contentious issues of carts and tracks.
- The approaches to the greens should be open, no forced carries . . .

All of these points would be further discussed and debated, but this was the music that Mike wanted to hear. It was clear that David, like Jimmy, was thinking of a course that would look and play like a true links course. It would be walking only. There would be no carts. The open approaches would invite a golfer to play low, running, under-the-wind shots. The most dramatic part of the property, the cliff tops, would be reserved for golf. Some of the Kemper people wanted the clubhouse located in a prime oceanside location (specifically, they wanted it where the 16th green now sits, the highest point along the cliffs), but the Kidds claimed that spot for golf. Though he didn't say so in the letter, David imagined the clubhouse and village as having an effect similar to the one that towns in Scotland had. In towns like Machrihanish or North Berwick or Carnoustie or St. Andrews, the golf course starts at the town's doorstep, so to speak, pushes off into the wilds of nature, and then, at the round's end, returns to civilization.

David's letter was six single-spaced pages in length, and it laid out a carefully staged process of design and construction. Altogether, there were five stages, with fees, rates, and expenses meticulously calculated. In effect, it was a multifaceted contract, and David and the others at Gleneagles Golf

Developments thought that it would be the beginning of negotiations. They certainly expected Mike to have questions.

He replied on December 12. His letter, in its entirety, read:

"Your proposal of November 11, 1994 is fine. Let's begin."

AND SO BEGAN the partnership that brought links golf to Oregon. The decision to hire Gleneagles Golf Developments might have seemed impulsive, but Mike had found in Jimmy a man he trusted and liked, and this—more than any assurances or guarantees about performance—was what he'd been looking for. This decision was about how, and with whom, he'd spend the next several years, and he started by traveling to Scotland in the summer of 1995 to make a tour of links courses.

Jimmy was the tour director, of course, and David tagged along, listening to the older men talk. Mike's first impression was that David was shy and reserved; he might be the only person who has ever used those adjectives to describe David Kidd. With Gleneagles as their home base, they sped—Jimmy, like Toad of Toad Hall, absolutely adores fast motorcars—around Scotland from one course to the next. At Turnberry they were treated like visiting dignitaries, but at Muirfield, the most famously stuffy and stiff-necked place in golf, they couldn't get in, not even with Jimmy's clout—he hadn't called ahead, so they had to peer at the course from over the wall. No matter. The moment when all of them felt that it was going to work, that Mike Keiser and the Gleneagles Golf Developments were meant to build a course together, occurred just down the road from Muirfield at North Berwick, a course that is a lot easier to get on and a lot quirkier, a course that many connoisseurs rank as their favorite unorthodox links course.

The 13th hole at North Berwick is known as the Pit. It is one of the most unusual holes in all of golf, a short par 4 with a green tucked behind a centuries-old stone wall. When a golfer tries to clear the wall with his approach shot, and fails to do so—well, there is no telling where the ball will end up. It could bounce anywhere. On the left side of the hole there are dunes and beach and the Firth of Forth, and nothing is out-of-bounds. Golfers either hate this hole, which defies just about every principle of modern golf course design, or they love it.

Mike loved it. He hit a monster hook off the tee, right onto the beach. He dug another ball out of his pocket and was about to tee it up when Jimmy stopped him. The beach was in bounds, he reminded him. The oldest rule of golf is to play the ball as it lies. Off he went, down onto the stones of the beach. He had a huge grin on his face, and the Kidds knew right then and there that Mike was a man after their own Scottish hearts. He wasn't another pampered American who paid lip service to the idea of links golf, but a player who looked forward to the chance to recover from the Firth of Forth at low tide. He didn't complain about stone walls or wretched lies, even lies on the beach. He accepted his fate with good humor and good grace. He liked his golf with the savor of surprise, adventure, and vicissitudes.

There was one more important stop on this trip: Machrihanish. This remote links at the southern tip of the Kintyre peninsula has always had a mythic reputation; the very name, Machrihanish, rolls around in the mouth like a smoky, peaty, pungent whisky. Built close to the open Atlantic, Machrihanish was known for the height of its shaggy dunes (they are as high as any in Scotland), its velvety turf, and its magnificent first hole, where a golfer must launch the round with a bold shot over the beach and the breakers. Over the years, the course has been tinkered with by various architects, and its closing holes have been eviscerated to accommodate a road, but the place has not lost its wild, unspoiled, end-of-the-earth feeling.

This was David Kidd's home course, the place where he soaked up his first impressions of what a golf course could be, where he absorbed the look and feel of the links, where he'd learned in his bones that the links was a place for play, discovery, and adventure.

Machrihanish wasn't the best golf course in Scotland, nor the busiest, but it was a place where the true seekers came to play the game. They came to pay homage to Tom Morris and to experience that strange exaltation, half joyous and half melancholy, that comes from playing where the earth meets the sea. The game can seem sublime in such a setting, or it can seem humbling, and often it seems both. In any case, neither Mike nor the Kidds could fail to recognize that there was a fearful symmetry in what they were about to embark upon. At the western edge of Scotland, where the country disappeared into the ocean, stood the links of Machrihanish.

Thousands of miles away, at Bandon, at the western edge of another continent, there would one day be another links.

10 | How the Permits Were Won

*Howard McKee is the reason this place is so pure and pristine. He's
also the reason it got permitted in the first place. The environmentalists
trusted him. A golf resort on the coast of Oregon? I don't think
anybody else could have gotten it done.* —STEVE LESNIK

OCTOBER. IT HAD BEEN a bluebird day at Bandon Dunes, a wonderful day
for golf, and the lodge was imbued with a fine sense of contentment as the
setting sun fired up the rim of the Pacific. Mike Keiser and Howard McKee,
studying the menu in the Gallery Restaurant, were frequently interrupted by
people who came over to the table to introduce themselves to Mike, and to
sing the praises of the golf courses.

Mike seemed almost embarrassed by the compliments, and he kept steer-
ing the conversation back to the menu created by Chef Paul Moss, the original chef at Bandon Dunes, the one who established the restaurant's balance
of hearty and elegant dishes. Mike ordered sturgeon that night, and Howard
had the Dungeness crab cakes; but the most popular item on the menu, and
one of Chef Paul's specialties, is Grandma Thayer's Meatloaf, which comes
with mashed potatoes, pan gravy, and haystack onions—a robust meal for
golfers who have just walked thirty-six holes.

Many local products are also featured on the menu. The restaurant offers
greens from Langlois (a town just south of Bandon), cheese from Tillamook,
locally caught salmon and shellfish, and wild mushrooms that have been
gathered on the South Coast. Similarly, the extensive wine list gives pride of
place to Oregon wines; and Howard, when he chose the building materials
and furnishings for the lodge, put the same emphasis on native products.

The chairs in the Gallery, he pointed out, were made of Oregon maple. The pale, clear-grained wood used as trim throughout the lodge was Port Orford cedar, a highly valued ornamental wood (it is widely used in Japanese temples) whose name came from the coastal town about fifty miles south of Bandon. On this subject Mike and Howard were in complete accord: They wanted visitors to Bandon to get the feel and flavor of this remote part of the world.

"From the start," Mike said, "our objectives were completely aligned. I was a golfer, and Howard wasn't, and he was an artist, and I'm not, but we had the same mission. Our attitude was, let's find something really good. Let's make something exceptional."

"We were in sync about the aesthetics of the place," Howard agreed.

"It was an adventure," Mike said. "I remember clawing through the brush at Crook's Point and suddenly seeing the Pacific Ocean in front of us. I felt as though we were Lewis and Clark. There was definitely a sense of discovering this part of the coast of Oregon.

"We're both environmentally inclined," Mike added, "though we don't always have the same views about the environmental movement. It's been hijacked by radicals."

"They didn't have much choice," said Howard, "since they were more or less forced into that position by uncompromising industrialists. But all the theory, all the politics, begin to seem irrelevant when you actually deal with these issues on the ground. What we've done is look for environmental solutions to practical problems, and by coming at them from two different points of view we've worked out solutions."

"This was a constantly evolving project," Mike said. "We didn't come out here and say, 'We're going to build a golf course.' Before anybody let us build anything, we had to have stacks of planning documents."

"You have to be patient," Howard said. "You can't get too far ahead of yourself when you're trying to develop a project like this, and with all respect, to get Mike to be patient took a lot of circular paths. Our ideas were big and ambitious but they were loose, and the challenge now that we had the property was to distill the dreams into what in architectural terms is called a program. We had to define the threshold development, and we went through an evolving exercise—"

Mike: "A group grope."

Howard: "—to come up with a plan that had a chance of success. If we were going to become a destination resort, for example, we would have to build accommodations for 150 people, and there were other requirements. We had to prove that there were wells that would provide enough water, and we had to design a water treatment plant."

Mike: "And we needed an entrance road—a two-mile entrance road."

Howard: "The initial investment had to increase."

Mike: "It quintupled. The golf course cost less than $4 million, and that was about 20 percent of the total."

Howard: "Mike wasn't going to do it on the cheap. If you're going to speculate, speculate. Go for broke."

Mike: "I believed in what I was doing, but the ante went way up. I had to quintuple my belief."

THE CONVERSATION THAT EVENING ranged over many subjects, as it tends to do when Mike and Howard are together, but mostly it hovered around the subject at hand. The effort to obtain permits for the Bandon Dunes resort, I came to realize, had much in common with a long military campaign. There were no bodies, but there were skirmishes and pitched battles, strategy and tactics, flanking actions and forced marches, and overall, the sense of a smaller, more nimble force, directed by Howard—General McKee—wearing down a large, entrenched adversary.

The permitting was Howard's subject, and he did most of the talking that night, usually emphasizing his points with his hands. His conversational style is animated, and he does not gloss over difficulties and complications. Often he seems to be moving large forces around by the sheer strength of his intellect, in much the same fashion as a lion tamer moves the big cats, trying to get them to sit still and behave. Mike—to continue this circus metaphor—picks and chooses his targets carefully. He is a knife thrower whose conversational daggers hit the spinning target with seemingly effortless precision.

"At the time I was trying to get permits for Bandon, I was also going to Moscow," Howard said. "I was trying to help them figure out how to become capitalists. That was my commercial project. This one was the soul project, the one that resonated with values that mattered."

Howard was racking up the intercontinental miles during the permitting period from 1992 to 1996, shuttling back and forth between Russia and Oregon. He was only half-joking when he claimed to be teaching the former Soviets how to become capitalists; he'd been hired to help transform antiquated buildings that had formerly housed the Communist bureaucracy into corporate headquarters with all the infrastructure, particularly the communications capabilities, necessary to do business in a high-tech economy. The job was even worse than it sounds: Howard's employers, it turned out, weren't really as interested in retrofitting old Soviet buildings as they were in *appearing* to be interested; they wanted to convince the International Monetary Fund that they intended to do the work in order to collect the large sums that the IMF was offering for precisely this purpose. They were, as Howard gradually came to realize, a bunch of brazen, world-class schemers.

The Bandon project, by contrast, seemed small, manageable, and pure. Even though the ultimate goal was to build a golf resort that would succeed as a business, Howard and Mike approached the project as a chance to build not just a golf course or even a golf course with a hotel, but a place that captured the mystery and beauty of this part of the world. They wanted to preserve the environment, stimulate the local economy, and generally fulfill the idea of stewardship that they both held dear. Many developers pay lip service to such lofty goals, but Mike and Howard really meant it.

Howard can be high-minded, but when it came to political maneuvering he was a hard-nosed realist. To get the Bandon permits, one of his first moves was to find a "facilitator" in the governor's office, someone who would put the state agencies on alert. There were going to be at least ten separate state agencies involved in the permitting process, and Howard didn't want them dragging their feet. From the outset his strategy was based on the recognition that he would have to overcome the inertia of the state agencies, who were institutionally opposed to development—and all they had to do to stop it was nothing at all. So long as they were passive, so long as they took no action, nothing could happen at Bandon.

So Howard pulled a string at the governor's office, and he got the major agency, the Oregon Parks and Recreation Department—the OPRD—which runs the state parks—to enter into a data-collecting effort with him. There was going to have to be a complete inventory of natural resources at Bandon, and since Mike's property (now owned by a company called the Bandon Dunes Limited Partnership) shared a long boundary with the state park at Bullard's Beach, Howard thought it made sense to share the data. To get off on the right foot with the OPRD, Howard purchased a 100-acre parcel that had belonged to a timber company, a chunk of land that knocked a hole in Bullard's Beach and that the OPRD had long coveted. Delicately, Howard opened conversations about ways in with the Bandon Dunes LP and the OPRD could cooperate, launching a joint planning effort that included a comprehensive resource inventory, the planning of nature trails, and even the siting of golf holes. At the very least, the OPRD could see that the new owners wanted to use land in a way that was compatible with the purposes of the park, and they began to regard Bandon Dunes LP as a valuable neighbor. (In one plan, a string of golf holes runs south from the Bandon property across the dunes of Bullard's Beach, all the way to the mouth of the Coquille River—an unbroken stretch of approximately four miles of oceanside golf.)

The cooperation of OPRD, Howard believes, was the key to securing the trust and cooperation of other agencies. In addition to state agencies, he was dealing with federal and county officials, not to mention local citizens, national environmental organizations, and Indian tribes. His ally in arranging tours for local groups was Shorty Dow, who stayed on as caretaker of the property and became a fierce advocate of the development plans. Sometimes, in fact, Shorty had to be restrained: When an agent from the Fish and Wildlife Department declared that salmon used Cut Creek for spawning, Shorty was appalled by the failure of common sense, since Cut Creek—which now runs past the lodge and borders the 18th hole at Bandon Dunes—does not flow into the ocean but disappears into the broad sands of the beach. "How do they get up into the creek?" Shorty demanded. "Salmon don't walk."

There were plenty of other skirmishes, but Howard and Shorty were an effective team. After their initial standoff, each had come to recognize the other's virtues. Shorty got a kick out of Howard's precise use of language. "There was a bunch of Indians coming out here one day, and I asked Howard how many. 'A whole *contingent*,' he said. That's the way he talked. He would say a whole sentence in one word."

Shorty, for his part, was effective in talking to local citizens, and their support was essential; nothing was going to happen unless the people of Coos County were won over. From both a political and legal point of view, the key task was to persuade the Coos County Board of Commissioners to grant an exception to the state law. Howard was the one who orchestrated the appeal, which had to meet very specific legal criteria. "We decided to seek approval as a destination resort," Howard said. "Mike kept saying that all he wanted was a golf course with a double-wide trailer for a clubhouse, but I don't think there's any way that we could have gotten approval for a golf course alone. Then, when I was trying to fulfill all the requirements for the application, I realized that no destination resort could be located within three miles of high value farming activity—and there were cranberry bogs close to our site. Well, the only way around that was to file for a special exception. So we were hit with a double whammy: We had to get approved both for a special exception and for a destination resort."

Through all the meetings, hearings, horse trading, and data gathering, Howard hewed to a strategy of persuasion and negotiation. He relied heavily on his land-use attorney, Al Johnson, whom he'd selected partly for his unflappable calm. ("Al wore sweaters like Mr. Rogers. He was the ultimate down-home lawyer, which was exactly what I wanted. We would never have gotten anywhere if we'd come off as hotshot city slickers. And Al's partner,

Corinne Sherton, had a Ph.D. in biology, so she was perfect for the job. Our opponents quickly realized they were up against an expert.")

Howard tried to avoid confronting the state agencies, including the all-powerful Land Conservation and Development Commission—even though the LCDC tried, in the middle of the process, to undermine the Bandon Dunes LP by rewriting its rules. Al was able to stave off the rules change, and Howard was tireless in seeking opportunities to give the state agencies things they wanted.

"We went in having nothing," he said. "We had no cards. There was nothing we could do as a matter of right. Somehow or other, we had to find a way that we could negotiate toward a plan in which we gave up certain things that were precious to others in return for concessions that mattered to us. As we studied the site, we learned that the environmentally sensitive areas were the forests of Port Orford cedar, active dunes, the wetlands, and the riparian areas, and we proposed an agreement that would protect those areas. In the end, we traded off about half the land, accepting constraints that would prevent it from being developed, in return for permission to develop the remainder of the property."

Howard did his homework thoroughly, and he lined up expert witnesses for the public hearings. He even called upon Jimmy Kidd, who flew in from Scotland to testify at a hearing of the Coos County Board of Commissioners. "Here was a significant figure in Scottish golf," Mike said, "telling them that the kind of course we wanted to build wouldn't have the adverse effect they feared. It was clear that Jimmy knew what he was talking about, and that their ideas about golf courses were knee-jerk. They just assumed that we were going to dump tons of chemicals everywhere. The resistance began to wane after that hearing."

Howard also produced careful studies to convince local opposition that the Bandon Dunes project would be an economic boon to the area. Bill Grile, the Coos County planning director, became a key supporter. On November 25, 1994, Crile sent the board of commissioners an update on the "Bandon

Coastal Dunelands golf course/resort project." He praised the quality of the
planning documents, and noted that the environmental problems—specifically, the potentially endangered silver phacelia—were "probably surmount-
able." Likewise, the issues of water availability appeared to have been solved.
The crux of Grile's memo was in the summary of the economic impacts:
"Jobs creation from the project is estimated at 450–850 during construction
and 140–175 after construction. BCD consultants cite research showing that
the development will likely contribute 1.5 to 7.5 times to public revenues what
it requires in cost of public services . . . The concept behind support of the
proposed plan amendment is that the project is needed 'to help Coos County
meet its [economic development goals]'." In a note jotted on the memo, Mike
reported to Pete Sinnott that "Our 1st big zoning meeting went v. v. well."

Beyond all the practical and financial considerations, however, there were
still intangible questions about the golf resort. One man who had to be persuaded was Don Ivy, the cultural resources coordinator for the Coquille Indian tribe, and, informally, the cultural guardian for the Coos tribe as well.
From an Indian perspective (there are over eight hundred Coquille Indians
nationally, and about three hundred in southern Oregon), the most vital
concern about the Bandon plan was whether or not it would preserve the
historical and archaeological sites important to the tribes' cultural heritage.
Don Ivy was aware the Whiskey Run Beach had been an important gathering place for the Coos and Coquille, and he knew that some Indian artifacts
remained in middens on the Bandon site, in locations that had been carefully
documented. The middens were little more than piles of shells and bones, but
for Don, and for the tribes, they told a "huge story": They contained a record
of continuous human habitation over the centuries. They also bore witness to
what Don called a "watershed moment, a moment in the archetypal conflict
between white settlers in search of fortune and Indians pursuing a traditional way of life."

Starting from a place of suspicion, Don came to trust Howard, whom he
saw as "passionate" and "proactive," and who convinced him that the Bandon
Dunes LP regarded the site in much the same way that the tribes had. "This

was never about money," Don Ivy said. "It was about bringing a vision into reality. Howard and Mike were concerned about legacy, and once you're there, a whole different set of values comes into play. The question is whether you're going to build something that will last. Before them, the Euro-American settlers came only to exploit the resources of the place. First they looked for gold, then they logged off the timber. They mined for coal and they looked for chromium. They put their animals on the fields where the camas grew, and the camas disappeared. It was replaced by the gorse that was of no use to anyone. And then they put up the windmills—they were going to harvest the wind. By then the only people who used the place were the ones who came in on their ATVs and ripped up the dunes even more. This place was completely depleted and degraded when Mike bought it. But now it serves many of the same purposes it did when the Indians came here. It's a place for people to gather and visit, and many come in search of renewal and sanctuary. They can find it here because the place has been healed. This area is closer than it has ever been to what it was when the Coquille and Coos came here."

By 1995, FOUR YEARS after Mike purchased the Bandon property, it was beginning to look as though the Coos County Board of Commissioners was going to approve the proposed amendment allowing the development of Bandon Dunes. All the right pieces—the support of the tribes, the negotiations with the state agencies, the endorsement of the planning director—were clicking into place. Mike, as we shall see, had been pressing forward with plans for the golf course, and Howard was trying to coordinate the work of botanists, hydrologists, geologists, and all the other experts and specialists whose contributions were needed to fulfill all the conditions required by state law. Approval seemed to be just a matter of time, but there was always another hoop to jump through, another T to cross. Not until July 31, 1996, did the Coos County Board of Commissioners come to an oral decision, and on August 21, 1996, the Coos County Zoning and Land Development Ordinance was officially changed to permit the building of the Bandon Dunes Resort.

For Howard, it was a hard-earned and personal victory. By the end of that year, as the project went from the permitting phase into an action mode, one that would require all the open-ended plans to be translated into specific buildings, roads, wells, parking lots, and other infrastructure, he was exhausted. His Russian adventure had also taken a lot out of him, and just after Christmas he was diagnosed with colon cancer. ("Considering all that was going on here and in Russia," he told me on another occasion, "I suppose I was lucky that it wasn't anything worse than cancer.") On that October night in the Gallery, he was the last to finish eating, and he was in a reflective mood. "This whole place was about serendipity. I wrote a paper once about it, about all the coincidences, all the serendipitous things that came together to make the project what it turned out to be. You couldn't possibly have scripted all the events that dovetailed. We made all the right arguments, we did all our homework, we talked to all the people we should have talked to, but in the end, I think the real turning point was the gorse."

The gorse?

"The gorse," Howard said. "What kind of serendipity is that? Here we are on the coast of Oregon, thousands of miles from Ireland, and we have a site covered by gorse that was brought over here by George Bennett, an Irishman. The local people regard the gorse as an obnoxious plant, since it's so prickly and so invasive. Even worse, it's highly flammable, and the town of Bandon has been destroyed twice by intensely hot fires.

"Gorse burns like kerosene, and it's spread all over this area. We were able to persuade the local people that the best way to eliminate the threat of fire was to clear the gorse and to plant grass, which is almost the only way to keep it from spreading. The Nature Conservancy had looked at this land to buy it, but they couldn't come up with a plan to control the gorse. We convinced Coos County that grass is the antidote to gorse."

Mike said, "So Lord Bennett of Ireland, when he brought the gorse, unknowingly enabled us to get our golf course built."

At that point Chef Paul and other members of the kitchen staff appeared, carrying a cake with candles. It was Howard's birthday, and they sang a spirited version of "Happy Birthday" as they presented him with the cake. The icing had been applied in the form of the new, enlarged kitchen that they wanted Howard to design for them.

That touched off Howard's infectious laugh, and Chef Paul had him and Mike doubled over with laughter when he cut them slices of cake, tiny slices. He said, "Those are budget cuts."

11 | More Serendipity

I want eighteen great holes, not nine great holes and nine that are only OK. Nobody is going to come here for average golf. —MIKE KEISER

SOME MORNINGS, DAVID KIDD had to take an extra turn on his pillow to get his geographical bearings. Was he in Oregon? England? Scotland? Nepal? The fortunes of Gleneagles Golf Developments had taken a quantum leap, and in 1995 David was all of a sudden leading the life of a globe-trotter. One week he would be at home in England, but the next he was back at the Sea Star in Bandon, and the week after that he'd find himself in the Yak and Yeti Hotel in Kathmandu, where GGD had been engaged to build Gokarna Forest Golf Club, the first regulation 18-hole golf course in Nepal, on land that had once been the hunting retreat of the royal family.

For a young man still in his twenties, this sudden opening of horizons seemed almost like a pipe dream. Not only was he engaged to design two golf courses in extraordinary locations, but one of them, Gokarna Forest, was going to be under construction as soon as he could get the plans drawn. The permitting requirements in Nepal were basically nil, and David was logging major air miles on Lufthansa, the German airline that flew to Katmandu via Dubai or Karachi.

The Gokarna Forest course was David's first true solo design, and he threw himself into it. Several holes were sited to frame views of the lofty mountains, others to incorporate historical features of the property. Leaving the 14th tee, for instance, golfers use ancient steps that were originally built to help elephants ascend the hill. To use these natural and cultural features in a way that enhanced the golf was one challenge; another, more interesting challenge to the young architect was to craft holes that expressed his increasingly bold ideas. He wanted to make a statement. Here is his own description, written for the course guide, of the 7th hole:

> The most demanding, challenging, nerve wrecking hole at Gokarna Forest Golf Club. Few leave unscathed. The green is dominated by a seemingly magnetic, huge, deep, wood-faced bunker that appears to sit right in the center. This novel C-shaped green is unabashedly contoured to attract everything towards its 10 foot abyss. There is no safety anywhere as creeks seem to crisscross every avenue. This is the type of hole where you cannot think too much. Keep your head down, hit the ball, and suffer the consequences. Consider a par on this hole a collectors item to be treasured.

David Kidd might have been a young man, but he obviously wasn't afraid to build unusual golf holes, and his brain was positively teeming with images of danger and disaster. He sounds like a wicked Captain Hook, twirling his mustache and cackling with glee, as he imagines the golfers headed toward the wicked snares he has set for them.

The Gokarna Forest project was on a fast track, relatively speaking; the Bandon project was still very much in the early design stages in 1995. Even though the permits hadn't been granted, Mike was proceeding on the optimistic assumption that they would eventually be forthcoming, and David—usually accompanied by Jimmy—spent weeks hacking his way through the gorse in an effort to get more precise information about the site.

The Kidds wanted to get rid of the gorse—all of it, all at once. But Mike and Howard resisted; the idea of clearing the entire site seemed premature, expensive, and radical. By temperament, they were both inclined to save trees, not destroy them. Mike did hire a crew to open up some sight lines, and Shorty Dow, putting his machinist's ingenuity to use, dreamed up an invention that was supposed to help in the reconnaissance of the property, a sort of crow's nest or flying bridge that he welded to a small bulldozer. David took one look at the contraption and advised his father not to climb up. "I told him he was out of his mind to get up on that thing, but he went right ahead. It almost shook the teeth out of his head. He climbed up there once, and that was it. He never went back up."

By June 1995, David had scrapped almost all of the holes on the original plan, talking through his ideas with his father. Philosophically, there was very little difference between them, but the specific design ideas originated with David, and Jimmy was careful not to poach on his son's territory. He still took the lead in talking to Mike, who came to Oregon twice that spring, both times with groups of retail golfers, to see firsthand what changes David was proposing.

He liked almost everything he saw, particularly the back nine. In fact, the routing plan that David completed in June 1995, two years before construction actually began, remained more or less constant. On the back nine, he had discovered a sequence that moved very nicely across the land and needed only to be tweaked and trimmed. The problems were on the front nine. The course was still designed in two 9-hole loops, and the front nine loop was squeezed up against the northern boundary of the property. With newly accurate information about the location of that northern boundary, David had been forced to shorten the course, and the new plan showed a total yardage of 6,780 yards. It remained a par 72, but only four holes were located on the edge of the cliff. Several inland holes on the front nine ran parallel to each other, and parallel holes have long been regarded as an ancient and evil curse; these holes were also on the flattest, dullest ground on the site. There was nowhere else to put them. This site that had originally seemed so ample and spacious was looking small and cramped.

"I want eighteen great holes," Mike told David over and over again, "not nine good ones and nine that are only OK. Nobody is going to come here for average golf."

But the site just didn't want to yield eighteen great holes.

The routing plan confirmed what Mike had sensed ever since he acquired the Bandon property. He needed the land to the north.

• • •

"I LUSTED AFTER that land," Mike said. He'd had his eye on it almost from the moment he bought his 1,215 acres. The neighboring parcel consisted of 400 acres, and it had once been a part of the original tract. The owner of the property was David Shuman, a California lawyer and businessman; he'd bought it from Duke Watson and his partners in 1989, just two years before Mike bought the rest of the property. Mike had kept close track of Shuman's activities, looking for some opening, some opportunity to acquire the place. He'd even gone so far as to hire a private investigator to do a background check on Shuman.

But Shuman demonstrated no interest whatsoever in selling. His property was called Varuna Farms, named for a Hindu deity. Ostensibly, the place was a horse farm, and according to an article in a local paper, Shuman had made a substantial investment in Morgan horses, a house, pastures, corrals, and a state-of-the-art barn with skylights, thirty-two stalls, a large arena, a breeding shed, tack rooms, grooming rooms, and a luxurious apartment for the ranch manager. The article suggested that Shuman hoped to set up a facility for handicapped riders—a laudable project, but one that didn't jibe with the local impressions of Shuman and his crew. Both Shorty Dow and Bob Johnson, Mike's real-estate operative in Oregon, had been rebuffed when they ventured over to say hello.

Mike had risked climbing over the fence to have a look at the land to the north, as had David. What they saw were ridges and hummocks and huge blowouts, places where the wind had scoured away the gorse, exposing stretches of rippled sand. You couldn't really say that these blowouts were bunkers, since they weren't part of a golf course, but to anyone thinking of golf they cried out to be used as bunkers.

As long as Shuman owned the place, those blowouts were off limits. Mike and David were like kids with their noses pressed against the window of the candy store.

STILL, THE 1995 DESIGN meetings were critical in many ways. Perhaps most importantly, they cemented the relationship between Mike and the Kidds, who realized they were of one mind in their approach to the design of the golf course. They spent long, dusty days together, tramping back and forth across the site, bonding in the anticipation and excitement of a new venture. At night they ate and drank at Bandon's best restaurants, the Wheelhouse and Lord Bennett's, and Jimmy often held court, regaling the assembled crowd with tales from his lifetime in golf. David also loved to spin a good story, but amongst the older men he felt like a youngster and was usually content to sit back and listen. When they were talking design, however, David had plenty to say, and he stated his views passionately. One of the things Mike liked about him was that he had the fire in his belly.

Those early, heady design meetings had a kind of first-tracks excitement about them. The landscape of gorse wasn't anything like a mountainside of pristine powder snow, but Mike and David and Jimmy had the exhilarating sensation of doing something new, of going where no one else had ever gone. They were dreaming, making it up as they went, and Mike, as we have seen, liked creative collaborations and open-ended plans.

He was more absorbed by golf than he'd ever been. On the Cascade Ranch, he'd been unable to keep his own design instincts in check, and he had spent several happy days with Pete Sinnott at his side laying out an 18-hole course (he calls it a "pasture course") that spreads out across the high meadows. He'd reluctantly sold the Pistol River property, but as Howard had pointed out, the ante was going up here at Bandon. He was committed to doing everything in cash, and he was going to need plenty of cash to turn this dream—this dream that kept growing—into a reality.

Mike's group of golf consultants now regularly included Pete Sinnott, Dick Youngscap, Steve Lesnik, and Jim Seeley, the chief of operations at Kemper Sports Management. A graduate of the Naval Academy and a former touring pro, Jim was perhaps the most orthodox of Mike's advisers, and he was certainly the one who challenged David most often. He was still a top-caliber player whose perspective had been formed by years of competitive play, and he questioned anything that might be perceived as unfair. He didn't like quirks or irregularities, wildly uneven lies, deep bunkers where you had to come out sideways. He questioned, in other words, just about every links feature that David was proposing, and he faced off with David when it came to walking. Jim had worked in and around golf operations for decades, and his experience told him that American golfers weren't going to be happy with any course that didn't allow carts.

The "retail golfers" who came out to Oregon with Mike weren't in the golf business. They were simply Mike's friends, and he regarded them as a representative sample of the golfers who would ultimately determine the success or failure of the place; they were the ones who'd spend their own money to come this far. Mike wasn't building a private club but a resort course, a course open for public play, and he was too much of a businessman to be indifferent to commercial success. He wanted more than favorable reviews; he wanted a course so spectacular and so irresistible that it would attract golfers to this place they'd never heard of. He wanted his golf course to make money.

In a sense, Mike was doing what he had done at Recycled Paper Greetings. He was conducting his own market research in an effort to come up with a product that would have a broad, popular appeal. A key difference, of course, was that RPG produced thousands of cards; not every card had to be a winner. The company could produce a hundred cards that failed miserably as long as one or two succeeded like "Hippo Birdie Two Ewes." Here he had just one shot at building a golf course, and he had to get it right the first time.

In the most specific ways, this emphasis on the retail golfer had far-reaching consequences on the design of the golf course. It meant, for instance, that the fairways would be wide and the greens would be huge. They had to be; the heavy coastal winds could knock a golf ball way off line. Mike and David agreed that they wanted a golfer to be able to finish the round with the same ball he started with. They also wanted him to have a chance to stop his ball on the greens, some of which would eventually measure sixty yards in length. Yet they didn't want a course where a player could simply whale away. David's approach was to design a kind of course-within-a-course, crafting holes that provided plenty of margin for the hacker but, for the golfer trying to shoot a low score, demanded a high degree of accuracy and the willingness to take a risk. There were no water hazards on the course, but David's bunkers were carved into the greens and fairways, not set back at a comfortable distance. Even on the schematic routing plan, they looked numerous and dangerous, and they were placed near the spots where a bold golfer would want to play. The essence of classic strategic design, of course, is that it requires a golfer to measure risk against reward on almost every shot, and provides many different routes from tee to green, allowing each golfer to chart his own way.

The roster of retail golfers changed from one trip to the next. Bob Peele, the tall, gregarious Merrill Lynch money manager who played golf with Mike back in Chicago and was a regular member of the grudge match foursome, logged the most trips to Bandon; others who made frequent visits included Larry Booth, the architect of the Dunes Club; Phil Friedmann, Mike's partner at RPG; and Warren Gelman, his old school friend from Buffalo. Alfred Hamilton, a friend from Mike's navy days, flew out in 1995, and much as he loved his golf, he admits that he didn't understand much of what he saw. "I listened to what they were saying, but honestly I didn't feel that I had much to contribute. Mike and David were consumed by what they were doing, and they were way out ahead of us."

Even if the retail golfers weren't always up to speed on matters of design, they understood marketing and realized that Mike was going to have a tough sell. They talked about ways he could get the word out, and they came up with many suggestions for names for the course. One name bandied about was Whiskey Run, but the name used on the 1995 routing plan, the name that was the leader in the clubhouse, was MacKenzie National. "MacKenzie was Mike's favorite architect," Alfred Hamilton said, "but I don't think Mike was ever completely happy with that name. I know he wasn't happy with the name that some of us suggested—Keiser National. Donald Trump puts his name on his courses, but that's not Mike."

IN THE FALL of 1995, as Howard was closing in on the permits, Mike was in Geneva, Switzerland, where he had taken his entire family for a year's sabbatical. With good memories of their European adventures during Mike's navy days, Mike and Lindy had decided to take the children to Europe, and they spent an entire school year abroad. Lindy and the kids thrived; Mike was impatient and ready to come home after two months. He worked almost every day. Through a combination of faxes and a daily FedEx delivery, he was able to tend to business, both RPG business and golf business.

Golf business included persistent efforts to acquire the Shuman property, though none of these efforts had gotten very far. The first glimmer of hope came when an employee of Mike's happened upon a short newspaper item noting that Shuman had filed for bankruptcy. Mike was on it like a flash. He didn't waste any time getting in touch with Bob Johnson, his Oregon real-estate agent, and discussing the terms of a formal offer. Shuman knew how much Mike wanted to buy his property, but he had always refused to meet with anyone to discuss a sale. This time he agreed to the meeting.

The meeting had plenty of strange vibrations. Bob was met by members of Shuman's staff—bodyguards, he thought—and led into Shuman's office, where he sat for a long while in complete silence, staring at some carved masks on the wall. He wasn't sure where they came from, only that they were weird and spooky. "They were voodoo masks," Bob says. "When Shuman finally came in and I presented the offer, he didn't look at me—he just looked up at those masks. Then he said, 'They say it's all right. I can accept the offer.' Those masks were giving him permission."

Once the voodoo powers had smiled upon it, the transaction was swift and smooth. Mike's little kingdom had increased by four hundred acres (and cost him another $2.3 million). That was a small price to pay for northward expansion. Those weak holes on the front nine could be replaced with new holes along the ocean.

Which is exactly what happened. In November 1996, Mike flew out to Oregon with several retail golfers for what was to be the final design trip. Permission to build the course had been officially granted earlier that year. David kept refining the design, but he hadn't yet extended the routing onto the Shuman property.

Mike and the retail golfers stayed in Oregon for several days, walking the property. They were even able to play construction golf, for the centerlines had been cleared and all the holes had been staked. Mike still didn't like the inland holes on the front nine. He wasn't ready to approve them, and he asked David to come up with a better routing. A young man named Troy Russell had just come to work on the project, and he attended the meeting at which David presented the latest iteration of the routing. "After that meeting, David went up to Mike and told him he'd done everything he could. He said he'd poured his heart out on that routing and he didn't think he could do any better. He told Mike that was the best he could do unless he had more land—and that's when the land magically appeared."

That is how Warren Gelman remembers it, too. "The holes on the front nine weren't working, and David and Jimmy went out one afternoon and staked the new holes. The next morning there they were—the 5th , 6th, and 7th holes, just like they are today."

Two of those holes, the 5th and the 6th, played right along the rim of the cliff, and they transformed the character of the front nine. With the additional land, David had also been able to bring the green of the 4th hole to the edge of the cliff. The previous routing had given the golfer teasing glimpses of the Pacific, but in this new sequence the golfer played three holes smack up against the ocean and stayed on the cliffs long enough to absorb the full force of the setting. This was neither a tease nor a glimpse; it was a full-on, flat-out, hang-on-to-your-Huggies climax.

The 4th, 5th, and 6th holes at Bandon are an unforgettable sequence, and they are the making of the course. Any one of them is enough to send a shiver up a golfer's spine; to play all three, one after the other, is both dreadful and exciting, almost more than a golfer can bear. They were the first crescendo of David Kidd's symphony. Trying to imagine Bandon Dunes without these holes is like trying to imagine Pebble Beach without the 7th and 8th, or Augusta National without Amen Corner.

Yet the course had been conceived and designed without them. It had been staked with different holes when, at the midnight hour, the Shuman land fell into Mike's hands

Howard had something major to add to his remarks on serendipity.

12 | Breaking Ground

We worked, drank, and bullshitted that week,
and I knew that we were going to have one hell of a ride together.
—JIM HALEY, SHAPER, AFTER HIS FIRST WEEK
AT BANDON WITH DAVID KIDD

WHEN COOS COUNTY gave its approval to plans for a destination resort at Bandon, the project entered a new phase—the action phase, for which, frankly, the Bandon Dunes Limited Partnership was not prepared. Howard had deliberately kept the planning as open-ended as possible, but when Mike returned from his year abroad in 1996, it was time to bolt down some of the plans and start moving dirt. Mike hadn't yet realized that his initial investment was going to quintuple, and he jotted down some ballpark estimates for what he expected the development to cost:

To Howard:
Here's what I see in Phase I.

1) Golf course—cost	1–1.5 MM
2) Clubhouse—cost	.5 MM
3) Max 10—4 BR modular lodging units	2 MM
4) Sewage treatment	——
5) Water system	——
6) ODOT Hwy 101 interchange	.1 MM
7) Construction contingency	.5 MM

8) Golf course architects

    Course #1 .4 MM

    Course #2 .1 MM

9) Other consultants .3 MM

10) Dick Youngscap—construction mgr .1 MM

    TOTAL (except for #4 and #5) 3.0–5.5 MM

Mike was capable of wild underestimates, but there was a rationale for all of his numbers. The cost of golf course construction, for instance, wasn't a guess. Even though most "average" courses, when conventionally built, cost in the vicinity of $5 million, Mike knew firsthand that the Dunes Club had been built for less than $1 million. The Dunes Club was only a 9-holer, but Sand Hills, a regulation 18-hole layout, had cost the same amount. Dick Youngscap, using Coore and Crenshaw as his architects at Sand Hills, had been able to avoid one huge expense of conventional courses: earth moving. As Ben Crenshaw said, "We only moved one teaspoon of dirt," and Youngscap hadn't been stuck with a massive bill for dozers, scrapers, pans, and all the other heavy equipment that usually takes over on a golf course construction site.

Furthermore, Mike hoped to build the course at Bandon without a huge outlay for drainage or irrigation. He expected the sandy soil to drain naturally, and the climate seemed damp enough to save him from having to install wall-to-wall irrigation. He was wrong on both counts, but this early, back-of-the-envelope budget does show one thing: He didn't think that the way to create a destination resort was to throw a lot of money at it. He was thinking of a place that would be plain and simple, a resort that wasn't going to be festooned with bells and whistles.

He had flown Dick Youngscap out to Oregon several times to look at the property. As the memo to Howard indicates, he wanted Dick to be his construction manager. By this time it was clear that Gleneagles Golf Developments, based in Scotland, wasn't going to be able to build the golf course, and that he, Mike, would preside over the construction in much the same way that he had at the Dunes Club. Such an arrangement gave him both financial and artistic control, and Mike wanted to hold the reins. He had asked Youngscap to be his on-site construction manager, even though Dick's role in his own projects had been far more comprehensive. In the end, that was the consideration that kept them from coming to an agreement. "I'd watched him work at Sand Hills," Mike said, "where he built one of the great golf courses without spending a lot of money. Impressive. But he turned me down, and it was probably a good thing that he did. Dick likes to have control over a project, and I don't know how well we would have worked together."

Mike next turned to Pete Sinnott, who had become a friend and regular companion since their collaboration at the Dunes Club. Pete had accompanied Mike on his Oregon trips more frequently than any other golf consultant, and he wasn't a retail golfer; he was a veteran of the golf business, a professional with years of experience in golf course construction and maintenance. Meticulous, thorough, systematic, and completely reliable, Pete had the kind of work ethic that Mike admired, and the two men simply enjoyed each other's company. As the number of decisions about Bandon piled up, Mike—who was still running RPG—asked Pete to consider moving to Oregon to supervise the construction.

In a memo dated January 1997, Pete reluctantly declined. He was already actively engaged in advising Mike about the construction, and he wrote, "Bandon is probably the most exciting golf undertaking in the country, and I would love to participate. Some options that come to mind: 1) We could place a strong superintendent and staff on site at the appropriate time in the construction schedule. I would go frequently during development and grow-in . . . 2) The second option would be that I go out as required with a specific assigned mission as directed by you. . . . Of utmost importance please be assured that our friendship and current business relationship are separate from your decision in this matter."

Mike chose the first option, and Pete's company, Serviscapes, became the general contractor for the golf course. By that spring, Pete had hired a superintendent, Mark Shepherd, and he was fully engaged in the run-up to construction.

With regular, on-site reports from Mark, and by making frequent trips from
Chicago to Oregon, Pete monitored and coordinated the myriad operations
that had gotten under way. There was site cleaning and preparation, which
involved not only clearing the gorse and timber but root-raking, applying
fertilizer, and double disking the ground to keep the soils from compacting;
developing plans for an irrigation system and soliciting bids for it; meeting
with the local fire departments to devise a safety system; bringing an electri-
cal system onto the property; figuring out how to manage effluent; staking
wetlands; developing and licensing wells; reviewing plans for pond development; and on and on and on. Every single item on the list involved meetings,
coordination with contractors and/or state and local agencies, and all the
attention and energy that Pete Sinnott could bring to bear. He wasn't the
kind of man to let things drift. He liked to run a tight ship.

One of his earliest exercises was to prepare a detailed budget for Mike, a
budget that would supplant Mike's hasty, horseback estimate. By early 1997,
hydrologists had disabused them of their original assumption that the site
would drain naturally. Water did run straight through the sandy soil, but the
water table was only a few feet below the surface in some parts of the property, and they were going to have to install extensive drainage. Furthermore,
given the dry summers and fierce winds, they were going to need a full-scale
irrigation system. Both items were reflected in the budget that Pete drew up
for the back nine, the nine that would be the first built. For the irrigation
system alone, he budgeted $549,000, and he estimated the cost of drainage
at $52,600 (in the final budget, for all eighteen holes, the cost of drainage
came to $490,124).

Other major items in Pete's 9-hole budget were clearing ($165,000), shap-
ing and fine grading ($202,000), and seeding ($150,000). The amount of
$77,000 was budgeted for cart paths; the question of making the course
walking only was turning out to be one of those pesky questions that just
couldn't be settled once and for all. When it was all added up, Pete thought
the back nine could be built for $1,330,452.

∙ ∙ ∙

"I'M THE ONLY ONE who sends Mike money," Shorty Dow liked to say. "Everybody else is on his payroll, but I'm sending him checks."

Shorty had contracted to clear the site of marketable timber, and he'd put together a crew to log off the stands of spruce, fir, and pine. Mike and Howard had finally accepted the necessity of clearing the whole site, leaving only a few ornamental trees, wonderful, wind-sculpted trees that have the dramatic shape of bonsais. The removal of the mature trees from the site didn't present any problem; they tended to grow in clusters, and in places sheltered from the full force of the ocean winds, but the logging operation didn't begin to solve the problem of the gorse, which grew thickly in the exposed areas. It wasn't impossible for a man with a chainsaw to take the gorse down, but he would have to fight the prickly leaves to lean in close enough to put his blade on the woody stem of the plant. The gorse was brutal, and Shorty had heard that some people who worked regularly in gorse had improvised clothing made of metal, like the Tin Man in *The Wizard of Oz*.

How to get rid of the stuff? There was no miracle method. Indeed, there was no known method that kept the workmen from getting mauled by the plants. Shorty didn't propose to make tin overalls for the workmen, but he and his son, Bud, did have an idea: On the front of a bulldozer, they'd rig a gizmo called a Hydro-Ax, a machine that was basically a giant lawn mower. A large rotary blade whipped around at high speeds inside a protective circular deck, pulverizing everything.

The system wasn't perfect. The Hydro-Ax was raised and lowered by a complex hydraulic system that, alas, tended to overheat. In the summer, with the gorse dry and highly combustible, splinters like kindling swirled through the air, and they frequently caught on fire. For the driver of the dozer with the Hydro-Ax, this was nerve-racking; if the oil on the machine caught fire, he was toast—badly burnt toast. One important part of his job was to keep the dozer cooled down by splashing buckets of water on it.

And then there was the problem of the pulverized gorse. The Hydro-Ax knocked the plants down and chewed them up, but it left behind a layer of organic duff that was a foot thick in some places. It was still as prickly as cactus, too. Crews of workers painfully collected the stuff any way they could—first with front-end loaders, then with rakes, and finally by hand. "In retrospect," said Troy Russell, who spent many days prying the last sprigs of gorse from the sand in which it had become embedded, "it might have been the worst possible way to remove the stuff. We'd have been better off cutting it cleanly and throwing the whole plant in the back of a truck and carting it off. The way we did it, we had to fool with all the bits and pieces."

TROY WAS ONE of the first locals to be hired at Bandon. He was a seed salesmen who had shown up one day at the trailer, known as the Design Center, that had become the headquarters for the project. As it happened, Jimmy Kidd was in the process of establishing test plots for various combinations of grasses, and he needed someone to look after them when he wasn't on site. Troy was his man.

Jimmy had taken a collaborative role in the early phases of the design, but what he really knew—what he understood inside and out—was how to grow grass. On one of the few level, open places on the Bandon property—a sheltered spot, once part of Varuna Farms, that had not only been cleared but also enriched with the droppings of Shuman's Morgan horses—Jimmy had started to do what he did best. He had started a turf nursery. He was growing grass—not just any grass, but several different blends; he wanted to see what kind of turf would grow in this climate. In particular, he wanted to see what combination of fescue and bent grass would work at Bandon. He met with various botanists and seed merchants in the region and laid out seven different test plots.

To most golfers, any turf talk makes the eyes roll and glaze, but out here in Oregon, Jimmy's experiments were of vital importance. The grasses on American golf courses, even on courses that call themselves links courses, are not the same as the grasses on the British links. Bent grass is the preferred grass in most of the northern United States; while bent grass provides a soft, velvety surface for fairways and greens, it doesn't allow for the kind of running shots that are essential to links golf. The blade of bent grass is just what the name suggests, a profile that is broad and flat; fescue grass grows in the shape of needles. Bent is flat, fescue is round. The difference in the playing qualities is that bent grass, unless shaved way down, tends to stop a ball. It acts almost like Velcro. By contrast, a ball rolls over fescue as though the surface has been oiled.

Jimmy rightly saw his test plots as vital to the building of an authentic links course, and Troy became their local caretaker. A graduate of Oregon State, Troy came from a family that had been farming in Coos County for generations. He was a hard worker, a practical joker, and an old-fashioned country boy who also happened to be completely up-to-date on horticulture and environmental science. After getting his degree, he returned to Coos County where he and wife had tried just about everything, including the planting of a small vineyard, to make ends meet, but it had been a struggle to make a living from the land. Troy was one of the first to decide that he wanted to throw his lot in with the Bandon project.

Troy knew how to plant and tend turf, and he did not lack for dedication and ingenuity. So that Jimmy could see just how the grass was growing, Troy got a hot-air balloon of the type seen above used-car lots, hooked up a camera, and sent it aloft at the end of a monofilament fishing line. He took his own aerial photographs and fired them off to Jimmy at Gleneagles.

JIM HALEY WAS OUT OF WORK. After eleven years of working as a shaper for architect Rees Jones, he had left the golf course construction business. A shaper is the artist of the heavy-equipment operators, the guy who creates the forms and final shapes of a golf course, the sculptor whose chisel is a twelve-foot dozer blade. Jim had decided that he wanted to become a shaper on a moonlit night in 1985, when he and a group of buddies, all of them students at the University of Nebraska, popped a few brews and ventured out to the site where architect Pete Dye was building a course called Firethorn (the developer, of course, was Dick Youngscap). Maybe it was the moonlight, or maybe it was the beer, or maybe a combination of the two—whatever, the shapes of the gaping bunkers and sloping greens looked fantastic to Jim Haley, and he decided right then and there that he wanted to be the one who made those shapes. Before enrolling at Nebraska, he had operated heavy equipment as a Navy Seabee, but the object had always been to make the earth flat and featureless. This golf course construction was exactly the opposite, and that was its appeal. "You could stand back and look at what you'd made," Jim says. "I thought, 'Whoa, that's pretty neat. It'll beat the hell out of selling seed corn for a living.'"

Jim loved the work, but he didn't care much for the constant travel. By 1997 he was married and living in Chicago, and he wanted to be around to see his daughters grow up. One day, his wife was getting her nails done by a manicurist whose husband sold fuel to Pete Sinnott's company, Serviscapes. The company was looking for a shaper to work on a small course in the Chicago area, and Jim sent in his resume; but he found out there was a catch. Serviscapes had just gotten involved in a course out in Oregon, and the Oregon course came first. Was Jim interested? Possibly. He agreed to go out to Oregon to have a look, and when he arrived at the Bandon site, he had the same kind of experience he'd had that night back in Nebraska. "I walked up to where the lodge is now, but then it was a huge ridge of sand. The whole place was like that, these huge ridges that looked like bulldozers had been working on them for years. I thought, 'I want to work on this,' and I called home that night and said, 'Honey, I'm gonna try to get this job.'"

He understood that he was there for a tryout. Pete and Mike wanted to see how well he worked with David Kidd (and David felt that he, too, was still auditioning, and that Mike and Pete wanted a chance to evaluate his work in the field). Working on a leased D7 with a wobbly blade that swung from side to side, Jim took the first pass at shaping holes No. 1 and No. 17, giving preliminary shape to the bunkers, greens, and the green surrounds. David made fun of the round, flat bunkers that Jim initially made—"satellite dishes," he called them. He wanted deep bunkers with ragged edges on No. 1, and a semiblind approach shot. For Jim, such forms and concepts were practically heresy, but he was excited; he was thirty-five years old, and David was thirty, and by the end of the week they were thick as thieves. "We worked, drank, and bullshitted that week, and I knew that we were going to have one hell of a ride together."

Before returning to Chicago, he went over to the Cascade Ranch and spent a week roughing in the tees, greens, and bunkers of the course that Mike had designed. In two short weeks in Oregon, he'd rediscovered all the old pleasures of pushing dirt into sculpted shapes, and he went home a happy man. He had gotten the job as lead shaper at Bandon Dunes.

THE FIRST SIGNS of conflict began to surface that spring.

David Kidd was still in frequent-flyer mode, traveling regularly to three different continents, but he wasn't about to become the kind of jet-set architect he deplored. He spent months at a time at Gokarna Forest in Nepal, and in 1996 he had also spent months in Bandon, learning the site, observing it in different winds and weathers, absorbing its intricacies, its features, its moods. Most of this time he spent alone, without Jimmy, and without his wife, Lyn, though she did make one trip to Oregon. The stress of travel and of rising to the career opportunities that now spread out before him had taken a toll on David, and on his marriage.

He had worked hard on the design plans for the golf course, preparing a highly detailed set of drawings for the design meeting in November. For the golfers who came to the meeting with Mike, a group that included Pete Sinnott, David had individual booklets made up, with each page showing a single golf hole and offering a brief description of its major features.

Pete reviewed all the holes with great care, and he set up a chart on which to evaluate them. In addition, he decided to rate each hole according to two different standards: the first was golf strategy, the second was what he called "visual appeal, landforms, comfort." Each hole was graded in each category, and overall Pete was a tough grader. For golf strategy, he awarded A's to only four holes; three holes got A's for visual appeal. Most holes got respectable B's, and Pete gave out ten C's. One hole, the 6th, pulled down a pair of D's.

David was fit to be tied when he got this report card. He wasn't happy with all of the holes, but he certainly hadn't expected to be graded on his work. He was stung to the quick, and though he didn't say anything to Mike, he began gearing up for what would be a pitched battle on several design matters.

It was clear that Pete was going to be more than a construction manager; he was going to have an important role in the decision making, and one of the first decisions was about the kind of grass to use on the golf course. This was Jimmy's area of expertise, of course, and it was also Pete's. He inspected the test plots that Jimmy and Troy had created, and he reviewed the whole issue from several angles, writing to Mike, "I like the fescue idea but it would probably not be the choice of American architects or players. It will be brown/gray/green, not the bright color of bent/poa annua. . . . Can we convince the American player at a top quality American course to buy our thinking? If yes, then let's do fescue fairways. If we think not, then maybe we should consider bent fairways and fescue rough."

His report was diplomatically worded and he deferred, as always, to Mike as the decision maker, but in effect he was stepping into the realm that had previously belonged exclusively to Jimmy. From both a marketing and a scientific point of view, Pete wanted—and got—other opinions besides Jimmy's about the use of fescue.

The matter came to a head in July 1997 when he held a meeting at which the final decision would be made about the blend of grass to be used at Bandon. Several seed consultants were present at the meeting, as were Mark Shepherd and Troy Russell, and the group reviewed results from the test plots. They decided on a mixture of colonial bent grass and fescue, blended with a species of brown top, that was very similar to the mix used on many Scottish links courses.

In a sense, Jimmy Kidd had prevailed—but he had been conspicuously absent from the meeting. He was in Scotland at the time, and there were pressing reasons to make a decision; Pete hadn't scheduled the meeting with the intention of eliminating Jimmy from the process, yet that was the effect. For all intents and purposes, Jimmy dropped out of the project after that, leaving Pete—and Mark and Troy—to make the calls on agronomy.

And leaving David, who believed that his father had been disrespected, with a growing sense of resentment.

13 | Do We Like It?

*I felt like the lead guitarist in a rock group. I had a hell of a band behind
me, and we were all playing the same tune.* —DAVID KIDD

ON A WINDY DAY in September 1997, on the site of the not-yet-built putting
green, Mike Keiser addressed the crew that had been rounded up to build
his golf course—a rough, ragged bunch of out-of-work loggers, former cranberry pickers, and hard-luck farmers, with a few Oregon hippies thrown in
for good measure. Most of them didn't know a golf hole from a gopher hole.
Even though the jumbled-up, half-cleared, fantastically shaped dunes served
as shelter, a north wind was blowing so hard that Mike's words of encouragement, when played back on tape, sound like they're competing with the
overflight of a jet fighter.

Nevertheless, his words made a lasting impression on several of the men.
"He told us that what we were going to build could last for five hundred years
if we built it right," Jim Haley recalls. "He got us pumped. He talked about
St. Andrews and how long people had been playing golf there. That talk really motivated the guys because we could see that Mike believed in what
we were about to do. He believed that this place was going to be something
special."

Jim Haley wanted to believe, but as the lead shaper and most experienced
member of the crew, he knew that they were facing a tall order, and he felt
the pressure. They all felt it. The goal was to build a world-class golf course,
and to build it in something close to record time. They were starting in September to take full advantage of the usually benign fall weather, and they

were going to try to complete the back nine—to have all nine holes drained, irrigated, shaped, and seeded—by Thanksgiving. Nine holes, start to finish, in two months. The pace was going to be breakneck. They were going to be working 24/7.

The construction plan was to focus on one or two holes at a time. Mike and Pete Sinnott would fly out at intervals, every three weeks or so, to check on the progress. As soon as a hole had won Mike's approval, the irrigation would be installed and the grass would be planted. Mike flew out on a private jet, often with people from Kemper or with retail golfers, and usually stayed for a few days. His standard question, asked over and over again, was, "Do we like it?" The phrase became a kind of mantra, and Jim and David, with their knack for mimicry, were able to capture the exact inflection of Mike's careful enunciation and unruffled baritone. Even when Mike wasn't on the site, his voice was there, asking for an appraisal, reminding them that they were aiming high. *Do we like it?*

Pete sometimes returned to Chicago with Mike, and sometimes stayed in Oregon a few extra days; but even when he was back in Indiana, at the home office of Serviscapes, he made daily phone calls to Mark Shepherd, his foreman, an experienced superintendent who was in charge of the day-to-day operations. Mark's job—a job that was difficult to start with and quickly became impossible—was to carry out Pete's orders while at the same time making sure that everything ran smoothly for David Kidd.

Altogether, there were about twenty men on that original crew, including Jim Haley, Troy Russell, and Troy's brother Tony, another Coos County dairy farmer who had the spirit of a merry prankster and an obvious talent with heavy machines; he was put to work doing rough grading and bulk earthwork—everything but the fine shaping. An ex-logger named Roger Sheffield, a guy who'd been on the clearing crew, turned out to have a deft touch with an excavator, and he became the chief bunker builder for the project. What he knew about bunkers could have been expressed in a single word—Zip!—but David showed him photographs of Muirfield and Gleneagles bunkers, and Roger caught on instantly.

Jim Haley caught on, too. He and David were obviously on the same wavelength; they were Butch Cassidy and the Sundance Kid, according to David (this was after I had called them the Lone Ranger and Tonto, and David corrected me: "Those two went around enforcing the law. That wasn't our style"). David and Jim were having a blast. At the end of the day, one of them would yell "Post Time" and they'd race to their vehicles and go fishtailing wildly through the sand, roaring across the site and down Route 101 to Bandon, where they were regulars at Lloyd's, one of the local watering holes. A good many others on the crew tagged along, and some nights they hoisted more than a few; David and Jim kept the pitchers coming. They just handed their plastic over to the barkeeps. They were demonstrating that the golf course really was going to be an economic boon to the town of Bandon, at least to the bars.

"We partied," Jim admits, "but you have to remember that we were working eighty hours a week. There wasn't that much time to screw off. And a part of what we were doing was trying to keep morale up. If the job had been run like boot camp, the way Pete was trying to run it, we would never have gotten the work done. There had to be some fun."

The tension between David and Pete kept bubbling, and the work, unquestionably, could be grim and miserable. During the clear days of September and October, the coastal winds blew steadily. On a site with exposed sand, this meant that crew members were pelted with blowing grains; they tried to cover their mouths and noses but still inhaled quarts of the stuff. They weren't exactly threatened by dangerous critters, but the site was overrun with porcupines, and the guys on the excavators got to be very adept at capturing them in their buckets and flicking them over the cliff edge (where many porcupines still live, though they rarely show their faces on the golf course). For the rake and shovel guys, who made up most of the crew, there was the seemingly endless task of getting rid of the gorse. Even worse, especially when the rains came in November, was the backbreaking wheelbarrow work, pushing the wheelbarrows loaded with turf from Jimmy Kidd's nursery through heavy, wet sand.

Sunup to sundown, day after day. They welcomed jokes, and David and Jim were the jokemeisters, with the Russells not far behind. One of the standing jokes was about a laborer named Kerwin, an elusive fellow who always seemed to go missing whenever there was a problem. So, naturally, he got the blame. "Where's Kerwin?" became shorthand for any sort of screwup. The one who was the target of most jokes, however, was the boss, Pete Sinnott. He was the lightning rod, the far-off taskmaster that the crew could complain about. They called him the Heat Miser, after the familiar figure in the TV commercial, a humorless character who was clearly modeled after the devil. During one of the many raucous nights on the town, somebody strung up a piñata, but it had been customized: a picture of Pete Sinnott was glued on, turning it into a *Pete-yata,* and it was gleefully smashed. And Pete didn't help his own cause when he climbed aboard a dozer to do some finishing work around the 14th green: The irrigation heads had already been put in, and in less than an hour Pete managed to hit three of them with his blade, mangling them. Troy Russell had the three heads with their twisted pipes fashioned into a kind of trophy and had a plaque made to go with it. The unusual trophy and plaque were presented to Pete, in commemoration of the feat known as The Hat Trick.

THE MAN WHO BELIEVED most passionately in Mike's vision was the one who'd been hired to execute it, David Kidd. By the time construction began, he'd been waiting for almost three years, and he had spent months—far more time than stipulated by contract—learning the site, absorbing its moods. The place wasn't exactly like Machrihanish, but it had the same rugged beauty and sense of wild isolation. David's imagination was on fire, and he'd lie awake at night thinking of the golf course he was about to build. Opportunity hadn't just knocked on his door but had pretty much blown it open, and his life had been turned inside out and upside down.

As long as he'd been around golf, *this* had never happened—this sense of passion, of brimming with ideas and inspiration, of being able to visualize exactly what he wanted to do. He was recovering all the messages that Machrihanish and Gleneagles had coded into his memory, into his subconscious, and he was hell-bent to inscribe those messages here on the Oregon dunes.

David had come to think of Bandon Dunes as *his* course, but every real designer feels that sense of possession. Ask any designer—not just a golf course architect, but anyone who designs anything for commercial use—about the greatest challenge of his job, and he will undoubtedly say, "Maintaining the integrity of the design." No matter what the product, the one who designs it feels that others are all too willing to tinker with it. Moreover, the designer knows that the smallest changes—a nip here, a tuck there—can put the project on a slippery slope. Designers are usually controlling people to begin with, and when they are astride a big project, and someone stands in their way, they can easily come across as monsters of ego. They can be rude, paranoid, defensive, petulant, belligerent, stubborn, selfish, and outrageous—and young David Kidd, at times, was all of those things.

He was also brilliant, charismatic, funny, inventive, and fiendishly inspired. He was determined to infuse this golf course with a sense of grandeur and exalted play, and he fumed inwardly whenever he encountered opposition or resistance. He was a thirty-year-old who knew that he'd been handed an opportunity to create something extraordinary, and his inner drama was heightened by the fact that his private life seemed to be falling apart. His wife, Lyn, his college sweetheart, had come to Oregon only once; she had remained in London while he traveled, and their marriage was buckling under the strain. For years they had tried unsuccessfully to have a child; twice, at great financial and emotional expense, they had gone through the process of in vitro fertilization, only to have it fail. In the fall of 1997, they were considering whether to try for a third time, and the uncertainties, anxieties, and fears were almost more than either of them could bear. Finally, in the desperate way of couples trying to will their future into the shape they wanted, they decided to make a third attempt—precisely at the moment when construction was about to begin and David was consumed with the need to make sure that his creative wishes were carried out in Bandon. He didn't feel that he could leave. It was an impossible dilemma, the kind of quandary that can ruin an artist or push him to new heights. Students of the creative mind may argue about whether the artist immerses himself in his work to escape from his personal demons, or whether these demons are somehow necessary to make the angels of imagination take wing, but many writers, composers, and painters seem to do their best work in a state of high turbulence.

David Kidd was discovering himself as an artist, and like it or not, he was in such a state. He was driving himself hard, and his emotions kept coming to the surface. The retail golfers, to put it bluntly, filled him with frustration; as far as he was concerned, they didn't have a clue. His rendition of *Do we like it?* carried undertones of defensiveness and exasperation. As a young man, far from home, he felt tremendous pressure to buckle when the consensus seemed to run against him. He and Jim Seeley, the head of operations at Kemper Sports Management, were often at loggerheads, and David had a huge dustup with a pro who came out with Mike on an early trip. The pro looked at the revetted bunker on the 12th hole, the first hole built, and declared that it was unfair. Was the Road Hole bunker unfair, David wanted to know. Was Muirfield unfair? Carnoustie? The pro said he wouldn't have a shot from the bunker, but David threw down a ball and demonstrated that there were several shots. He could get out sideways or backward. Who had decreed that a golfer who hits into a bunker has a divine right to advance the ball?

Fortunately, Mike was on David's side. They were building a links course here at Bandon, a course that really didn't have any exact models in the United States. There are plenty of courses that call themselves links, but David was trying to create the real thing, a seaside course that would be as true a links as anyone had ever built in the United States. He knew exactly how he wanted his golf holes to look. His attitude, he says now, was "Follow me or get the fuck out of my way."

MOST MEMBERS OF the construction crew were willing to follow, but it was clear that David was on a collision course with Pete Sinnott and his right-hand man, Mark Shepherd. There were plenty of small incidents.

David would ask a worker to do one thing, and Mark Shepherd would ask him to do another. There would be words, some of them heated, some of them expletives. Construction sites aren't known for their dainty language, and men in a power struggle don't usually display much sensitivity for the feelings of their adversaries. There were shouting matches between David and Mark Shepherd, but it was really Pete who, in David's eyes, had become the villain. From back in Indiana, halfway across the country, Pete seemed intent on thwarting him.

Pure and simple, this was a clash of wills. Throw in radically different personalities, and you have an explosive situation in which there were disputes about damn near everything, from the shape of a green to the right way to plant beach grass (David wanted it to have a random look, and Pete wanted the sprigs planted on 18-inch centers). The fact that Pete had a longer-standing relationship with Mike gave him a certain advantage; the fact that David had the allegiance of the crew dictated some of his strategy. One of David's ploys was to wait until the day before Mike was to visit before implementing last-minute changes; that way he never had to discuss the changes with Mark or Pete; if Mike approved, it was too late for Pete to stand in their way.

The conflict simmered throughout the fall and finally came to a head when the 16th and 17th holes were being built. Today, the 16th is one of the best-known and most-admired holes on the golf course, a short, slightly uphill par 4 bordered on the right by the Pacific Ocean. The green is on a cliff top, and the cliff edge is on a dramatic shelf of clay called redshot. In the prevailing north wind, a long-hitting golfer might be tempted to drive the green, but in order to do so he must carry a deep chasm and a long, diagonal ridge where the beach grass is deep and thick. With the ocean to the right, a gorse-covered dune to the left, and the chasm and the angled ridge in the line of play, this 16th hole is like no other golf hole in the world, a bold, original, and brilliant design.

In the earliest planning, remember, this high point was considered for a clubhouse site. Later, the 16th was designed as a long par 5. In a still later incarnation, it was drawn as a 385-yard par 4, a two-shotter with two distinct lines of play, the more aggressive line being inside a ridge running parallel to the ocean.

Parallel? So where did that diagonal ridge come from?

From David's imagination, that's where. He decided the 16th would be a better hole if the ridge was realigned. It was an impulse decision, made one day as he stood on the tee, and he constructed a model of the hole right there in the sand. He showed Jim Haley and Roger Sheffield how the hole would look if the ridge, then oriented like the hour hand of a clock at high noon, were moved to the two o'clock position. The strategy of the hole would change dramatically, for a golfer could now carry the ridge instead of having to play to one side or the other. The hole that had required a finesse approach, and perhaps a lay-up from the tee, now invited the golfer to attack with a mighty blow of the driver.

While he was at it, David had Jim shave off several feet of earth in front of the tee to make the chasm loom even more ominously, and he moved the location of the green back as near as he could to the cliff's edge. He knew that Pete and Mark wouldn't approve of these changes, so he got a group of his loyalists, his gang from Lloyd's, to plant the green at night, in the pitch dark, in the glow of the headlights from their cars and trucks.

By daylight the green was planted, and David had gotten his way, again.

THE PITCHED BATTLE came at the 17th hole. One of the most unusual holes at Bandon, the 17th is flanked on the right by a chasm formed by Cut Creek. The creek is small, but the chasm is deep, broad, and gorse choked. The hole is designed so that the chasm bites into the right side of the fairway at the place where a long drive would finish; on the left side there are deep, mean bunkers. The player who wants to attack this hole must hit a straight ball.

So much for the strategy. The problem was that the bank of the chasm was unstable, and the drop-off was steep. David thought he needed to shore up the bank in some fashion, and he decided to use railroad ties. These had already been used in several places to create walkways through the gorse or to move golfers from one hole to the next, but they hadn't been used vertically, for bulk heading, as David was now proposing. Scratch that: He did not *propose* to use them to stabilize the bank. He went ahead and installed them.

This use of railroad ties had not been approved. Phone calls were made. Pete Sinnott was informed, and so was Mike. Mark Shepherd took pictures of the vertical ties, which had been driven into the ground but not sawed off. They stood at various heights, ragged and snaggletoothed. In the pictures, taken from below, they loomed up, Troy Russell says, "like the peaks of the Andes." Faxes flew back and forth (since the age of the cell phone was still in its infancy and there was no signal on the coast) from Oregon to Illinois. Mike, upset, wanted to know what railroad ties were doing on a links course. Pete wanted to know why David had gone ahead without permission.

David wanted Mike to understand that plenty of links courses used railroad ties to shore up bunkers, which was part of what he was trying to do. There was a bunker below the ties to catch drives that were wide right. Furthermore, he intended to saw off the ties at ground level, not leave them as they appeared in the photograph. When the job was finished, he insisted, most golfers would never even know that the ties were there. And *something* had to be done to keep that bank from collapsing.

Stalemate. The project ground to a halt until Mike could get out to Oregon to see with his own eyes what David had done. People did keep working, but on minor things, waiting for the outcome of what everyone on the ground understood to be the decisive engagement. And when Mike did arrive, he took David's side. He saw that the ties, when they were trimmed, would be almost invisible. He ruled that they could stay.

"From that moment on," David declares, "I was able to be freer. That whole episode was hugely frustrating, but it was liberating, too. And not long after it all happened, Mike took me aside and said, 'I just held you up for ten days, didn't I?' After that, he had more faith in me."

BY THANKSGIVING, EVEN with the delay on the 17th hole, the back nine at Bandon Dunes was completed. The crew had worked for fifty-seven days without a break. The golf holes were shaped, the irrigation and drainage were installed, and the grass was planted. The breakneck pace had yielded results, and Jim Haley, who'd never been on a links course and never seen anything like what he was being asked to build, was turning into a true believer. In December, when Mike rewarded him and David with a trip to Scotland and Ireland to play the great links courses, Jim had a kind of awakening. "Frankly, I'd been scared shitless by what we were doing. I'd been around golf for years but never seen anything like what David wanted. After that trip, though, my idea of golf was just thrown into a complete tailspin. I said to David, 'What the hell, we can do whatever we want.' We saw all these famous links courses, and our site was just as good as any of them. I never doubted what we were doing after that, and I told David that our elevator was going up. We were going to the top."

Something else happened on that trip. Just before Christmas, at St. Andrews, David got the news that his wife, Lyn, was pregnant. The third attempt at IVF had succeeded, and the whirlwind journey to the meccas of golf was interrupted by many wrenching, emotional phone calls. By this time, David was drained, personally and professionally. He was simply exhausted. He was only thirty years old, he was doing the most inspired work of his life, he was going to be a father, and his marriage was in a shambles. He took some time to try to gather himself.

When construction resumed in the early spring of 1998, David was back in Bandon, and he was back on a creative high. He hadn't resolved all the issues with Lyn or his impending fatherhood, but he knew exactly what he wanted to do with this golf course. The holes on the back nine had grown in, and there was no longer any doubt about how this golf course was going to turn out. Josh Lesnik had moved to Oregon as the first general manager of the Bandon Dunes Resort, and he was putting together a publicity effort. The buzz had already started, and a trickle of visitors—local pros and writers, a few people from the Oregon Golf Association and the USGA, all of them deep-dyed golfers, the kind of folks whose opinions carried some weight—

made the trek to look at Bandon Dunes. They registered surprise and awe. That "Wow" factor was huge. David realized that he was riding a tiger.

During the second phase of the construction, he felt that he could do no wrong. By this time the slackers and nonloyalists in the crew had mostly fallen away, and the gang building the second nine knew what they were doing. Jim Haley and Roger Sheffield were still on board, of course, as were the Russell brothers, and they understood what David wanted. This core group had bonded together, and there was a flow to the work, a camaraderie, a shared sense of accomplishment. As a sign of solidarity, they all started wearing the same kind of sunglasses, big, blocky Ray-Bans, the kind worn by country-music star Roy Orbison. David, naturally, was the one who bought the glasses and decided who got to wear them. "I felt like the lead guitarist in a rock group," David says. "I had a hell of a band behind me, and we were all playing the same tune."

Sometimes David was the errand boy for the others. They were on the machines all day long, and he was the one who went into Bandon to get lunch and, sometimes, to do Jim Haley's laundry. He could leave the site more easily than they could. What was required of him was to keep coming up with ideas, and they were just pouring out of him. The front nine, with the addition of the holes on the Shuman land, was sound in its sequence, but David kept adding and refining, making changes—some small, some large—that gave character and definition to the holes. For instance, he changed the location of the tees on No. 2, a sturdy par 3. From the original tees, the green benched into the ridge presented a sidehill shot, and the left side of the green fell away to a large, sandy waste. David rotated the tees by ninety degrees, placed them atop dunes, and completely changed the golfer's perspective of the green, requiring a tee shot directly over the waste area. Both holes are good, but the new version was decidedly more dramatic. Mike liked the change, and he gave it his blessing.

And so it went throughout the construction on the front nine. At No. 7, David built a roller-coaster green inspired by some of the wilder Machrihanish greens, the greens that were designed by Old Tom Morris; this 7th green has tremendous slopes off of which a golfer can bank his approach or pitch. At the 8th, the tee shot is played over a double row of severe bunkers. "Mike called me and said he was looking at pictures of the Hell Bunker. 'I like them,' he said [David just can't resist imitating Mike's deep voice]. 'Let's do something like that.' So I was looking for a place, and this was it."

When they got to the 9th hole, Jim Haley said, "What else can we do?" He thought that David had used every trick in the book, but he hadn't. He wasn't going to finish on a meek note: He put the bunkers right in the middle of the fairway—not just to make a statement, but to give the golfer something to think about on both the drive and the second shot, making this par 5 a stronger hole.

This nine took longer to build, but by June 1998 the golf course was finished. The sand was in the bunkers, the irrigation lines were in the ground, and the grass was growing in beautifully. The project ended, as golf projects do, not with a bang but with a long winding down and the constant play of sprinklers on maiden turf. Piece by piece, the leased heavy equipment disappeared, and the men who tinkered with the final details were not part of the construction gang but members of the grounds crew. Mark Shepherd had left, and Troy Russell, the local boy who had decided to hitch his wagon to the Bandon star, had been installed as the first superintendent.

David Kidd and Jim Haley had left, too, but not before coming up with a T-shirt to pass out to the survivors of this adventure. No one wants to take credit, or blame, for the entries on the shirt, but it has the telltale characteristics of a Kidd-Haley production. The front of the shirt showed the Bandon logo, a tufted puffin, and the back read:

Bandon Dunes Construction

Top 10 List

10. Inhaled Sand

9. Post Time

8. Porcupines

7. Where's Kerwin?
6. The Keiser Effect
5. April Fools—Payback
4. Night Seeding
3. Does your <u>blank</u> hurt?
2. BHP
1. Hat Trick

Attentive readers will get nearly all of these jokes, but there are a couple of entries on the list that no one wants to explain. Even though many years have passed, there are some things that the Bandon Dunes crew would just as soon keep secret. No one would tell me what a <u>blank</u> was? "You can guess," one source said, "but you'll guess wrong. You'll be close, but wrong."

As for BHP, that does need explication. It was a favorite expression of David's, shorthand for a term of approval and admiration. It was used to describe a man who had the courage of his convictions.

The man to whom the term was most often applied was Mike Keiser.

BHP stood for Big Hairy Pair.

14 | The Anti-Resort

It's all about the golf.

—Josh Lesnik

JOSH LESNIK WAS AT his desk at Kemper Sports Management when he got a call from Mike Keiser. He was twenty-nine years old, recently married, relatively new to the golf business, and Mike had a proposition for him: How would he like to move to Oregon to work at Bandon Dunes?

Josh was flabbergasted, and his first reaction was not to leap for joy. Oregon? He thought of himself as a city kid, and he liked bright lights. He liked streets and traffic and crowds and the Cubs and the Bulls. He and his wife, Judy, had just bought their first house; their first son, Jake, had been born in November 1996. Now, less than a year later, was he really prepared to pick up and move? And why had Mike decided to call *him*? They barely knew each other, and Josh didn't have the kind of experience that suggested that he was ready to become the general manager of a resort. His first assignment at KSM had been "assistant to the assistant PR guy" for a minor-league basketball team, the Sioux Falls Skyforce. He had then gone to work for his father-in-law, managing accounts for the sale of automotive products like sound systems and security systems, before returning to KSM to develop new business and market new properties.

Naturally, he suspected his father, Steve, of having influenced Mike—and indeed he had, though not in the way that Josh imagined. "I can't even remember whether Josh and I had met," Mike said, "but I'd heard about him from Steve, and I'd concluded intuitively that I wanted to hire him. I was able to filter out the dad-bragging and I had a hunch about Josh, the way I did about David Kidd. I knew that Steve thought Josh had good PR sense, but mostly Steve talked about how much everybody liked him. 'Why does everybody like him?' he'd say. 'Everybody loves Josh. They love Josh, and they love [my wife] Mady. Why don't they love me?' Steve couldn't figure it out. And the other thing I knew was that Steve and Judy's dad had competed for him. I decided I wanted to get into the fray."

A few weeks after that out-of-the-blue phone call, in September 1997, Josh flew out to Oregon for his first look at Bandon; it was also his first trip on a private jet. He and Mike were the only passengers, and they got along famously. Mike made it clear that he wanted Josh to take over as general manager. Josh asked, "Can I see the place before I decide?"

At Bandon they went straight to the 12th hole. Josh met David Kidd and Jim Haley, and he started taking pictures. He'd never been to Scotland or Ireland, and never seen a links course, but he liked this golf hole on the bluff over the ocean. The hole wasn't seeded, but its shapes were apparent, and the dune at the right of the green reared its brushy head. Josh kept taking pictures as he and Mike walked the site, heading south toward Bullard's Beach and what is now the 17th tee. He responded, as everyone does, to the wild beauty of the place. He was a long way from the corporate world, and he liked being outside in jeans and work boots. By that night, after Mike threw a beer-and-pizza party for the crew, he was almost ready to sign on. It would take another trip to persuade Judy, but once she'd been to Bandon—and after Mike had promised that the job would only last two years—Josh Lesnik became the first general manager of Bandon Dunes Resort.

His task, as Mike described it later, was "to create something out of nothing." When he moved to Oregon in May 1998, a year before the golf course opened, the only building on the property was the trailer known as the Design Center. Josh had a desk, a phone, a computer, and a wastebasket. He shared the space with Howard McKee—and with David, Jim, Mark Shepherd, Troy Russell, and other members of the crew, all of whom used the Design Center as a shelter and base of operations—and started thinking about how to spread the word about Bandon Dunes. "We never had a stated goal," Josh said. "Mike never said we have to do this or that to make this a Top 100 course. He didn't say, 'Josh, this is going to be big.' If he had, I'm not sure I would have taken the job. But he made it easy for me to operate. It was never overwhelming. We talked on the phone every day, and he'd ask me questions I could answer, like how's the weather out there? He kept it caveman simple. When we first started talking about how to market Bandon, I sent him a fax with some ideas, and about ten minutes later the fax comes back. Mike had written on it: *Great golf + great food + great people = our marketing plan.*"

Though Mike never appeared worried, he knew that Bandon Dunes faced daunting odds. At the same time that he was offering Josh a job, he was signing another deal with KSM, this one making them the manager of the resort. KSM had been in a consulting role all along, and Mike and Steve felt a bond of loyalty to one another. But Gleneagles Golf Developments wanted to make its case for managing the hotel and resort, and Howard thought GGD deserved the opportunity. Mike: "Howard wanted to interview Gleneagles and other potential managers, and we did talk to Ian Ferrier. The Gleneagles position was that we're Scottish, and can run it like a Scottish hotel, with bagpipers in kilts, that kind of thing. But it wasn't as if we had ten companies to choose from, all of them eager to do something in Oregon. At that time, remember, it was a folly, not a phenomenon. Nobody knew how much money we were going to make, or if we'd make any money at all. The one thing I did know was that Bandon Dunes wouldn't be just another property for KSM. They'd give it their full attention."

Hiring Josh, in the opinion of Jim Haley, was a way of making sure that KSM focused on Bandon Dunes. "We used to joke," he said, "that Mike's deal with Kemper was, 'OK, you get the management contract, but I want your firstborn.'" Josh was a few years younger than Jim, and the same age as David Kidd; he brought, as they did, a spirit of youthful optimism and energy to the project—though he occasionally got a rude, forceful reminder of just how tough a sell Bandon was going to be. When Josh went to Portland in the fall of 1998 for a small golf exposition, he set up a booth with several pictures of Bandon, and the only people who stopped by for a second look did so in order to needle him. Were the pictures retouched? How'd he get the sun to shine? Everybody knew that it rained 365 days a year on the Oregon coast! Josh had weather data to prove the scoffers wrong, but he realized—as everyone at KSM had realized all along—that a lot of people associated the coast of Oregon with wet, gray, grim weather.

The number-crunchers at KSM headquarters in Northbrook factored that into their budget projections. They were trying to calculate just how many golfers might show up at Bandon Dunes. As a basis for their projections, they assumed that a modestly successful golf course in a place with a season of seven or eight months might play 25,000 rounds.

Since Bandon Dunes would be a start-up in a remote location, fighting the perception of lousy weather, the KSM analysts sliced that number in half. For the first year of operations, the budget projection was 12,466 rounds at $35 per round.

GIVEN THOSE PALTRY NUMBERS, and all the other expenses that Mike had to incur before the opening of the golf course, Josh didn't have much of a marketing budget. There was next to nothing for advertising. Mike: "I don't believe in advertising. I love PR, but I think most advertising is a waste of money." As always, his concept was to "concentrate on what you're good at," and he was good at making cards. His experience at Recycled Paper Greetings had taught him to rely on images ("In the card business, I learned about the impotence of words, and too much information just leaves me slack-jawed"). When he and Josh tackled the question of how to publicize Bandon Dunes, they decided quickly on their first tactic: Send the message in a greeting card.

"I'd seen enough press releases," Mike said, "to know they were eminently tedious. The fancy folders that some courses put out have to be expensive— they must cost at least ten dollars—and most of them go straight into the trash can. For a few thousand dollars, we could send thousands of cards. Our idea was to send a card that contained just enough information to make people want to know more. We wanted them to open the card, look at the picture, say *Wow!*, and call Josh for more information."

The Bandon Dunes style would be understatement, not overkill, and it prevailed in every marketing decision and every effort to define and establish the "brand." Mike and Josh selected a picture for the front of the card and a few carefully considered words for the message. Josh: "I wrote the cards, and at first it was hard to be brief. I was used to writing longer stuff, so it was good discipline. If you have only a few sentences, you have to be clear about what you want to say. There's no place for nuance or braggadocio—that's a word I learned from Mike. As in, no braggadocio. Everything was about the place, and the golf. That was it. What we had was golf and the ocean."

The first card they designed showed just that. The front was a picture of the 12th hole, that par 3 hard by the Pacific Ocean. The card was sent to every member of the Golf Writers Association of America, and to the presidents of golf clubs in Oregon, Washington, and northern California, who were invited to bring a foursome to Bandon for a preopening round. The intent was to stir up the interest and support of the "bell cows," the ones who lead the rest of the herd.

Both Mike and Josh believed that anyone who came to Bandon and saw the place would react like Brian McCallen, the veteran travel writer from *Golf Magazine,* a guy who'd been everywhere and seen everything. He wasn't a gusher, but when he showed up at Bandon that June, he was blown away. David Kidd was still in town, putting the finishing touches on the course; the front nine wasn't open yet, but Brian and David and Josh played the back nine over and over again, finishing in the moonlight. They went into town and dined at the Wheelhouse and did oyster shooters and Brian ended up spending the night at Josh's house. In May 1999, the month Bandon Dunes opened, Brian published his review, and he was one of the first to trumpet the beauties of the place: "No finer piece of land has been made available for a golf course in America since Alister MacKenzie (another Scot) was shown the site for the Cypress Point Club on the Monterey Peninsula." And the headline for the article was: "Oregon's Answer to Ballybunion?" It was by no means the only time that writers would reach for heroic comparisons in their attempt to convey the potent allure of Bandon Dunes.

Timely though it was, the *Golf* article wasn't the first rave. Several writers from *Golfweek* had been in Washington State for the 1998 PGA Championship, played at Sahalee Golf Club and won by Vijay Singh, and Josh persuaded them to stop at Bandon on the way home.

Josh treated their visit as a make-or-break event. These were senior golf writers, guys like Dave Seanor and Jeff Rude, whose opinions carried weight. Altogether, there were eight writers, and Josh turned to his staff—at this point, a volunteer staff of one, Bob Gaspar—to arrange for caddies. A Bandon resident, former teamster, and member of the Coast Guard Reserve, Gaspar knew just about everybody in Coos County, and he had decided the day he read about Bandon Dunes in the local paper that his future was linked to the future of the golf course. "I was working in the cranberry bogs when I read about the work that was going on. They weren't hiring yet but I decided to call anyway. I left a message. The next day I was standing in the bogs in a pair of waders when the boss came up to me and said Josh Lesnik was on the phone, and I put my shovel down and never went back." When Josh said that he couldn't give him a full-time job, Bob said he'd come in anyway and make himself useful, and he became the Design Center's all-purpose factotum.

He also became Bandon's first caddy master. He'd never caddied before, but Josh gave him a tutorial, and Bob passed along the lessons to the people he recruited. When the *Golfweek* writers arrived, he happened to get Dave Seanor's bag. Dave took one glance at him and said, "You look just like Willie Shoemaker. From now on, your name is Shoe." Bob is a slight man, and he does look like the great jockey, who had always been a hero to him; just like that, the caddy-golfer bond was formed. Dave, like the others from *Golfweek*, knew that they were discovering an extraordinary place. "At dinner that first night," Dave told me, "we sat around and talked about our favorite holes. We'd played the whole course, and everybody had a different favorite hole. Anybody can see how beautiful it is, but that's when it started to sink in just how good it was. Most courses are lucky to have one or two great holes, but Bandon Dunes has a bunch."

The *Golfweek* writers were sure of their opinions, and in March 1999, two months before Bandon Dunes opened, the golf course made its debut on the magazine's list of America's Greatest Courses. It was ranked No. 10. The *Golfweek* list is divided into two sections, Classic and Modern, and the ranking was on the Modern list, among courses built since 1960, but it was still an astounding vote of confidence.

The buzz had started. Rather, the national buzz had started; the local and regional buzz was already going strong. The people in Coos County had been reading about the golf course for years, and the mailing to golf club presidents had produced a strong response. People wanted to come to Bandon to claim their preview rounds. The course raters from the Oregon Golf Association had come to rate Bandon Dunes; among the insiders, the hard-core golfers who pride themselves on keeping up, the word was spreading quickly that this new track in Bandon was a must-see. On the December day that a favorable article by Bob Robinson appeared in the *Oregonian,* the phone rang in the Design Center. Shoe answered. At the other end of the line was a golfer who wanted to reserve a tee time. Josh listened—"my heart was pounding I was so excited"—to the conversation, and Shoe took down all the information by hand, doing his best to act as if he was used to taking these requests.

When he hung up, he and Josh whooped and hollered and danced around the room. They had just gotten Bandon Dunes' first customer. As a commercial enterprise, Bandon Dunes was up and running.

From that day on, the phone kept ringing. They would need, of course, to get a computerized reservation system in place. Shoe would become a regular employee, a fixture at Bandon Dunes, the smiling man in the sky-blue Bandon cap who greets guests outside the lodge, many of whom know his name—and he knows theirs. And the advance interest in the golf course was enthusiastic enough to make the businesspeople go back and look at their numbers.

They decided to set the green fee for the first season at $100.

THAT WAS THE FEE for out-of-state golfers. There was a different, much lower fee for Oregonians, a fee that varied according to the day of the week and the month of the year, but it was usually less than half of what the out-of-staters paid (it still is). KSM intended, as a matter of good business and good community relations, to price the course so that it would draw regionally. And when Mike said he wanted a public course, he had always meant a course that the members of the public could at least *think* about playing. In places like Scottsdale and Palm Springs, the price of public golf had ramped up steadily; in 1999, the green fee at plenty of resort courses was closer to $200 than $100, and Pebble Beach was charging $325. Compared to those prices, Bandon's fee structure was more than reasonable. It was positively modest.

Mike talked over decisions about price with Josh, Steve, and Jim Seeley, the chief of operations at KSM. In the KSM organization, Josh actually reported to Jim, but even as the opening day approached, the planning was conducted along the established lines of the group grope. On this point, Mike couldn't have been more clear: "I'm not a planner. I don't know why people bother to try to plan things out when so much always comes between the plans and the reality. How many meetings does it take to catch up? I tried to keep the focus on what we were going to do right now." His resistance to planning sometimes frustrated Howard, a planner by instinct and by training, and it ran counter to the corporate protocol of KSM—but Mike was the boss. Bandon Dunes was his resort. He was paying the bills, and he was calling the shots.

His preference was to feel his way forward, allowing plenty of room for change—for imagination, discovery, serendipity, and inspiration. His MO had always been to solicit and welcome ideas from all quarters. On the key decision about making the golf course walking only, he had asked for the opinion of the retail golfers, the construction guys, the KSM people, and everyone else he came into contact with. David Kidd had always been dead set against carts, and Mike preferred walking—but Dick Youngscap had warned him that he'd turn away golfers if he didn't have carts, and Jim Seeley could put his finger on a budget line and show him how much revenue he'd give up without carts. Troy Russell had set up test areas with several kinds of cart surfaces, and David had hidden a few cart paths on the golf course; they were natural paths in the sand, tucked away behind ridges or walls of gorse in places where there had to be some kind of passage. Legally, the resort was going to have to provide carts for golfers with disabilities or medical conditions (today, the resort does own a few carts, and players who qualify to take a cart must also take as their driver a caddy who knows the whereabouts of these paths, and the places where a cart may not be driven).

Mike, who has always loved hiking and walking, agonized over this decision, and neither he nor anyone else can remember the exact moment when the hammer fell. As the point of no return approached, Mike did make a late-night call to Steve Lesnik—that might have been the moment when the matter was settled. But the discussion had gone on for so long, with the sentiment for walking gathering weight and momentum, that this decision seemed to make itself, and one day Mike realized that he no longer had a choice. The moment when he might have bought a fleet of carts had passed, and when the first visitors were starting to arrive at Bandon, Josh and Shoe fixed them up with caddies.

It was all about the golf. That's what he and Josh kept saying to each other as they worked on a way to present Bandon to the public, and that's what Mike believed. The statement was disarmingly simple, considering all the time, effort, and money that had gone into the development of the golf course, but Mike was determined to keep *everything* that way. Every image, every statement that Josh wrote, every building that Howard designed, every stick of furniture for the guest rooms, every meal served on the property—everything started with the fact that *it was all about the golf.*

The resort was there to enhance the golf experience, not get in the way of it, or provide a dozen different kinds of diversions and activities. Mike was more interested in comfort than in luxury, and—this was a man whose favorite accommodations were the austere rooms at Sand Hills—he didn't feel any need to pamper the clientele. This was Bandon, Oregon, after all, not

Palm Springs. Bandon Dunes was all about the golf, and the golf was walking only, and that decision told golfers a lot about what they could expect. The resort took shape as a no-frills, no-fuss, no-apologies kind of place, a place with its own ethos and character. In other words, it was the opposite of the kind of corporate resort, a Marriott or Ritz-Carlton, where a concerted effort is made to anticipate the guest's every need and cater to his every whim, with the result that the service often comes across as insincere and over-the-top and the "product" is usually sleek, bland, impersonal, and predictable. At Bandon, nothing was predictable, not even the weather, and the place reeked with personality—with several personalities, actually. The golf course was an expression of David Kidd, the buildings and the overall plan were an expression of Howard McKee, and the whole operation, top to bottom, was an expression of Mike Keiser.

WHILE JOSH WAS TRYING to get out the word, Howard McKee was gearing up to build a lodge and all the other buildings and infrastructure required at a resort. During much of 1997, he'd been undergoing chemotherapy for his colon cancer and he had to schedule his work carefully, but in 1998 he was back at full throttle. His response to the disease and the treatment had led down some unusual paths. As a part of his spiritual healing, Howard had gone on a retreat to practice Vipassana meditation, a rigorous and ancient technique that aims at mental purification. "I went to a retreat that lasted ten days. Each day we sat meditation for eleven hours. There was no speaking. The meditation technique was to focus on this place just below the nose and above the lip, to be aware of this specific point at a molecular level. Once that was mastered, we focused on different parts of the body. It was like a scan, and part of the lesson was to realize that we are in a constant process of change. There might be pain in the arm, for instance, but if you accept it, if you simply observe it, it goes away. It transforms itself into something else, and this happens all the time. Ultimately, the goal of Vipassana is to achieve a kind of detachment, a freedom from desire or any effort to control an outcome, a state in which I believe we have a taste of our eternal existence.

We have energy before we're born, and energy after death, and I believe that's our true essence, something that exists apart from out physical being. The purpose of the meditation is to align ourselves with whatever happens."

From the beginning, Howard had regarded the association with Mike and the return to Oregon as his chance to do soul work, and now, having confronted his mortality, and having completed the most tedious and bureaucratic parts of the project, he was ready to build. The time had come to give shape and form to the vision that had been outlined on a couple of sheets of paper a full decade earlier, a vision that was now becoming tangible. Out on the land, the vision was turning into the reality of a golf course, and somehow or other Howard had to translate Mike's desires—and those of Steve and Josh and Jim and all the others—into structures. In a way, the task was akin to that of Daniel, the biblical prophet who was called upon to interpret the dream of King Nebuchadnezzar. The problem was that Nebuchadnezzar couldn't remember his dream. Mike hadn't forgotten his vision, but the vision had always been about golf, never about buildings.

Now the group grope was going to have to yield some specific plans, and Howard would occasionally need all the patience, calm, and balance he could summon. He was managing a multitude of projects that all had to be completed before the opening of the resort. The only construction project not under his direction was the golf course itself; everything else—the maintenance building, the water treatment plant, the entrance road, the lodge, the cottages, the restaurants, the parking lots, the landscaping, the arrangements with all the local vendors and inspectors—was in Howard's domain.

Regarding the lodge, the most prominent building, a consensus was starting to emerge. It hadn't come easily. Mike had sought the advice of not only the people at KSM but also the retail golfers, one of whom was Larry Booth, the architect who had designed the charming, cottage-like clubhouse at the Dunes Club. A man brimming with creative energies, Larry had participated actively in the design of the golf course by touching up photographs of the land under construction; using his Sharpie, he added vegetation, bunkers, and rough to transform the bare, shaped earth into recognizable golf holes.

He had taken it upon himself to enter the discussion about the course logo, and had suggested, after a trip to the Bandon museum, the use of an unusual sea bird, the tufted puffin. Today, Bandon's orange-billed puffin logo is recognized everywhere in golf. Most of all, Larry wanted a chance to contribute to the design of the lodge, and he came up with a daring plan, a high-concept building that used modern materials and was, Howard said succinctly, "indefensible."

Mike thought so, too, but the exercise of considering an unworkable design had nudged them closer to the right one. No one wanted a building that stood out and called attention to itself. It was all about the golf, and the buildings "should just disappear." (This principle was carried through in the use of natural grasses for landscaping around the lodge: The grass connects the building to its surroundings, whereas a formal flower bed would have screamed a different message. Likewise, the hard surfaces around the lodge lead into a roadway of pavers that heads out to the golf course; the road soon splits into two paved tracks, and then into a grass track, and finally peters out entirely.)

In the spirit of keeping it simple and keeping it classic, Mike was leaning toward a clubhouse that would evoke the first American golf clubhouse—the one at Shinnecock Hills, a graceful, colonnaded, shingle-style building designed by Stanford White. The idea was to build a lodge that would blend easily into the natural environment and to make it intimate in scale. This was partly a matter of economics—Mike had already dug deep into his pocket—and partly a matter of preference. To meet its obligations as a "destination resort," Bandon would have to provide a certain number of beds, but erecting a monster hotel was never an option. A big building would have looked silly out on the dunes, and it would have worked against the kind of comfortable, intimate, low-key, no-fuss atmosphere that Mike knew he wanted. Even the original design for the lodge, calling for a building three stories in height, seemed too large, and David Kidd thought it overshadowed the golf course. He added his voice to those who wanted a building with a lower profile, and to prove his point, he and his sidekick, Jim Haley, rigged up sections of PVC pipe topped with bright orange flags. They then attached the pipe to the excavator buckets, positioned the excavators on the site of the lodge, and hoisted the buckets as high as possible so that the flags were way up in the air—up at the height of the roofline of a three-story building. They got Howard and Mike to look at the flags from various places on the golf course, and they agreed: Three stories was too high.

The lodge would be only two stories high. Howard did the preliminary drawings for the building, but he had so many balls in the air that he hired a Portland architect, Bill Church, to do the construction drawings. Church wasn't a golfer and had never seen the Shinnecock Hills clubhouse, but Mike had given him pictures of it, and Church—as Howard knew from his work—was comfortable working in the shingle-style as it had adapted itself to the Pacific Northwest. The lines were a bit different, less formal than the geometric colonnades that were such a conspicuous feature at Shinnecock Hills; indeed, for Howard and Bill Church, the more relevant model was the Newport Casino in Rhode Island, where Stanford White had used green trim, softened the lines of the building with porches and rounded extensions, and softened the texture by using shingles with rounded edges.

The lodge was designed with twenty-one guest rooms, two of which were suites, and with a restaurant, two bars, and a pro shop. Not long after construction began, Howard was bucking to get work going on the other accommodations, the Lily Pond Cottages, four separate, unobtrusive buildings also in the shingle style, arranged around the lake. With his passion for detail, Howard couldn't help getting involved in all the finishing touches for all the buildings, and he put his stamp on everything from the design of the furniture in the restaurant—it was custom designed, made of Oregon maple—to the chrome pull chains for the blinds, to the ironwork that adorns the lobby in the form of gates and stair rails and whose Celtic designs are intended to make subtle connections to the British Isles, the home of links golf.

The problem was that the lodge wasn't going to be ready for the date— May 2, 1999—that had been chosen for the golf course opening. The coast of Oregon is warm enough to grow grass all twelve months of the year, and the golf course had grown in solidly during the winter; come spring, it was going to be ready to go. Mike wanted to get in as much golf as possible in his first season.

He decided to open Bandon Dunes without the lodge.

AS OPENING DAY APPROACHED, the pace of work at Bandon Dunes accelerated like a river headed toward a rapids. More and more writers showed up, wanting to ask questions, wanting to get in on the story. The phone in the Design Center kept ringing, and KSM was trying to get the kinks out of a computerized reservation system. Groups of golfers, led by the "bell cows," showed up for their preview rounds, and Shoe scurried to make sure they had caddies. Finding enough caddies, good caddies, was clearly going to be an issue, and Shoe was put to the test when Mike came out in April with a group of forty-eight Chicago golfers.

For this trip Mike had chartered the Madison Square Garden jet, a plane that was outfitted to carry professional athletes in comfort and style. And when Shoe started recruiting caddies, the word spread all over Coos County that a group of golfers was coming out for a kind of preopening blowout. As often happens, stories about just who might be coming got wildly speculative. The fact that the plane often carried basketball players and that it was arriving from Chicago somehow added up to the expectation that Michael Jordan was going to be on board, and there was a small, excited crowd waiting at the North Bend airport when the passengers came down the steps. Mike Keiser had to make a short, impromptu speech, an apology for not producing any NBA all-stars.

However, his Chicago friends, some of them friends of friends, were not disappointed. Josh and Shoe humped their bags from the hold of the plane and loaded them into the vans; everyone went straight to the golf course. The area around the lodge was a building site, but there was a shed (now the St. Andrews Room) with a few coolers of beer, soda, and turkey sandwiches. The weather was warm and sunny. The golf course was in perfect shape, and that night, when Mike's guests sat down at the Wheelhouse restaurant, there was enough euphoria in the air so that it could have been bottled. What was it like to fly to the edge of the continent and take the first divots on their pal's golf course? "Absolutely unbelievable," said Bob Millman, a stalwart member of the Dunes Club, one of the happy forty-eight.

They loved the simplicity and informality of the whole experience. The weather remained ideal, the golfers played in shorts, and the caddies made out like bandits. If there had been any questions in Coos County about how much money caddies could make, the generous tips at the end of that visit went a long way toward answering them. Josh and Shoe and the newly appointed director of golf, twenty-four-year-old Matt Allen, were pleased and relieved by how well this shakedown visit had gone; they'd gotten a big reassurance that even for sophisticated golfers—and the men on the plane were definitely sophisticated—their approach could work. As a matter of fact, they got their first inkling that some of these sophisticates might be a little jaded and that the simplicity, the lack of fuss and folderol, had an appeal of its own. They'd been to plenty of five-star resorts, but not to many places where the only building was basically a garage and the accommodations were in the Harbor View Motel. There was a kind of reverse mystique at work, a sense of roughing it and doing without, of getting back to nature, stripping away all the distractions and diversions, getting back to the essence of the game.

It's all about the golf.

Josh hadn't had any trouble getting that message across to Matt Allen, who was about as deep into golf as a young man could be. He was a scratch golfer who had started out as a caddy, won an Evans Scholarship, and become an active member of the Oregon Golf Association. He had come to Bandon Dunes not in search of a job but as a course rater. Josh and Mike had discussed the kind of caddy master they wanted and agreed that their model was Greg Kunkel, a mountain of a man, the caddy master at Sunset Ridge and a well-known figure in Chicago golf. Josh: "One day I'm in my office in the Design Center, and suddenly there's no light coming in through the doorway. Total eclipse. This guy is standing there, and he fills the door frame. I think, 'He's here. My caddy master just arrived.'" But it wasn't quite that easy. Matt was flattered by the offer, but not overwhelmed. He wanted to think about it. He came back to Josh with an alternative proposal: He wanted the position of director of golf, and he got it.

Mike was worried about opening day, but Josh was watching the reservations add up, and he knew that people were going to come. Some of them were people like Gary Chang, the owner of the Wheelhouse, who'd become the friendly and unofficial caterer for Bandon Dunes; most were simply local residents who loved golf, had followed the course's progress for years, and wanted to be among the first to play it. Josh had a special opening-day scorecard designed, and he ordered two hundred special ball markers. Made of burnished gunmetal, they were a little bigger than silver dollars, with the tufted puffin logo on one side of the coin and the date on the other: May 2, 1999.

A cold, steady rain was falling that day, but there was only one no-show. From seven-thirty that morning until after three o'clock that afternoon, foursome after foursome of golfers, bundled in raingear, stepped to the first tee. For Josh, this willingness to play in lousy weather was a good sign, an early hint that the golfers who made their way to Bandon Dunes were an especially hardy lot. He kept busy that day, making sure that there were plenty of turkey sandwiches and hot soup for golfers as they made the turn.

On the first tee, a photographer was on hand to take a picture of each foursome; by the end of the round, the pictures had been developed and each golfer received one as a souvenir. The pictures are standard shots of golfers leaning on their drivers, and every foursome has the same guy standing in its midst, wearing a blue and red rain suit and grinning from ear to ear.

That was the owner, Mike Keiser. And if you ask him what day at Bandon Dunes was the best day, he'll say, "The day the golf course opened."

HE HAD BUILT IT, and they came. They came in a steady stream, so many of them that the numbers seemed too good to be true. For golf courses, like restaurants, there is a honeymoon, a period of time when everything seems to come up roses and everybody is blissfully happy—but the Bandon

Dunes honeymoon just kept going. The first articles had made it into print, and the phones kept ringing. Most of the golfers that first summer were from Oregon or northern California, but more and more reservations were coming from people in other parts of the country. By early summer it was clear that the totals for the first year were going to exceed everyone's expectation. The KSM break-even scenario had called for 12,466 rounds, but Josh and Mike and others had made their own predictions. Troy Russell, who'd taken over as superintendent, had been the most optimistic, guessing that Bandon Dunes would do 18,000 rounds of golf in its first year. He was about 4,000 rounds short of the mark.

On July 1, the lodge opened. Both Josh and Howard had been in overdrive trying to make sure they were ready. For Josh, the principal task was now the hiring of the hundred-plus people needed to staff the lodge and the golf operations. On the golf side, he had Matt to help him; on the hotel side, he had Don Crowe, an experienced manager. One of the most important hires, obviously, was the chef, and the competition came down to two men. There was a cook-off, an evening when each man was given free rein, told to invent menus that would be appropriate for the resort, to prepare everything from soup to nuts, and to choose dishes that would display his talents. Chef No. 1, with a resume that listed big-time resorts, put on a fabulous feast that would have been right at home in Las Vegas. Chef No. 2 was an Oregonian, Paul Moss, and he prepared excellent but heartier, humbler dishes; his showstopper, and the dish that got him the job, was Grandma Thayer's Meatloaf.

The decision to hire Paul Moss spoke volumes about the kind of hospitality that Bandon Dunes would offer. He could cook more than meatloaf, but the menu was characterized by simplicity and authenticity—the same qualities that characterized the design and furniture in the Gallery restaurant, the Tufted Puffin Lounge, and the guest rooms. The menu emphasized local produce, fish, and wine; the building showcased local craftsmen and the beauty of native woods.

Perhaps the most arresting objects in the lodge are the four stone monoliths in the lobby. They are the unique and central feature of the lodge. They are not, strictly speaking, local stones; they are basalt columns that were quarried in the state of Washington. Positioned on a tan carpet that is a representation of sand dunes, the stones range from five to eleven feet in height, and they have a massive presence. For most visitors, they evoke mythic sites like Stonehenge and Avebury, though a Buddhist might think first of the rock gardens of Kyoto.

"Intelligent life on this planet does two things," Howard McKee told me when I asked him about the stones. "It plays golf, and it creates patterns of upright stones."

Howard, obviously, had often been asked about those stones, but he warmed to the opportunity to explain them. "It was originally Bill Church's idea—he's the architect who did the design for this building, and he'd always been fascinated by standing stones. Back in the office we have an easel with an overlay that he made up, showing the golf courses in Scotland and Ireland and the prehistoric sites that have standing stones. It's quite remarkable how the two coincide—the golf courses were often built in the same places where earlier people had created ceremonial sites with stones. You often find cathedrals in these spots as well. Some people believe that you can chart the location of these places with lay lines, which aren't marked on any map but which nevertheless seem to have been generally acknowledged. They were spiritual corridors, like the song lines of the Aborigines. It's interesting that, today, these lay lines can actually be picked up by magnetic devices. I'm not a golfer, but we wanted to emulate the British tradition, and we also wanted to acknowledge that Bandon, with all those huge formations and sea stacks in the ocean, was an unusual site, one that seemed to have its own sacred associations. Bill found out about a quarry up in Washington where we could get these stones—they weigh between eight hundred and a thousand pounds per lineal foot, and we had to have the floor of the lobby specially reinforced to hold them. They're only slightly less hard than diamonds. The crane that lifted them into place almost tilted over. But we got them in, and they're standing in a true north-south, east-west configuration, marking the cardinal points of the compass. I know we had Mike worried while we were putting the stones in, but he indulged us."

Mike had built his throwback golf course, a course that could claim kinship with the "ancient" courses of Scotland and Ireland, courses that were a century old. Leave it to Howard to find a way to link Bandon Dunes to prehistory, to the oldest myths and most enduring symbols of the human quest for spiritual fulfillment.

The rugged par-3 11th hole at Pacific Dunes looks completely wild,
but the bunkers were fashioned by Renaissance Golf Design.
Photo by Wood Sabold.

Tom Doak was a talented young
designer who hadn't yet worked
on a major site when Mike Keiser
commissioned him to build the
second course, Pacific Dunes.
Photo by Wood Sabold.

From left to right, Jim Urbina, Tom Doak, David Kidd,
and Jim Haley in the Bunker Bar—one of the rare meetings
of the designers of the first two courses at Bandon Dunes.
Photo courtesy of Bandon Dunes Resort.

One of Doak's favorite holes, the 2nd at Pacific Dunes, is a short par 4 that showcases the rugged elements that give the course its character—dunes, gorse, shore pines, and huge natural blow-out bunkers.   Photo by Wood Sabold.

With the green and fairway perched over the Pacific Ocean,
the 4th hole is one of the most dramatic par 4s anywhere.
Photo by Wood Sabold.

The giant sandhills are the few hazards dramatic enough
to steal attention from the hazard on the other side—
the Pacific Ocean.   Photo by Wood Sabold.

Key members of the team that created Bandon Trails, from left to right:
Tony Russell, Jim Craig, Bill Coore, Dave Zinkand, Ben Crenshaw, and Jeff Bradley.
Photo by Chip Simons.

Many holes at Bandon Trails, like the 13th, are snuggled into
a Pacific Northwest rainforest.   Photo by Wood Sebold.

Towering dunes frame the 2nd hole at Bandon Trails...

... and the 3rd hole moves into a distinctly different "meadow" environment.

Photos on this page by Wood Sabold.

The tee of the 17th hole at Bandon Trails is close to the place where Mike Keiser had his *Eureka!* moment and decided that this was where he wanted to build his dream course.
Photo by Wood Sabold.

Bandon Dunes

Printed: 06/09/2010 2:01:00 PM

Outlet: Bandon Dunes Golf Shop
Register: COUNTERBANPRO3
Ticket #: 441588 Clerk: BAN 1 AM

Shirt - Millar MS09K38
  23935 - 1 @ 94.00   94.00
01 Discount: 50% DISC   -47.00
Sweater - FG 811195 Adm
  21921 - 1 @ 160.00   160.00
01 Discount: 50% DISC   -80.00
Book - Dream Golf
  12058 - 1 @ 24.95   24.95

                    Sub-Total: 151.95
                         Tax: 0.00
                       Total: 151.95

Payments/Refunds
          CREDIT CARD-VISA   151.95
CC#: ************3227
Card Name: Goold/donna L

    Thank you for visiting Bandon Dunes
888-345-6008 www.bandondunesgolf.com

I agree to pay the above amount in
accordance with cardholder agreement

Signature: _____

Print Name: _____

15 | David at Bandon Dunes

When people ask me if this is true links golf, I say the only difference
between here and Scotland is we don't have the skylarks.
—GRANT ROGERS, DIRECTOR OF INSTRUCTION AT BANDON DUNES RESORT

JUNE 2004. DAVID KIDD was jet-lagged and happy. Greeting old friends in the lobby of the Bandon Dunes Lodge, he announced with a huge grin that he'd come back to Oregon to be with Jill, his second wife, and their brand-new daughter, Ailsa. "She didn't wait for me," he said, and mother and daughter, after a couple of rough days, were doing fine. Ailsa—he pronounced it liltingly in his Scottish brogue, and spelled it out for those who'd never heard the name—was born prematurely, while he was still en route to Oregon from South Africa, where he was remodeling one of the courses at Fancourt, a leading golf resort in that country.

The success of Bandon Dunes had put David's career into a global orbit, and he had rearranged almost every aspect of his life. He was now the proprietor of his own company, DMK Golf Design, and he had designed high-profile courses in Ireland, England, and Hawaii. He was named the architect for a new course in Machrihanish, his childhood haunt, and he won a commission that stamped his career with the seal of high approval: He was chosen as the architect for a new course at St. Andrews. For a young Scotsman—for that matter, for any golf course architect—there could be no greater affirmation than to be selected to build a course in the cradle of golf.

David had coveted the commission and he had labored for weeks on his presentation to the St. Andrews Links Trust. Aware that the Links Trust would be reviewing several designs, having been informed of the constraints of the site and warned that his presentation must not exceed an hour, David decided nevertheless to throw caution to the winds. When he appeared before the Links Trust, he spoke for three hours, arguing that no one could build a first-class golf course on the site as offered. He urged the Links Trust to acquire additional land, and he got the job.

David Kidd, in short, was still brimming with confidence and energy and ideas. Yet for those who have observed his career over the years, he seems to have grown more centered and disciplined. The personal turmoil that came with the end of his marriage to Lyn took its toll, and David laments the fact that he sees so little of his son, Campbell, who lives in the United Kingdom with Lyn. As hectic as his schedule is, David tries to make sure that he and Jill are together as much as possible; his marriage to her has provided a fixed point on his personal compass. Jill is from Oregon, and she has strong family ties there. During this visit to Oregon, in fact, David was trying to cement arrangements to build a course in northern California. The site was near San Francisco, some four hundred miles from Bandon, but to a man who flies as often and as far as he does, that was practically in his backyard.

Meanwhile, David's partnership with Jim Haley remains securely in place. Jim was the best man at David's wedding, and he has worked on every one of David's projects since Bandon. Like David, Jim has started his own company, Highland Construction, which contracts its services to DMK and, occasionally, hires out to others in need of creative earthmoving. Both Jim and David speak of their time at Bandon with a kind of nostalgia, like respectable grown-ups recalling the high combustion of their youth, and they both maintain that they've done a lot of growing up. They no longer feel that they have to be the ones who close the bar. The younger guys on Jim's crew kid him about his tendency, after a day of hard work, to doze over dinner. Perhaps David and Jim reflected on the end of *Butch Cassidy and the Sundance Kid* and decided that they'd rather avoid the fate of their favorite outlaws, or perhaps they simply realized that if they wanted to have the careers that were open to them in a competitive, far-flung business, they were going to have to trim their sails. They have years to go before achieving the status of elder states-men, but they definitely project the air of purpose and success of high achiev-ers in midcareer. With Bandon Dunes and several other courses already on their resume, with courses at St. Andrews and Machrihanish ahead of them, they have established themselves as significant players in golf course design and construction. They are making their mark.

IT WAS A GLORIOUS DAY for links golf. A fresh breeze was blowing, and the coastal air tasted like an elixir, pure and invigorating, with a tang of salt and pine. I had set up a game with Kidd and Grant Rogers, who had somehow never met. Grant is the local guru, the director of instruction at Bandon Dunes and a links aficionado, and I thought David would like to see how a true shotmaker played his golf course. Though Grant was born and raised in California, he has made more than twenty trips to Scotland and Ireland to play links golf, and he has command of a repertory of golf shots that most of us can only fantasize about. To put him on a links course is like putting a guitar into the hands of Eric Clapton, or passing a cello to Yo-Yo Ma.

Grant was dressed in his usual outfit—well-worn khakis, scuffed shoes, wind jacket zipped all the way up to his throat, khaki-colored cap pulled low over his deep-set blue eyes. His personal look is weathered, and that extends to his stand-up golf bag, which has faded to the timeless gray of an elephant's rump. David, by contrast, was hatless, and he arrived on the first tee nattily dressed in a lightweight burgundy fleece, creased black pants, and shined shoes. His clubs—the latest Titleists, custom-made—were bright and gleam-ing. His driver was the Titleist 983K with a blood-colored shaft, a serious weapon, and David swung it with serious intent as he loosened up. He is over six feet tall, and when he gets his arms fully extended his club creates that loud, air-splitting *whoosh!* that only occurs when titanium is moving at high speeds. He pulled his first shot into the high grass well left of the fairway.

"Not where you want to be," David said, and off we went.

Hole No. 1. Par 4, 398 yards. (Yardage is from the tips, though we played from the green tees. At its full length, Bandon Dunes is 7,212 and it can be stretched even farther; we played it at 6,732 yards.)

The ideal tee shot hugs the right side of the fairway and provides the best angle of approach to the elevated green. To the right of the fairway, a grassy ridge separates the golf course from the buildings of the "village"—the pro shop, McKee's Pub, and the new administration building—but every now and then a monster slice goes sailing over the ridge and dings the tin roofs. David is all in favor of relocating the first green to a position farther to the left, so that the golfer on the first tee isn't tempted to cut the corner but has to play away from the buildings. He takes the attitude that a golf course is constantly evolving—several changes have already been made to Bandon Dunes—and he doesn't regard this hole as sacrosanct. Indeed, some changes had already been made to the 1st hole, including the removal of a bunker on the left side of the fairway to encourage golfers to play down that side, away from the village.

"At the time we built the first hole," David said, "we knew where the lodge would be located, but it wasn't clear where the other buildings would be located, or that there would be so many of them. What we wanted was a first hole that wouldn't be too difficult—a nice, friendly handshake to get the round started. The fairway is wide and the hole isn't very long, and we were working with a natural green site up on the ridge and a couple of blowout bunkers to the left of the green—they're almost the only natural blowout bunkers on the whole course."

A friendly handshake? Those blowout bunkers are deep, and fringed with beach grass, and they are frightening enough to make average golfers like me play the approach shot well to the right. Grant kept me company in the bailout area. From there, the situation calls for a classic links shot—the long approach putt from off the green. Given the size of the greens at Bandon Dunes—the first green is 54 yards long—this shot requires a great touch. Even Grant was unable to get up and down for his par. He putted with his left hand low, and he missed a 4-footer. He looked shocked. He is usually deadly from short range.

Hole No. 2. Par 3, 220 yards.

This hole is a full right angle, different from the way it was originally drawn. As we left the first green, David pointed out the original tees that are benched into the slope above the putting surface. From these tees, the golfers played to a green that sloped precariously off to the left, down to a large sandy waste.

By moving the tee 150 yards to a slightly elevated, gorse-lined knob, David made the hole into a frontal assault. The tee shot must now carry the waste area. The grassy slope that rises up out of the waste area and leads to the green isn't as steep as it used to be; it has been softened so that a short ball will not trickle, sickeningly, back down into the sand.

The green sits in a bowl, and the prevailing summer wind, coming from the golfer's left, pushes a good many shots into the collection area to the right of the green. We were playing the hole at 190 yards, and David told me that I might need an extra club, but his eyes popped wide open when Grant pulled out his driver.

With no explanation, with a buttery smooth half-swing, Grant hit a low-ish shot that flew straight as a clothesline toward the pin. "I think the bunt driver is the play here," he said.

He admitted that he worked on this shot, the bunt driver, as the ultimate wind-cheater. Like all links freaks, Grant welcomes the wind. "Sometimes when I come out, I just practice until the wind gets up. That's the time to play, when the wind's blowing. I like the bunt driver because it holds its line so well. The ball is spinning slowly and that makes it heavy in the wind."

David was amused. He was in a talkative mood on this banner day, glad to be renewing an acquaintance with the course he hadn't seen for a while. He noticed places where the gorse is growing back; it had been completely cleared when the course opened. When Grant almost holed his putt for a 2, David asked us to note the contours of this green. "You're a writer," he said to me. "How can a golf writer come out here and play a round of golf and say these greens are flat? They may not be as undulating as Tom's greens [at Pacific Dunes], but flat they are *not*."

Hole No. 3. Par 5, 563 yards.

From the height of the third tee, we were looking directly west, directly at the shining ocean, and we could hear the boom of the surf. From both the first and second green, there are teasing glimpses of the ocean, but here, on the highest point of the course, the needle jumps into the red zone of the "Wow!" meter. Not only does the ocean fill the horizon, but the landscape reveals the golf holes that lie in wait. It is the first of the many "crescendos" that David wanted to orchestrate, though he used a different metaphor in our round. "I always knew that this spot was a dramatic vista," he said, "but I didn't want to get here right away. I didn't want to show everything all at once. You don't take your knickers down right away—there's got to be some foreplay."

He was loosening up and finding his groove, and he caught hold of this drive, sending it far down the fairway. This par 5 was definitely a birdie hole (for us it played about 500 yards), and David is the kind of player who likes to attack. This was my first round with him, but we'd talked a lot of golf, and I said, "I get the impression that the driver is your favorite club. Do you think you design with the driver in mind?"

He admitted that he loved to hit his driver, but our conversation had to be put on pause as he stepped up to lash his 3-wood—wide left, alas, but he couldn't be accused of playing safe.

David, of course, is aware of the theory that golf course architects de-sign courses to suit their own game. C. B. Macdonald was famously a slicer, and his courses are forgiving of slices—but hard on hooks. Donald Ross built courses that required precise, well-struck iron shots and rewarded the player who can chip. Alister MacKenzie was known for his wildly undulat-ing greens, and while he wasn't a particularly strong ball striker, he was a skilled, confident putter. By then, Pacific Dunes, the companion to Bandon Dunes, had been completed, with Tom Doak as architect. Doak, I speculated, seemed to be a lot like MacKenzie in placing a premium on putting, but David often talked about strategy from the tee and the sheer joy of belting the ball.

"I wouldn't say that I design for long hitters," David said, "but I do think that Bandon and Pacific are very different golf courses. Bandon is much longer—it's 7,200 yards and Pacific is just over 6,600. I spent so much time here, and saw how the winds varied from day to day, and I wanted to create tees that would require full shots even from the top players. Maybe I do emphasize the driver more than Tom does, but I didn't want to take the driver out of a player's hands. The way I'd put it is that we both built links courses, but Bandon is a modern links. It takes modern equipment into account. Bandon looks forward, whereas Pacific looks back to the historic links and plays more as they do."

Hole No. 4. Par 4, 443 yards.

Here the crescendo builds. After that first sight of the ocean from the 3rd tee, the golfer descends to the fairway, and the horizon disappears from view. The 4th tee is still at little more than fairway height. The hole plays between a pair of gorse-covered ridges that bend to the right, and when the golfer walks down the fairway toward the place where his drive has finished, he suddenly rounds the bend and—boom! The ocean smacks him in the chops. The green sits on the edge of the cliff, the edge of the continent.

Awesome.

David was looking at the hole far more critically. He had been involved in all the ongoing changes to the course, and he was concerned about whether or not the maintenance road to the right was visible from the tees (I never saw it). But he clapped when Grant pulled off the approach shot that the design of the hole suggests, a low trajectory iron that comes in from the right, getting a kick and roll from mounds that were built for precisely that purpose.

His shot illustrated, among other things, that a "modern" links course still had plenty of classic links shots.

Hole No. 5. Par 4, 445 yards.

The 5th is perhaps the most familiar hole on Bandon Dunes, the one whose image is most frequently reproduced. The hole plays along the edge of the cliff, with the ocean on the left, and the fairway is dotted with small, tufted mounds. The green is nestled down between two gnarly ridges. Like the 4th hole, the 5th is another original. Nowhere in the world is there another golf hole anything like it.

On days when the prevailing north wind blows, it plays like a tiger. The green is closely guarded on both sides, and for the golfer who has a long approach shot—that is, for most golfers—the 5th is a real gut check.

"This is one of the holes we made on the land Mike bought [from David Shuman], and it was the hardest hole of all to build. There wasn't any soil here, just the redshot. We had to bring load after load of sand so that we could grow grass. But the mounds were always there—and we had a row about that. There were people from Kemper telling me I couldn't leave the mounds, and that I couldn't leave the bunker by the green, another natural blowout bunker. It was hard to stand up to them. I was a youngster, and they had been in the golf business for years, and sometimes I gave in. But on this hole, I held out for the mounds and the bunker, and I'm glad I did."

One of the fairway mounds has indeed been removed in order to give a golfer on the tee a less obstructed view, but the others have all stayed. And just to the right of the green, David pointed out a blowout bunker, the object of another battle. This bunker may be the most beautiful on the course. You have to be glad that David didn't back down.

Hole No. 6. Par 3, 217 yards.

Another hole playing into the wind, another deep green. The pin was all the way back, and for our tees, at 165 yards, Grant hit another bunt driver, a bullet of a shot that rolled dead about 20 feet from the cup.

Playing conventional iron shots, neither David nor I managed to hit the huge green. The wind just stopped our balls and swatted them to the right of the green, where they fell harmlessly and well short of pin high. "The wind," David said, and that's all he needed to say. What had been a one-club wind back on the more protected part of the course was at least a two-club wind here on the cliffs.

That right-hand side of the green, by the way, has been made less steep than it was when the course opened and when balls used to bound down into the sandy stuff. Like all the changes to the course, this one was made to make Bandon Dunes more player-friendly.

Hole No. 7. Par 4, 411 yards.

Admittedly, I felt a certain letdown when the course turned inland and we left the ocean behind. The 7th hole at Bandon Dunes is a very sound golf hole that has the misfortune of coming after three spectacular holes, rather like a drink of a decent whisky after three splendid single malts.

This winding down was part of David's master plan, his symphony. The next five holes, from the 7th through the 11th, are all inland holes, and they form a movement that is distinctly quieter, though the golf is demanding. Indeed, David was well aware that these inland holes had to have a strong character of their own to stand alongside the ocean holes.

The 7th appears to be a straightaway, medium-length par 4 (from our tees, 380 yards) with a wide and generous fairway and an elevated green, but the hole is full of deceit. The best line of play is down the left side, to a piece of fairway that is hidden from the tee; the wind and appearance of the hole both conspire to push balls to the right, and the golfer who strays right has to approach over a deep swale that protects the most radical green on the golf course, a three-tiered green where putts can break 180 degrees.

Grant posed a question: How could you hit this green in regulation, two putt, and make a double bogey? He had seen it done.

Answer: The first putt rolled off the green and all the way to the bottom of the swale. The next shot was a chip that didn't quite make it to the putting surface and rolled back down to the golfer's feet. The fifth shot reached the green, and the sixth shot—and second putt—went in for a double.

Grant told the story as he was holing out for his own routine par. David acknowledged that this green had some of the daring of the greens that Old

Tom Morris had designed at Machrihanish. A par 4 of this length seemed like just the right place to introduce these dramatic undulations since, presumably, good players would be coming into the green with short irons. And after the drama of the ocean, the heaving green provided drama on a more intimate scale.

Hole No. 8. Par 4, 385 yards.

Another hole that seems like a breather, although the cross bunkers—the bunkers that David designed in response to Mike's desire to do something like the Hell Bunker—get a player's full attention. The carry is only 180 yards, and the best line of attack is down the right side—where there are a couple of distant bunkers that catch many balls.

"Those bunkers are there for a purpose," David said. "They're not there for looks. I wanted to give the better golfers a challenge. If the course was going to be as open as Mike wanted it—this fairway is a hundred yards wide—the question was how to defend it. And the answer was bunkers. I wanted the good player to have to deal with the bunkers if he was going to take an attacking line, and we had fights about the bunkers. The old Scots were canny, Dad taught me, and they formalized their bunkers. They made them deep, with steep faces. A bunker like that doesn't get eroded in the wind, and if a player hits into one, he often has to come out sideways or backward. He loses a shot. Jim Seeley [from KSM] told me these bunkers were so unfair that we were going to have to fill them all in, and I told him he was thinking like an American. The great thing about Mike was that he supported me. He wanted me to try things that people didn't see every day."

Hole No. 9. Par 5, 520 yards.

This is not a hard finishing hole, provided that you avoid the pot bunkers in the center of the landing zone and the bunkers positioned to catch second shots. The green complex is one of David's favorites, with slopes that blend into one another seamlessly and create rolls that aren't immediately apparent. With the hole cut in the far right, it looked as though Grant should play his third, a shot of about ninety yards, to the right edge of the green and let it come back to the center.

Grant, however, knows the course and he knows his game. He chose to play a low, running shot with a club he identified as his "daughter's 7-wood." The ball carried fifty yards and rolled another forty, expiring a few feet from the cup. He holed the putt for a birdie and he was out in 35.

David said, "It's fun to watch an exhibition round on my golf course."

Hole No. 10. Par 4, 380 yards.

The 10th fairway sprawls across the landscape, and the temptation is to launch the drive straight at the green—though both Grant and David played well out to the left. The terrain on this hole has been left pretty much as David found it, and the green is tucked behind a formidable knob. To the golfer approaching it straight on, the shot to the green is blind; from the left, the green opens up and the backside of the knob can provide a favorable kick. "There were two natural ridges here," David said, "and I just tried to use them. You couldn't possibly draw this hole."

The 10th is another hole where the drive is the key (some players, from the forward tees and playing with a tailwind, have driven the green). It illustrates a couple of other Kidd principles, too. One is that these vast fairways, while they let long hitters air it out, have the virtue of letting everyone else figure out their own best route; there are many strategies here, many paths to the hole. Another is that David Kidd does not fear a little blindness. On the contrary, the blindness adds a strategic element, since it pushes the decision back to the tee. Do you prefer a shorter approach shot that is blind? Or a longer shot where you can see the flagstick?

Hole No. 11. Par 4, 351 yards.

Before hitting our tee shots, David took us to the back tees—the way-back tees. They measure out at more than 450 yards, but they are rarely used. "Most people don't notice how many tees there are, and how they're situated to change the way the hole plays. Today we have the prevailing wind, but when the wind is out of the south and this hole is downwind, it's a pussycat."

I wasn't convinced. The 11th is another hole where David says he didn't have to do a thing. He built a green into a natural shelf, put the fairway in a small valley that had been cleared of gorse, and got Roger Sheffield to build a couple of bunkers—but what bunkers! The bunker at the green is a deep sod-faced bunker, a bunker to avoid at all costs. Since the green slopes from right to left, and the opening to the green is left of the bunker, the best line is down the left side—which brings the fairway bunkers into play. They are not sod-faced, but they will quickly gobble up strokes.

If the 10th hole allows the golfer many strategic choices, the 11th narrows those choices to a tight set of risk-reward factors. How much do you want to flirt with the fairway bunkers? Then, assuming you have avoided them, how close do you dare come to the sod-faced bunker?

Grant solved the strategic puzzle by pulling his drive well to the left of the bunkers. He was almost in the gorse, but he had a full swing and a perfect angle, and he hit an iron shot that came out low and ran right up onto the green.

"That's why all these greens have openings," David said.

Hole No. 12. Par 3, 238 yards.

We have reached the hole that first made Bandon famous. Although Hole No. 1 was the first to be roughed in, the 12th was the first to be seeded and played. Early visitors to Bandon were brought to gape at this small creation, an artful composition of grass, gorse, sod, and sand against the backdrop of the ocean and the sky. The picture is gorgeous, but what makes this hole such a perfect encapsulation of Bandon Dunes is not merely the grand view but the weaving of a few man-made elements into the natural tapestry.

There is, of course, the contrast of the tight, tended fescue turf with the tufted beach grass. There is the relatively flat surface of the green surrounded by humps and mounds. And there is one sod-faced, sharp-edged bunker scooped into the flank of the green, a bunker that does for this hole what a similar bunker does for the Road Hole at St. Andrews: It rearranges everything. It is a tiny part of the whole picture, but it asserts itself as the center and focal point of the entire composition, the piece that means as much to this arena as the matador's red cape means to the bullfight.

When you stand on the tee and prepare to hit a shot, you can't tear your eyes away from it.

There are only four of these sod-faced bunkers on the golf course, and all four are located with malice aforethought. They are intended to mess with a golfer's mind and trigger his, um, puckering mechanism.

David's decision to deploy such obviously man-made features on a links course has its precedents: Sod-faced bunkers can be found at Muirfield, St. Andrews, and many other links courses. But he was aware that his willingness to use this style of bunker put him in a different camp from Tom Doak, who tried to avoid any appearance of artificiality. "Bandon has a more groomed appearance than Pacific," he said. "Mike was willing to go with a degree of ruggedness at Pacific that was beyond anything here, and Bandon Trails is another several degrees more rugged than that. But the site here was flatter to begin with, and it didn't have the huge blowouts that Tom had at Pacific, so we were always thinking of a course that had a less wild look to it. Some people have said that Bandon is more Scottish, and Pacific is more Irish—well, laddy, that's as it should be."

Try to hear those last words in a Scottish burr.

I probably don't have to tell you that David and I, playing the hole at 175 yards, both hit windblown iron shots that fell on the wrong side of the bunker and required us to fashion a most delicate pitch over the bunker onto the green—a shot that proved beyond our poor powers. It is no easy thing to hit feathery wedges or lob shots from the tight turf at Bandon. Grant, of course, hit another bunt driver that ran safely up the right side of the fairway and rolled to stop in the mathematical center of the green.

Hole No. 13. Par 5, 553 yards.

What makes this hole is the fabulously rumpled fairway.

"When we cleared away the brush and saw these hillocks and hollows, we didn't know what to do—they're quite extreme. Nearly everyone who saw them said they'd have to go. They said you can't play golf on ground like *that*! But Mike never wavered, not for a moment. He said they'd stay, and they did."

The heaving, bucking ground runs right through the green, and the deep swale to the right of the green gobbles up many an approach. To the left of the fairway lies the only wetland on the course, and David can't walk past without a laugh. "The day the wetlands inspector was to come, we had a crew clearing some brush around it and loading it up in a truck. Well, they weren't the most careful crew, and as they were leaving they drove right into the wetland and got stuck. When the inspector got here to see that we were treating the wetlands properly, he saw a truck in the midst of it, up to its axles in the muck."

Hole No. 14. Par 4, 390 yards.

"Architecturally, this is my favorite hole," David said. "This was a hole we had to build—it was a blank stretch of ground to begin with. There was nothing here except that ridge. I knew I wanted to use that as a backdrop for the green—and look how the gorse has come back on the ridge. We cleared it completely when the hole was built."

The green does snuggle into the ridge like a puppy trying to hide behind a couch, but the first order of business is to figure out where to hit the tee shot. The wide fairway is all dings and dents, and there are five oddly shaped bunkers that seem to have been randomly placed. Beyond them, for the player who can really launch the ball, are two more bunkers in what would otherwise be a prime landing area.

This short par 4 is another hole where a bold, successful drive sets up a chance for a birdie.

Hole No. 15. Par 3, 206 yards.

When the golfer stands on the 15th tee, the final movement of David Kidd's symphony begins in earnest. Once again the Pacific Ocean looms as a backdrop, and the familiar elements—gorse, beach grass, sand—are combined in a manner that is gothic in its power to intimidate. A long ridge forms a wall along the left side of the hole, but there's no bailout to the right, where the green falls away to a huge bunker, the deepest bunker on the golf course. The green seems to hover in midair, and the longer you look at it, the more impossible it appears that a ball could actually land on its surface and remain there. Hard to believe that this is another hole where an attempt has been made to reduce the severity by pushing back the trouble on the left.

David, however, hits a very sweet 5-iron that holds its line in the breeze and settles down nicely. Grant goes with the bunt driver, a shot that looks too far left to me, but it bounces in from the slope as though pulled by a cord. He has gone 4-for-4 with that shot.

But the shot that really interests him on this hole is my second shot, from behind the green. The first was long and left, and the preamble to the second shot was my complaint, made directly to the architect, that the second was insanely difficult—a short shot from thick rough up and onto a green that then sloped precipitously away.

David just smiled a villainous grin. He obviously intended for golfers like me to find their short second every bit as taxing as the first shot on this hole. Grant said, "I love shots like that. You could make a 3 or a 7 from there." And he added philosophically, "Whichever you make, you'll remember it. I always tell people that they don't remember the routine pars. Hit the fairway, hit the green, two putts—that's not much of a story. But from a lie like that, to get the ball to run up the bank and just over the lip, then die at the cup—that's the kind of shot you just have to love."

"You like it more than I do," I said. "Why don't you play it?"

David seconded the suggestion, and Grant knocked the ball up to the cup just as pretty as you please.

"Has anyone ever called you Shivas Irons?" David asked.

Hole No. 16. Par 4, 363 yards.

Wow. That's about the only syllable that develops as your mind tries to take in this hole, its entire length visible from the tee, another hole that has no precedent, another David Kidd original. On a clear day the long view goes all the way down the coast to the rock formations at Bandon and then to the horizon, and the near view is of a chasm and a cliff of redshot clay.

"This is the hole where we had such a big fight," David said. "I had drawn it several ways, and then one day I was standing right here and I decided to rearrange things a bit. I made a model in the sand, and Jim and Roger built the hole just as I had imagined it. But I was terrified that Mike wouldn't like it. He came out the day after we finished the changes, and I didn't want to be with him when he saw what we'd done. I sort of hung back over the hill and watched him, trying to read his body language. He was with Mike Davis that day, from the USGA, and they didn't really stand on the tee that long—Mike looked for a moment and just turned away. And I thought, 'Uh-oh, I'm in the deep stuff now, he hates it.' So I avoided him for hours, but finally he caught up with me and it was Mike Davis that shook my hand and congratulated me."

The 16th, from the forward tees, is only 315 yards long, and the drive is one of the great shots at Bandon. Even semilong hitters, with a tailwind, can think about reaching the green with their drive. Since so many people like to take a big swing here, the fairway has been widened and an open grassy area added for drives that stray to the left. Still, the 16th is another hole where you can make a 3 or a 7, for that green—the one planted by headlight—is pressed hard against the abyss. If the approach is a touch too strong, it's gone.

Grant's drive finished about thirty yards from the green, which slopes away. For most players it would have been a pitch, but for Grant, naturally, it was a putt that skirted the sod-faced bunker and trundled right up to the cup.

Hole No. 17. Par 4, 405 yards.

From the tee, we turned to face the ocean and performed what has become a Bandon ritual: We each fired a shot into the Pacific.

We then made an about-face and confronted another formidable tee shot, with bunkers left and the chasm of Cut Creek to the right. There's actually plenty of room over there, and the controversial railroad ties shore up a bunker that is positioned to catch balls that would otherwise run down into the chasm. And way off in the rough, on high ground not far from the bunker, is a tee that is rarely used.

"That's Mike's tee up there," David said. "This is one of his favorite holes, and he thought we could play it from that tee sometimes. It's a par 3 from over there, a strong par 3 with a carry over a canyon."

We walked over to have a look, though the par-3 tee has never been used for regular play. The shot of about 175 yards over a sea of gorse looks like nothing else on the golf course—but then neither does the approach shot when the hole is played by the book as a par 4. The gaping canyon gives it a different feel, and if the drive is right, or even in the right-center of the fairway, half of the green is hidden by the gorse that has grown up. Add to this blindness the fact that the green is 60 yards long, and deceptively uphill, and a plateau green with Rossian contours and the kind of devilish chips that Ross liked to devise—yes, it is easy to see why Mike has such a high regard for the 17th.

Hole No. 18. Par 5, 558 yards.

"This hole has been the most criticized on the golf course," David said. "I can't tell you how many times I've heard people say that it's anticlimactic, but I don't see it that way. You can't have every hole on the ocean. I think of this hole like the 18th at St. Andrews or North Berwick, where you're returning to the village. At St. Andrews you aim at a steeple, and here you pick out a rooftop, or the cupola on the pro shop—the thing that looks like a rocket. You're returning at the end of your journey."

David has made changes to the 18th to improve the lines of sight, for the hole was originally a double-blind one, with the landing area for both the drive and the second shot partially hidden from view. Now the fairway is plainly visible from the tee, and David socked one last drive to Position A as if to defend the concept of his design. With my questions to distract him, he hadn't played a stellar round, though he had relished the exhibition put on by Grant. The links guru drove into the rough on this hole and had to lay up, and he was looking at a third shot of about 100 yards into the green. He reached for a wedge.

"Not a wedge," David said, "not at the end of this round. You can't do the predictable thing now."

"You're right, you're right," Grant said, and he replaced the wedge in his bag. His hand hovered over his fairway wood, then moved toward his putter.

"I don't often see a man trying to figure out whether his next shot is 3-wood or putter," said David.

It turned out to be a putter, and Grant played your ordinary 100-yard putt with about 20 yards of break to about 15 feet.

David just laughed. "I tried to imagine all the shots that people could hit out here, but that's the great thing about links golf. I could never have imagined that. People come out here every day and invent shots I never dreamed of."

Part Three

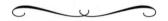

Pacific Dunes
and Bandon Trails

16 | The Boy Wonder

Here was this young man ... and he absolutely knew his stuff. Even at that age, you could see the genius in him —BILL SHEAN, ON TOM DOAK

TOM DOAK WAS ELEVEN years old when his father, an executive for Lever Brothers, took him along on a business trip to Hilton Head, South Carolina. The boy was a fledgling golfer, and he'd never taken any particular notice of golf courses, but the just-completed Harbour Town Golf Links made a profound and lasting impression. The effect wasn't quite the same as the apple falling on the head of Isaac Newton, but Harbour Town did set young Tom Doak on a path from which he has never wavered.

Doak was going to design golf courses, and the best way to understand his passion and commitment is to think of Tiger Woods. Tiger didn't just dream about doing it, or wonder if he had what it took to get on the Tour; he prepared himself, and he expected to excel. In his mind, he was always competing with the great ones, Nicklaus and Hogan and Jones. Similarly, Tom Doak began to study golf courses and the history of golf course architecture. He didn't just want to build golf courses but to build great, enduring courses. He didn't just want to earn a living as a golf course architect but to be regarded as one of the best who ever lived.

He was born on March 16, 1961, in New York City, and he grew up in Stamford, Connecticut, one of two boys in a bookish family. The first golf course that he got to know was Sterling Farms, a muni not far from his home. His father, a sometime golfer, took him on business trips to Pebble Beach and to Pinehurst, to anyplace where there was a golf course. His father's friends, once they realized the depth of the boy's interest, began passing along books on course architecture; his mother, a journalism major in college, and a lover of language—it was she who always encouraged his writing—ordered copies of hard-to-find books on the subject through interlibrary loan. She always made two copies of each—one for Tom, one for herself to read. With her encouragement and companionship, Tom read classic works by George Thomas, Robert Hunter, and the man who became his idol, Alister MacKenzie. She also encouraged the intellectual curiosity of Tom's younger brother, who grew up to be an archaeologist, and she is on record as having said, "I have two sons who dig dirt for a living."

Tom says that he had "memorized" most of the *World Atlas of Golf* by the time he was a teenager. First published in 1976, the *World Atlas* was and remains a definitive book on the subject of golf course design, and it is easy to imagine how its sumptuous illustrations and lyrical prose could have inspired a sixteen-year-old boy. This is a book that leaves no doubt that the design of golf courses is a high, epic calling. In the introduction, Alistair Cooke wrote, "Let us turn these pages and read and weep. Here are the power and the glory, the fine flower of many landscapes."

When Tom said that he memorized it, he probably wasn't exaggerating. In matters of golf design, his memory is close to photographic, and he's always been able to remember numbers. His SAT scores were in the upper brackets: 800 in math, 690 in verbal. He was admitted to MIT, where he quickly realized that there was only one thing that he really wanted to study, and that was golf course design. Since no undergraduate institution in America offered a program that fit his exact needs, Tom decided that the best place for him would be Cornell, where the motto was that any student could fashion his own curriculum. He transferred after the end of his freshman year.

Cornell also happened to be the college attended by America's most famous golf course architect, Robert Trent Jones, Sr., who had taken similar advantage of Cornell's flexibility half a century earlier. Tom's affiliation was with the landscape architecture department, but he was emphatically not schooling himself to become another RTJ; he was already drawing his own conclusions about golf course design, conclusions that would place him at loggerheads with Trent Jones and many other modern architects.

At Cornell, Tom began to spread his wings. He wasn't satisfied with reading about the great courses; he wanted to see them, so he put his writing skills to good use, composing letters to clubs like Pine Valley, Merion, and Seminole, explaining that he was a student of golf course architecture and requesting a chance to visit. One recipient of a Doak letter was Bill Shean, the pal whom Mike Keiser called "Mr. Chicago Golf." Bill was a member of both Butler National and Chicago Golf Club, and he was won over: "The letter was neatly typed, and it intrigued me. Here was this young man who said he was studying the best courses and that he'd like to play ours, if we'd permit it, or photograph it. That's what set the hook. I wanted to know if he really would be content to take pictures, or if he was just scheming to get out and play. But he was sincere. We did play when he came to Butler National, and then he said that if we didn't mind, he'd like to go back out and take some pictures. It was getting late in the day, and the light was right for photography, and he went off with his camera. By then I was convinced that he was into the study of golf courses up to his eyeballs, and when he came off the course, he asked us if we'd like to see any of his slides. In the trunk of his car, he had three thousand slides of golf courses, and we sat there for five hours in the clubhouse at Butler National looking at them and listening to this kid talk about them. They were great slides, too—he was a wonderful photographer, and he absolutely knew his stuff. Even at that age you could see the genius in him."

In Bill Shean, Tom had found a staunch supporter, and he won several others during his college years, firing off letters not only to golf clubs but to influential figures in golf. He wrote to several golf course architects, including Geoffrey Cornish, one of the few who took the time to write back, encouraging Tom to pursue a career in the field. Because he had read that Ben Crenshaw, then one of the young stars on the PGA Tour, was a lover of golf history and a student of traditional courses, Tom wrote to Ben; he received a gracious reply, and a lifelong friendship was formed. George Peper, then the editor of *Golf Magazine,* was another recipient of Tom's letters; though he had the innate skepticism of the veteran journalist, Peper was impressed by the young man's brashness, his persistence, his prose, and his already considerable knowledge. In 1980, *Golf Magazine* ran a sidebar that Tom had written, and in May 1982 his first feature appeared in the magazine, earning him an A+ for his Writing for Magazines class at Cornell.

The letter-writing campaign also wore down the resistance of Pete Dye, whom Tom had decided he wanted as his mentor. Dye, of course, was the designer of Harbour Town, and in 1981 he was in the red-hot center of his career. Tom besieged Pete with letters requesting a job on his crew; he now believes that Alice Dye, not Pete, finally took pity on him and relented. In the summer of 1981, while he was still at Cornell, Tom took a summer job as a menial laborer on the crew building Long Cove, in South Carolina. "Most of the other guys on the crew thought it was funny that I was studying to be a designer," Tom says, and initially he couldn't help pestering Pete with more questions than Pete wanted to answer. After Tom had been on the job for a few days, Pete waved him over to look at a green site and asked for his ideas. Tom knew that he was being put on the spot, and the site looked like nothing but a big pile of dirt to him, but he realized something about his new boss: Pete Dye wasn't afraid to take suggestions. He was searching for an idea, and if the kid from Cornell had come up with one, he would have used it. "One of the main things I learned from him," Tom has said, "is that it takes a lot of people to build a golf course. Many people can make contributions, and if the head architect is smart enough, he'll take the best ideas and incorporate them into the course."

By the time he was a senior at Cornell, a great many people at the university and in the world of golf knew that Tom Doak was a disciplined, serious, passionate, and completely driven student of golf course architecture. The landscape architecture department offered a traveling fellowship for an outstanding graduate, and there wasn't much question about who'd get it: Tom Doak, who wanted to extend his knowledge of golf course design by visiting the classic courses of Great Britain. His application was supported by letters of recommendation from George Peper, PGA Tour Commissioner Deane Beman, Ben Crenshaw, and Pete Dye.

HE MADE A BEELINE to St. Andrews, where he lived in a B & B and worked as a sort of second-string caddy, the one who got a loop in the afternoon after the locals had gone out. His original plan had been to work on the grounds crew, and he did become a friend of Walter Woods, the green keeper at St. Andrews, but caddying turned out to be a perfect way to learn the golf course. By carrying the bags of people of all different skill levels, he got to see just how many ways there were to get around the Old Course. He looked at some famous hazards from perspectives he might otherwise never have imagined. What fascinated him was the infinite complexity of the place, the "million strategies already out there on the ground."

The experience at St. Andrews was mind-expanding. Here was a completely different approach not only to course design but to the playing of the game, an approach that seemed to contradict almost every principle of modern design. The Old Course hadn't even been designed in the usual sense of the word; it was a stretch of dimpled, rumpled linksland where golf had been played for centuries and the holes had slowly evolved. The holes didn't conform to any "rules" regarding length, or the placement of hazards, or the best route to take from tee to green. There was nothing orthodox about the golf course that had been the source of so many ideas about golf course design, ideas that the student-caddy believed had been increasingly and arrogantly brushed aside by contemporary golf course architects. Visits to many other British courses (171 other courses, to be exact) on this year of postgraduate study in Great Britain only confirmed the lessons he had learned at St. Andrews. He took thousands of photographs and made extensive notes, and he was formulating the principles that would become the bedrock of his own design philosophy.

One cardinal principle was that a golf course must be interesting for all classes of player. As simple and self-evident as such a principle might sound, it put Tom at odds with the designers of modern "championship" courses, which were invariably long and difficult, and sometimes unplayable for any golfer of ordinary skills. A second principle—that the natural features of a landscape should be preserved, not obliterated—was equally at odds with modern course design.

In Great Britain, Tom was discovering the virtues of classic golf course design. Here he was looking at golf courses that had been around for decades, or for centuries, and they had changed very little. They hadn't needed to change. They were very different from the courses that most modern architects were building in the United States, but the more he studied them, the more he came to believe that far from becoming obsolete, these older courses actually required shotmaking skills of a high caliber—and they were also, unlike so many modern courses, just plain fun.

Like many other Americans, Tom was exhilarated by his first exposure to the courses of the British Isles. With his analytic turn of mind and his already extensive knowledge of classic American courses, he couldn't stop trying to interpret and evaluate what he was seeing. For Tom, the precedent for his discovery was nothing less than what had taken place in fourteenth-century Europe when thinkers and writers "discovered" the arts and culture of the Greeks and Romans; that discovery ignited the Renaissance, a period of immense intellectual ferment and creativity that drew its energy and inspiration from classical sources.

Tom was still a few years away from designing his own courses, but when the time came to start his own company, he would name it Renaissance Golf Design.

FIRST, THOUGH, TOM wanted to earn his stripes in the field. The research phase of his quest was not complete—there would always be more courses to see—but it was time to switch gears. It was time to leave the sepia-tinted past and come back to the here-and-now. It was time to get his hands dirty and learn exactly how people built courses in the golf boom of the 1980s in the United States of America—and not just ordinary golf courses, but the most original, high-profile, and provocative courses.

In other words, Tom went back to work for Pete Dye, where he got an up-close-and-personal look at how the postmodern golf courses were designed and constructed. In *The Anatomy of a Golf Course,* Tom wrote: "Of all the things that I learned from Pete, the most important was just how much work is involved in getting a great golf course from the dream to the ground." To the world, Pete Dye might have seemed headstrong and ornery, but he took a humble approach to golf course design, not the Great Man approach in which all concepts and ideas must come from on high. As Tom saw repeatedly, Pete Dye was sometimes willing to admit that he was stumped. He was always looking for fresh ideas, for ways to compound the intricacy and complexity of his designs. His best holes teemed with strategic options. He was genuinely receptive to ideas from his crew, and the business—with Alice as a daily partner, and his sons Perry and P. B. actively involved—was very much a family business. Pete liked to work in the field on one course at a time, immersing himself completely in the project at hand; this was in contrast to those architects who spent a lot of time in their offices (or playing competitive golf), relied on associates to draw detailed plans, and used golf course construction companies to get their courses built. The golf world was rife with stories about Pete Dye, the mad genius who made it up on the fly, the guy who didn't hesitate to rebuild a hole if he didn't like it, and sometimes tore it apart and rebuilt it four or five times before he was satisfied; to work for him was to be present at and to participate in the messy, exciting act of creation.

At ground level, Tom saw how some of the knotty issues of design were actually resolved. For example, how was the need to make a course challenging for a top player balanced against the desire to make it playable for the weekend golfer? Answer: by tinkering with all kinds of details, and by having a voice like Alice Dye's in the architect's ear. "The whole time I worked for Pete Dye, he was caught up in tournament play, and yet I thought the best course he built in that stretch was the one I started on, Long Cove, where Alice was reminding him every day that he wasn't building for a tournament anymore and he had to accommodate the seventy-year-old woman member. Long Cove is full of features that are fun for the average golfer."

Tom was realizing that he was temperamentally more interested in designing for regular golfers than for the pros, and he was absorbing the lesson that a little controversy isn't a bad thing. He was also observing a working method that he would emulate. Gradually, as Pete came to realize that Tom carried around in his head an extensive and detailed archive of great golf holes—including holes of Pete's design—he was entrusted with greater and greater responsibility, and he worked on a variety of projects, following the Dye star from Long Cove to Plum Creek and Riverdale Dunes, with brief stops in California (where he drew the first plans for PGA West) and on Long Island (for the renovation of the Piping Rock Club, a classic design by C. B. Macdonald).

Perhaps the most important event in his apprenticeship to Pete Dye occurred at Plum Creek, in Colorado, where Tom got to know a dark-haired, bearish shaper named Jim Urbina. A teacher by training and a big-time sports fan, Jim realized that he'd met his match when he failed to stump Tom with baseball trivia. He and a buddy even resorted to taking out an almanac filled with obscure, arcane baseball facts—and Tom knew the answer to every question they threw at him.

As far as Jim Urbina was concerned, Tom was a guy who didn't know much about construction but knew a whole lot about baseball—and about classic golf courses, too, as Jim discovered the following summer at Riverdale Dunes. Jim taught Tom how to operate a bulldozer, and as a kind of quid pro quo Tom began to show him slides of the courses he had visited in his travels. They talked a lot of golf that summer. For Jim, who didn't have much of a golf background, this brainy young dude was a trip, someone who could put any kind of problem into a much larger historical and aesthetic perspective; for Tom, the solid guy on the bulldozer was a practical genius, someone who could translate ideas into tangible shapes. Riverdale Dunes was being built on flat farm ground, and the young crew members had some creative license. They began to use some of Tom's ideas in the shaping, and Jim Urbina still believes that Riverdale Dunes contains some of the most imaginative shaping that has ever been done in the Denver area.

That collaboration in 1985 between the whip-thin apprentice and burly ex–football player was the start of a long partnership. Fifteen years later, at Pacific Dunes, Jim and Tom would still be talking to each other about the best way to shape golf holes, pushing each other to find the best way to make the ground express their vision.

WHILE HE WORKED for Pete Dye, Tom kept an eye on what was happening elsewhere in the booming American golf business, and he didn't like much of what he saw.

In Scotland, the game of golf was the national pastime, a popular, affordable, walking game played on courses that had been built at little expense on land well suited to the purpose. In the United States, the game was increasingly played by people who paid hefty fees to ride in golf carts on courses that had been built at great expense on land poorly suited for the purpose.

Even worse, many of the expensive courses being built advertised themselves as Scottish. "When I returned from overseas my first reaction was disappointment, in that most of the new courses were being sold as 'Scottish style' courses," Tom said in an interview with *Golfer* magazine. "That just sounded so hollow to me. They were nothing like Scotland—they just built artificial dunes to create a look. A lot of what happens in American golf is marketing driven, and I feared that many golfers might actually believe these courses accurately reflected the courses in Scotland."

To Tom, steeped in the virtues of classic courses, most of the new courses coming on-line, whether or not they were described as Scotish, seemed predictable, unimaginative, ticky-tacky, homogenized. They seemed always to be arranged in two loops of nine holes; the holes were the prescribed length; they played to a par of 72, always with the same balance of par-3, par-4, and par-5 holes; they seemed to follow a set of "rules" about how holes should be shaped, how hazards should be placed, and so on. They were soulless creations, and they made him cringe.

He was in his early twenties, but he knew he wanted a chance to build courses of his own. "I believed absolutely that the golf course architects of the

1980s weren't building as interesting courses as the architects of the 1920s, and I thought I could do better." But who was going to hire him? How was he going to get from the Dye crew to a design commission of his own? Golf course architecture wasn't exactly a closed profession, but he couldn't just hang out his shingle and expect clients to show up. One of the best ways to enter the field was to become a professional golfer and win a lot of tournaments; this was the route followed by Jack Nicklaus, Arnold Palmer, Tom Weiskopf, and many other players whose names were certain to add to the appeal of a new course ("No golf course architect is as well known as Davis Love"). Another was to be born into a design family, like that of Robert Trent Jones, whose sons Rees and Robert Trent, Jr., followed him into the business; or the Fazio clan, where Tom had inherited the practice of his uncle, George; or, closer to home, the Dye family, where sons P. B. and Perry were carrying on the family tradition. ("I didn't really set out to chart a course of my own, other than recognizing that there a lot of styles of great golf courses and I shouldn't try to copy Pete Dye's. If you wanted that, you would hire his sons, not me.")

So Tom began to write about golf course design, both privately and publicly. From his first feature article in 1982 until his last in 1998, he was a regular contributor to *Golf Magazine,* writing a couple of features every year. He was never actually on the payroll ("I should have had a better agent, I guess, but I was just grateful that George Peper had given me a platform to write"). In 1983 Tom started keeping track of the rankings of the Greatest Courses in the world; in those precomputer days, Peper remembers, Tom manually and flawlessly tabulated thousands of votes. When his own design career started to gather momentum, and his courses became eligible for coverage in the magazine, there were a few grumbles about possible conflicts of interest. ("It was quite a while before anyone started to look at my role in the rankings as a conflict of interest because obviously I wasn't taken seriously as an architect when I was twenty-two. However, when High Pointe [Tom's first design] made *Golf's* list of the best courses in 1993, a handful of architects—not the big names—were upset about that, and suggested that it was only because

I was adding up the ballots. I was upset that someone would question my integrity, and George defended me and kept me in charge. By 1997, though, it was clear that some people considered my work for *Golf* a conflict of interest, and perception is everything. If *Golf* wrote something about one of my courses, it was perceived as being because of my relationship with *Golf*; and my relationship with *Golf* made the other magazines reluctant to write anything about my work as a designer.")

Most of Tom's writing for *Golf* was analytical, restrained, and objective. He wrote, for instance, in "Killer Pins at Augusta," about the way a pin placement changed the strategy for the big guns, or, in "The Untouchables," about unreachable par 5s. A potentially more controversial assignment was an appraisal of Jack Nicklaus's growing body of work as a golf course architect, a feature included in a special commemorative issue of the magazine intended to honor Nicklaus as *Golf*'s "Player of the Century." It would have been rude, to say the least, to knock the Golden Bear, and the article is respectful—but not fawning. Tom might have been a kid, and Nicklaus was one of the most powerful men in golf, but he couldn't help noting that Nicklaus said his ideal course would have "18 downhill holes"—and remarking, drily, that "this is seldom possible." He also takes Nicklaus slightly to task for designing courses that "require exorbitant sums to build and maintain—and, therefore, to play."

The *Golf* articles were for public consumption and his criticism was muted. Privately, he was a lot more explicit about what he liked and didn't like. The notes and observations that he had been compiling ever since he first started visiting golf courses were taking on a shape and life of their own, for Tom copied and circulated the notes to friends. He didn't try to water down his opinions, and his prose was no-holds-barred. He wasn't afraid to slam architects whose work was often considered sacrosanct. He dismissed one course by Tom Fazio as "absolutely vapid." He called a Desmond Muirhead design in New Jersey "the most ridiculous course I've ever seen." He called Sherwood, a much-praised Nicklaus layout with not one but a multitude of artificial waterfalls, as "classic Nicklaus-client overkill." And he singled out another Nicklaus design, Bear Creek, as the place where he "suddenly takes a turn toward the marketable, including features that would scream, 'This is where he sold out.'"

Hard words, but *The Confidential Guide,* as these private notes were called, was intended for friends' eyes only when it was first circulated in 1988. Tom had printed up about fifty copies for his pals. But the copies were passed around among golf insiders, and got people talking. They didn't always have nice things to say about the young man, who sometimes came across as a smart aleck and a know-it-all. Tom resisted making the book generally available, for he didn't want to make his name "as a critic first and a designer second," but in 1996 he finally agreed to let Sleeping Bear Press publish *The Confidential Guide,* and he wrote an introduction that acknowledged his misgivings: "Much of the controversy that surrounds this book stems from the fact that I am not only a critic but a budding architect as well . . . In the private edition I made some funny and insulting comments about other architects, and I apologize if any were taken in the wrong light."

The Confidential Guide made waves when it came out in public form, even though Tom had edited his prose to remove some of the most provocative comments. The book contains descriptions of 854 golf courses, all of them rated according to Tom's own 10-point scale. Many of the usual suspects— Cypress Point, Pine Valley, Ballybunion, and St. Andrews—are awarded perfect 10s, but some hallowed tracks, like Augusta National, didn't earn that highest grade. Tom's "system" was admittedly personal and idiosyncratic, and he chose to restrict his list of thirty-one favorite courses to one course per architect, stating explicitly, "I didn't want anybody to mistake this list for my selection of the world's 'best' courses." As a result, this section, called "Gourmet's Choice," includes several little-known British courses, like St. Enodoc and Woodhall Spa, but not Muirfield, Portrush, Cypress Point, Royal Melbourne, Winged Foot, Augusta National, or Shinnecock Hills. Altogether, *The Confidential Guide,* with its idiosyncratic "Gazeteer," listing Tom's choices for clubs with the best lunch, best halfway house, most hospitable clubs, and Dumb Blonde Awards—for places that are pretty but lacking in substance—comes across as a shrewd, crotchety, opinionated book. For the reader who takes the time to read it, as opposed to skimming it for its withering remarks, the book actually contains a clear, unshakable idea about what matters in golf. "I believe that real golf," Tom wrote, "is about interesting and exciting golf holes."

That idea is articulated at greater length in *The Anatomy of a Golf Course,* published in 1992. For students of golf course architecture, this book stands as one of the most reasoned volumes ever written on the subject. Far less flowery than the *World Atlas*—Tom just doesn't have it in him to be flowery—and far less provocative than *The Confidential Guide, The Anatomy of a Golf Course* is as thoughtful as the title suggests. In a sense, it is a manifesto for Tom's "minimalist" design philosophy, and it makes its argument by tracing minimalist principles back to their source. Yet the tone is always personal, and Tom assumes throughout the book that the reader is as completely and utterly enthralled by the subject as he is.

That is his usual assumption, come to think of it. He can and does talk about other things, but nothing fascinates him as much as golf course design, and he is neither shy nor self-conscious about laying out his ideas and opinions. Why should he be? He knows the subject backward and forward, and he believes that any undertaking worth its salt deserves debate and discussion. In his willingness to criticize and dispute, he violated the unspoken rule that golf course architects would praise each other's work and refrain from uttering a single syllable that could be construed as critical or controversial. Some professional associations thrive on the give-and-take of opposing points of view, but the American Society of Golf Course Architects is perfectly discreet and remains high above every fray. (Let it be noted in passing that Tom Doak is not a member of the ASGCA.) By daring to knock the work of his elders, by praising his own work in both the *Confidential Guide* and *The Anatomy of a Golf Course,* by setting himself apart from the trends and fashions of golf course design, Tom set himself up as a target. People said he was arrogant. Vain. Egotistical. A self-promoter.

"Tom was guilty," Mike Keiser said, "of scandalous honesty. He modeled himself after Alister MacKenzie, who was also outspoken. The difference was that MacKenzie was a middle-aged man at the height of his career, and Tom was still an unproven young man." George Peper thought that Tom had a more complete archive of golf holes in his head than anyone else in the field, but doubted whether he could succeed in a profession that required getting along with others. "In the beginning, he had the people skills of an ostrich," George said. "He was like a mild version of an idiot savant."

He was starting out with a reputation as a young man who thought for himself, a maverick in a profession that tended to be chummy and clubby. He wasn't afraid to lob a few grenades at golf's established figures. He was known as golf's enfant terrible.

NEVERTHELESS, TOM HAD a band of loyal friends, and they were people who believed in him absolutely. One was Fred Muller, the pro at Crystal Downs, the Michigan course designed by Alister MacKenzie. When Tom left the Dye crew, he spent some time hanging out and playing golf at Crystal Downs; the course wasn't well known at the time, and Tom prevailed on one of his old pals, Ben Crenshaw, to come up and have a look. Ben played a morning round at the Buick Open, flew up on a private plane, loved Crystal Downs, and returned to the tournament singing the praises of the golf course and hitting the ball with gusto and confidence. (He won that 1986 Buick Open, by the way, and Crystal Downs has become a perennial in the upper echelons of the Top 100.)

Tom got his first design job when Fred Muller recommended him to a developer in Traverse City. The area of upper Michigan around Traverse City and Gaylord is now home to more than fifty courses, but when Tom was hired in 1986 to design a daily fee course, High Pointe, the course in the local news was The Bear, a heavily promoted Nicklaus design at the Grand Traverse resort. It was the kind of "Scottish" course that Tom disdained, a "links-style" course with lots of mounds and deep bunkers, as well several water hazards and woodlands—features that simply do not occur on authentic links courses. Nicklaus's crews had moved mountains of dirt in construction.

Tom, naturally, did something completely different. His site had a ridge on one side and a valley on the other, and he decided that he wouldn't move much ground. He wouldn't build deep bunkers or mounds, but would try to design a course on which the greens and fairways followed the natural terrain. Working completely solo, doing most of the shaping himself on the back of a bulldozer, he delivered a reasonably priced golf course that was a showcase for his kind of architectural minimalism.

"Minimalism begins with common sense," Tom often says, meaning that it begins with a decision not to move dirt when you don't have to. Minimalism was not just a style, or a look, but a disciplined, principled approach to golf course design, one that began with a careful study of the available land and evolved a design to fit it. The goal was to retain as much as possible the flavor and local character of the land. It was the opposite of the "rape it and shape it" approach of many designers, where the idea was to flatten the land and then mold it in whatever forms the architect fancied.

Ironically, Tom's next job was on a flat site in Myrtle Beach, South Carolina, where developer Larry Young wanted him to build a Scottish course. Young had shaken up Myrtle Beach by departing from the tried-and-true formula of building absolutely basic, cut-and-fill golf courses, as many of them as possible and as close to major highways as possible, and running golfers through in turnstile numbers. His courses put an emphasis on imaginative design, and at his flagship Legends complex, he wanted a course that would capture the essence of Scottish golf. He asked Tom to design it for him.

The site was flat as a tabletop, and Young had hired a lead shaper of the old school who didn't like having the young whippersnapper messing with "his" work. Tom insisted on being allowed to go back and shape the green contours and do all the detail work himself. He gave Larry Young the huge greens he wanted, but the undulations are Tom's, and he was able to re-create several holes that successfully evoked the spirit of British originals. He resisted creating a lake on the course, designing the obligatory water hazard as a burn. He used several features—including occasional blind or semiblind shots, bunkers in the center of fairways, and green complexes that encouraged play along the ground—that were familiar to Scots but not to Americans, and which provoked plenty of discussion in the enormous stucco clubhouse, a Myrtle Beach approximation of St. Andrews' Royal and Ancient, that dominates the Legends complex.

Heathlands was well received. It won Best New Course honors in *Golf* and attracted attention from other magazines. Tom was invited to do another course for Young, the Parkland course. "I thought Larry would give me a lot of freedom on that one because Heathlands had turned out well, but he had moved his office to the Legends so he was on site every day and he didn't like what I was doing—too subtle. There wasn't one particular argument. He had just lost confidence in me and had decided to wave his hands around and tell the shapers what to do, and I didn't want to put my name on that. We were ready to start Stonewall, so I suggested we just part ways."

By this time Tom had incorporated, and his first associate was Gil Hanse, a young man who'd worked on the crew at High Pointe, returned to school, and came back to work as Tom's first associate in 1990. Hanse shared Tom's views on minimalist design. Before beginning work on Tom's third course, Black Forest in Gaylord, Michigan, the two of them made a trip to California. "We stopped in at San Francisco Golf Club, Cypress Point, The Valley Club at Montecito and others, just to look at the MacKenzie bunkers. We realized that no one was building bunkers like those in 1990, and that they had a great style to try to emulate." Gil Hanse did a lot of the shaping at Black Forest, and at Stonewall, a private club in Pennsylvania.

Both courses showed Tom Doak hitting his stride, combining a minimalist approach with an ever-increasing repertory of traditional shapes and features. He was happy with the way that Stonewall turned out, and he had high hopes that the course would get some publicity on *Golf Digest*'s "Best New" ranking, but the course was left off entirely. Not enough raters had visited it. The fact that Stonewall was ignored was a "definite low," and the period that followed tested his patience. "The truth is that it's easier to attract the first course than the third or the sixth, when your novelty factor has worn off but you're still far less experienced than your competitors. Our one real slow time was between 1993 and 1995."

LIKE ALL GOLF COURSE ARCHITECTS, Tom was the proprietor of a small business, and he had a payroll to meet. By 1993, Jim Urbina was on that payroll, along with Bruce Hepner and Tom Mead. Gil Hanse left to go into business for himself. Although Tom always worked in the spirit of Pete Dye, using design ideas from everyone on his crew, and although all his associates made essential contributions, Gil was the only one who got design credit. In the readjustment that followed his departure, they all agreed that it was in the best interests of Renaissance Golf if only Tom's name was on all future designs.

Tom had to scramble to get work in the mid-90s. Even though the golf boom was rolling right along, the best commissions went to the big names— to Jack Nicklaus, Pete Dye, Tom Fazio, Rees Jones, and a few others. The sheer cost of golf course construction went into the stratosphere, and there was hardly an upscale course that didn't have its waterfall, its stone bridges, and its bagpipers. There were a few courses, like Sand Hills, that bucked the prevailing trend and made the case for minimalism, but Renaissance Golf Design wasn't exactly flourishing.

Tom Doak needed a place where he could show the world what he could do. There was a cutoff age beyond which he could no longer be regarded as a boy wonder. He'd always had a brilliant future, but he was approaching that dangerous point at which his brilliant future might lie behind him. He'd looked at one site where he might have a real chance to make a show of his talent, and he'd met a developer who was just enough of a risk-taker to hire him.

The site was in Oregon, and the developer was Mike Keiser.

The man who'd put them together was Bill Shean. He'd told Tom about Bandon, and Tom had asked Mike if he could go out and have a look. Given the green light, he went to Bandon in February 1994 and got the tour from Shorty Dow. Mike didn't yet own the land that would become the site of Pacific Dunes, but Tom remembers peeking across the boundary fence at the tall, shaggy dunes; they made an impression, and he wrote Mike a long letter telling him how much he'd like to be involved. He lobbied hard for the commission, and he had powerful advocates in Dick Youngscap and Bill Shean. Mike admired Tom's writing, and he accepted an invitation from Tom to take a look at Stonewall. On that trip, they got to know each other much better, but Mike had already begun to talk to David Kidd, and he was afraid that Tom had offended too many people. In 1996, Mike invited Tom to join a group traveling to Ireland, and they played golf together at Royal County Down and Portrush.

"I thought Tom had too many negatives to do the first course," Mike said, but he was close to making up his mind to hire him to build the second course at Bandon. When he made another trip in 1997 to spend time with Tom at Crystal Downs, he and Tom shook hands on it: He would get a crack at building the second course.

There were a couple of caveats. Mike didn't know exactly when he'd want to get started, and it was clear that he wanted the same sort of arrangement that he had with David, one in which he could always change his mind. And his decision to go with Tom wasn't a no-confidence vote in David, who had completed the routing for Bandon Dunes and was just getting ready to begin construction. The original intention had been to have David—or, to go back to the first plans, Gleneagles Golf Developments—design two courses at Bandon, but Mike had come to favor the variety that a different architect could bring. And as Mike would tell David, he was almost certain to fail if he designed the second course; how was he going to surpass his first effort? A second course would be a standing invitation to negative comparisons. Better to bring in someone else, and to let David stand back fully vindicated as the designer of the first course at Bandon Dunes.

In any case, Tom was willing to wait. He had recognized the potential of the coastal site in Oregon. Bruce Hepner, who'd gone out with him on that first visit, came right out and said, "This was going to be our Sand Hills. It was going to be our chance to prove ourselves."

17 | The Moons Are in Alignment

If Bandon Dunes was Pebble Beach, then we were going to try to do
something different. We were going to be Cypress Point. —TOM DOAK

ON THE NIGHT of September 29, 1999, the construction of Pacific Dunes
got off to an auspicious start when the site caught on fire.

Mike Keiser was on the 18th fairway at Bandon Dunes, completing a
round with friends from Chicago, when he first saw the smoke. It seemed
safely distant, but he talked to Troy Russell and Josh Lesnik about the potential danger before he went back to his room to change. It was late in the day,
and people outside the lodge were glancing apprehensively at the heavy bil-
lows of smoke rising into the evening sky. Everyone knew how dangerously
flammable the gorse was, and Mike was reassured that the local fire crews had
been alerted. Nonetheless, by the time Mike came down for dinner the fire
had obviously spread, and the flames were shooting high into the night sky.
The summers are dry on Oregon's South Coast, and September is the driest
time of all; the Bandon fire of 1936 had occurred in September. There was a
light breeze from the north, and the fire was advancing slowly and erratically
toward the golf course and lodge, leaping ahead in some places, hesitating in
others, exploding when the resin in the stands of gorse suddenly reached the
combustion point. *Whummmpppff!* The air crackled and the huge flames
sent up a dazzling spray of sparks.

The theory that a golf course could extinguish a gorse fire was about to
be tested.

While the local fire crews were trying to put out the fire, Mike was talking to members of the maintenance crew, and to David Kidd and Jim Haley, about measures they could take. David and Jim were in Oregon to build the driving range, and they were ready to get into the battle. While members of the grounds crew turned on the irrigation on the northernmost holes of Bandon Dunes, the 6th, 7th, and 8th, to make sure that the turf would be soaking wet when the flames arrived, David and Jim set out to build a firebreak.

All the equipment—a couple of dozers and two excavators—from the range construction was mobilized as the drivers set out to the north. Jim took his D8 bulldozer up into the gorse-covered dunes near the present site of the 8th tee at Pacific Dunes; working in the dark at furious speed, he began to clear a swath with his twelve-foot blade. David stayed nearby on a high piece of ground so that he could keep an eye on the advancing fire. He and Jim and the others had walkie-talkies, and David felt "like a general on a battlefield," trying to keep an eye on his field units and on the movements of the enemy. It was full night by now, but the fire lit up the landscape in bursts, with bits of burning gorse raining down "like shrapnel," in Troy Russell's words. Jim, driving his blade into a wall of gorse, couldn't always see where he was headed, and David sometimes lost sight of him when he went down between dunes or tunneled deep into the brush. "I knew I must be near the edge of the cliff," Jim said, "but I couldn't tell how near I was in the dark, and with all the brush in front of me. I'm pushing, pushing, pushing with the blade, and the next thing I know the blade is free. It's just swinging in thin air, hanging over the edge of the cliff. I came that close to going over."

The firebreak seemed to work, and Troy and the others thought that the fire had been contained, but then the backfires set by the local fire crews got out of control. Mike, David, and Jim stayed awake all night, watching as the original fire and backfires joined forces, consuming in all some four hundred acres. The flames advanced wherever they could, seeking out stands of gorse and shore pines, at one point dipping down over the cliff into the heavy vegetation on the ocean slope, where Roger Sheffield, the bunker expert, drove his bulldozer into the gorse. Working at a 45-degree angle, he managed to cut a wide swath, and the fire gradually ran out of sustenance. By daybreak there were only a few smoldering embers.

The danger had passed. The fire was out, the lodge was safe, and the golf course had indeed proven to be a kind of firewall. Beyond that, the fire had accomplished in one night what had taken months on the Bandon Dunes site. Here at Pacific Dunes there would be no need for the Hydro-Ax to chop gorse, no need to hire crews to remove the nasty stuff, piece by prickly piece. The job was done. The fire had saved Mike Keiser hundreds of thousands of dollars, and it had cleared the site for Renaissance Golf Design.

David Kidd would later say, jokingly, "No one knows how the fire started, but I'd like to know the whereabouts of Tom Doak earlier that evening."

"ON CHOICE PROPERTY," Tom wrote in *The Anatomy of a Golf Course,* "architects must discover the correct routing through the natural terrain, and thereby claim its advantages . . . But the architect cannot decide upon his best alternative until he has put together several different schemes. To discover all the potential options is the true skill, and knowledge in two areas is key—the ability to visualize existing features from the topographic maps, and to make mental comparisons with the best holes one has seen or played in the past."

Long before August 1999, when he spent more than a week communing with the site, wandering through the sandhills and mulling over the various possibilities, Tom had been thinking about the routing for Pacific Dunes and the kinds of holes that he wanted to build. The site lent itself to a rugged, wild "look"—the kind of look that he and Mike had both admired at Royal County Down and Portrush on their trip to Ireland in 1996. To convey his ideas, Tom put together one of his slide shows and presented it, in the Bunker Bar in the basement of the lodge, to a group that included Mike and several officers from Kemper. He had deliberately arranged the slides so that the presentation began gently but edged gradually toward the extreme. The bunkers got deeper, the greens got wilder, and the golf holes generally started to look more like moonscapes. "Jim Seeley was the first to crack," Tom says. "He finally just couldn't take it. He said, 'You can't do that here.'"

But Tom was beginning to know just what he wanted to do, and he had a rationale for every decision, including his determination to avoid the predictable routing. "It's almost a cliché," he said, "to route a seaside course in two nine-hole loops, with the first holes inland and the finishing holes of each nine along the water. That was the one thing I knew I was *not* going to do."

This discussion, too, harkened back three years to Tom's Irish trip. Both Tom and Mike had preferred the routing of Portrush, where the golf course moves toward the sea in the middle holes of each nine, to that of Royal County Down, where the course moves progressively inland after starting holes along the sea. The Portrush routing builds to a pair of crescendos, the first coming at the 5th and 6th holes, the second coming at the 14th, the hole known as Calamity Corner. In its pacing and psychology, the Portrush sequence was similar to Bandon Dunes, another course that was uppermost in Tom's mind as he made his plans.

While he wanted to make sure that Pacific Dunes differed from its sister, Tom wasn't worried about any general similarities in the routing. The specific differences were going to be pronounced. Here, again, Tom had Mike's strong backing; Mike had cast his vote in favor of a distinctively different course when he decided to hire Tom, rather than David Kidd, to design the second course. He always knew that he wanted to avoid the sameness that is the flaw of resorts where one course blurs into another, and, at the end of the day, guests can't even remember which course they played.

All along, Tom had felt that the property he'd been given was better than the Bandon Dunes property—and even David, when he looked at the height of the sand dunes and the natural blowouts on Tom's site, had conceded this point. The two of them sat down for dinner together that fall at the Wheelhouse in Bandon. David was there to build the range, Tom to make another pass at the routing. David told Tom, "I've already holed my putt, and left you a gimme."

The natural differences, Tom had decided, were going to be underscored when Pacific Dunes was built. "I remembered something that Pete had told me about Harbour Town, which he built when Trent Jones was building Palmetto Dunes on the other side of Hilton Head. Pete drove by the site every morning, and he decided that he was going to make his course the opposite of Palmetto Dunes. . . . Working on a site so different from David's, I decided that I was going to do most things differently."

So while the general configuration of Pacific Dunes was roughly similar to that of Bandon Dunes, in that there were dramatic holes in the middle of each nine playing along the ocean cliffs, the details of the routing had very little in common. "Our routing kept looping, looping, looping," Jim Urbina said of Pacific Dunes, and the routing does have a more maze-like, labyrinthine quality than that of Bandon Dunes. Bandon was arranged in two loops, with the 9th and 18th both returning to the lodge; Pacific never returned to its clubhouse. Bandon went to the cliffs on the 4th, 5th, and 6th holes, on the short 12th, and for a seaside climax on the 15th and 16th; Pacific's seaside holes were the 4th, the 10th and 11th—a pair of back-to-back par 3s—and the sensational 13th. Bandon had a standard balance of holes, with each nine consisting of five par 4s, two par 3s, and two par 5s; Pacific had a highly unusual sequence of holes, particularly on the back nine. Finally, while David had built a golf course that could be stretched out to play at 7,200 yards, Tom built Pacific as a much shorter course with a total length of 6,633 yards and a par of 71. Tom had never gone along with the trend toward longer and longer courses, and here at Pacific he didn't have to; the land provided him with several situations that seemed ideal for par 3s and for a kind of hole he loved to design—the short par 4.

Not that he had decided a priori on the length of the golf course, or that he'd made up his mind to build any specific hole, or kind of hole, before he "found" it. For Tom, as for any lay-of-the-land architect, the process of routing a course is a matter of getting to know a site and discovering what it has to offer. On the site of Pacific, where the land was so rough-and-tumble, the question was how to make the best use of the sand hills, the ocean vistas, and the sandy blowouts, but a couple of holes immediately suggested themselves to Tom's imagination.

One was the 13th, the par 4 with the ocean on one side and a monster sand ridge on the other. "That hole was just waiting there," Tom said, and he wasn't the first to discover it. Indeed, the story of the 13th hole at Pacific Dunes is another study in Bandon serendipity, or perhaps symmetry: Most of Pacific Dunes is laid out on the land purchased in 1996 from David Shuman, which had been vital to Bandon Dunes as well, providing David Kidd with land on which to build his 5th, 6th, and 7th holes. Tom Doak seemed to have enough land, but he, too, looked longingly at property north of the property line. There was a mammoth sandhill up there, one of the biggest along this stretch of coast, and a spit of land between the sandhill and the oceanside cliff. Mike, too, had seen the potential of this piece of land on his walks with his retail golfers, and he acquired it in 1997 as part of a large tract purchased from Pacific Power and Light. In 1999, when Tom was feeling the need to annex the parcel, Mike went ahead and gave it to him—a gift that was as important to the final design of Pacific Dunes as the Shuman property had been to Bandon Dunes.

Another hole that was quickly discovered, and became a fixture in all routing possibilities, was the 16th, a short par 4 where a tumbling stretch of ground turned right in a natural dogleg, against the flank of a sandhill into which a green could be shelved. On the other side of the sandhill was a hollow that seemed to cry out for a par 3. Here was a natural pairing, and there was another pairing on the cliffs, where the back-to-back par 3s, the 10th and 11th, were located. In the earliest planning these holes weren't numbered, and Tom tried out many sequences, but these holes kept reappearing in every version. One early routing plan called for a course that played to a par of 34–37, which was lopsided enough to make Mike nervous; he didn't like the numbers, or the fact that the short par 4s on the plan played downwind while the long par 4s were into the wind.

Tom kept working, adjusting the sequence, trying out new holes. As he mulled over the natural sites, and grew more and more committed to a handful of holes, he came up with a routing that he knew was unusual; he couldn't think of any precedents among the great courses. The course did not return to the clubhouse at the 9th (though the 7th green wasn't too far away from it), and the card looked like this:

$$445 \quad | \quad 434 \quad | \quad 444 \quad | \quad - \quad | \quad 36$$
$$335 \quad | \quad 435 \quad | \quad 435 \quad | \quad - \quad | \quad 35$$

The front nine was unorthodox, but the back nine was off the scale. With four par 3s, two of them back-to-back, and three par 5s, it was a bird of a different feather. Tom was afraid that Mike would object, but on the day they walked this sequence, from the first hole to the last, Mike loved it.

Tom could breathe a little more easily. He'd just learned, if he hadn't known already, that his boss really was ready to take risks and do things differently. The routing of Pacific Dunes was now set, and the back-to-back par 3s were going to be built. Inevitably, they would remind golfers of another pair of back-to-back par 3s that were built on cliffs above the Pacific by Tom's hero, Alister MacKenzie.

Those par 3s were, of course, the 15th and 16th at Cypress Point.

WHEN CONSTRUCTION OF Pacific Dunes began on January 3, 2000, the man in charge was Jim Urbina. He was one of four people on the payroll of Renaissance Golf Design who had the title of "design associate," and all four were indeed designers, though they made their contributions in different ways. Jim's way was to serve as a field commander, working not out of an office but from the center of the action—i.e., the front seat of his Wagoneer—making sure that all the myriad parts of the construction stayed on track and that the course was built to suit the eye, and the ideas, of the boss. He was the guy who hired the labor force (mostly young and inexperienced kids), drew up the daily work schedules, designed the drainage plans, saw to it that all the necessary equipment, pipe, and fuel was delivered to the site, coordinated his crews with the irrigation subcontractors, worked with the course superintendent, Ken Nice, and the turf consultant, Dave Wilber. As if that weren't enough, he occasionally climbed on a bulldozer to shape a green or two.

In other words, he was the rock. As Bill Coore, a longtime observer of Tom's career, puts it, "Without Jim there, Tom's operation would have had a wheel in the ditch pretty quick." Bill knew whereof he spoke, for Coore-Crenshaw and Renassiance Golf Design operated in a similar fashion; both companies carefully built their crews not on the corporate model, with hierarchical structures and chains of command, but as teams of artisans. The chief designers had trusted associates to whom they could not only give responsibility, but on whom they relied for creative collaboration. Tom and Jim's relationship had evolved since the days when they both worked for Pete Dye, but they both believed in giving crew members the same latitude that they'd enjoyed as young crew members.

Jim's role at Pacific Dunes included the duties of construction supervisor, the role that Pete Sinnott had played at Bandon Dunes. Initially, Mike had wanted to have Pete on hand as overseer at Pacific Dunes (Tom had asked David Kidd about Pete when they had dinner together, and David "just growled"), but Renaissance Golf had established a track record of building courses on schedule and on budget. "I felt instinctively that Tom was a tight-wad," Mike says, and his quiet due diligence had yielded strong endorsements of Renaissance Golf in general and Jim Urbina in particular.

By this time, Mike had known Tom for several years, and he was prepared to give him a freer rein than he had given David. He would still have to approve each hole, as he had at Bandon Dunes, but he trusted Tom's bold design ideas and he was comfortable hiring Renaissance Golf to build the course on a time-and-materials basis rather than on a fixed bid. To encourage frugality, the contract was set up so that Renaissance would get a bonus if they could build the course for less than $3.5 million, the cost of Bandon Dunes. In the end, Pacific Dunes cost almost exactly the same amount, though Jim Urbina had worked hard to earn that bonus; one of the running jokes on the site was that they were spending *his* money, not Mike's.

All of the Renaissance men had a hand in the work at Pacific Dunes, but the key associate, the one who put in the most days on-site, was Brian Slawnik, a shaper who had worked with Tom long enough to have absorbed his aesthetic principles, and who had the kind of finicky, perfectionist tendencies needed on every crew. Two other Renaissance design associates, Don Placek and Bruce Hepner, spent more than forty days on-site, doing regular shaping and logging hundreds of hours on a sand pro, the small machine used for finish work. Their willingness to do this detail work was both a testimony to the importance of the project to Renaissance Golf and an illustration of how the company carried on the everybody-down-in-the-dirt tradition that Tom had absorbed during his years with Pete Dye. Another key shaper who came to work at Pacific Dunes was an Oregonian named Kyle Franz, an intense young man who had once played golf on 478 consecutive days and who couldn't get over the fact that he was now working for Tom Doak, whose every word he had read and studied. On the crew, Kyle was called Dr. MacKenzie, or Alistair MacFrancis, since he was always reading or talking about the man who was the tutelary divinity of Renaissance Golf.

And there was one more indispensable crew member: Tony Russell. Having earned his stripes while working at Bandon Dunes, Tony was now a godsend to Jim Urbina, since he could not only operate heavy equipment but also owned some of his own, and he knew other equipment operators as well as other locals who might need a job. Beyond that, he quickly proved to have an uncanny feel for the kind of bunkers that Tom wanted. At first, Tom flagged the bunkers for Tony and hovered close by when he dug them, but it soon became clear that Tony had an instinct for the work, and he was given more and more creative license. "Tony was doing cutting-edge stuff," Jim said, "and he didn't even know it." Using an attachment called a "knuckle bucket," Tony could give the bunkers the internal contours that would otherwise have to be created more slowly and expensively by hand. At Bandon Dunes, Tony had done the routine grading, the less demanding jobs around the tees and on the fairways, but at Pacific Dunes he did artistic work, giving the bunkers their irregular, scalloped shapes and edges.

Though Jim was at Pacific Dunes for long, unbroken stretches, Tom's plan was to visit the site every three weeks or so. In 1999, as the work was getting under way, Tom was entering a new phase of his personal life. His first marriage had ended in divorce, and he wanted to spend as much time as possible at home in Traverse City with his son, Michael. At an ice cream parlor, he met Jennifer, the woman who would become his second wife. "I was happy again after the year or two of struggle which most divorces produce," he said. "Jenny never came out to Oregon while we were working on the course, nor did my son, Michael. But I was in love, and my work showed it."

The frequency of his visits also suited what he had come to recognize as the right pace for him. "I work best," he said, "when I'm working fast and excited about what I'm doing, but I understand that construction can't really move that fast. When I was on-site every day, I would get too tied up emotionally in every little detail of our projects, and I would get impatient. I would micromanage things that Jim would do better on his own. I've found that being away from the site off and on gives me a better perspective on how we're doing, and I can still think plenty about the design while I'm waiting to go back."

Mike tailored his schedule so that his visits would coincide with Tom's, and while there was no owner's rep on the project, Troy Russell, now the superintendent at Bandon Dunes, was always nearby, casting his glance on the project and helping Jim with nuts-and-bolts construction matters. And the superintendent of Pacific Dunes, Ken Nice, was involved, too, talking to Jim and Tom and Mike about all the details that would affect the maintenance of the golf course—about where golfers would walk on and off greens and tees, what features would need particular care or attention, what would need to be done to keep the golf course playing as Tom intended. Ken Nice, as it turned out, was every bit as consumed by the project as Jim Urbina or Brian Slawnik, and a fanatic when it came to putting the finishing touches on the design.

The plan was to build several holes that spring and to have them completed—shaped, irrigated, and seeded—before dry summer weather began. During the dry summer months, there would be a lull in construction so that the north winds didn't blow sand everywhere, particularly not onto the golfers who'd come to play Bandon Dunes.

Throughout the spring, the work went about as smoothly as it possibly could. There were no big glitches or setbacks, no nasty surprises or unforeseen problems. For years, Jim Urbina had fantasized about a project such as this, on which all the elements meshed smoothly: a great site, a client who shared the vision, a crew that took care of business, weather that cooperated. He took to saying, "The moons are in alignment," and Don Placek, a Renaissance associate with a talent for illustration, drew a picture of the universe on the whiteboard in Ken Nice's office that showed the planets spinning in balance and harmony.

WHEN TOM WENT to Oregon, he didn't go just to check up on things. He'd usually spend four or five days, trying to finish up the last details of the holes that had been started on his previous visit and getting started on the next set of holes. In addition to reviewing the work with Mike, he spent a lot of the time in the vicinity of Tony Russell ("He would shape bunkers with me standing there watching him and moving flags, and then when I'd leave he'd go back to drainage and irrigation main lines and all the other stuff that had to get done").

If he wasn't with Mike or Tony, he was usually deep in thought, cogitating around the greens. He could spend hours tinkering with greens and green surrounds, working with the slopes so that approach shots and recovery shots—not to mention putts—presented golfers with an array of opportunities. In *Anatomy*, Tom's chapter on "The Green Complex" carries as its epigraph a quote from C. B. Macdonald: "Putting greens are to golf courses what faces are to portraits." Greens are, in other words, the most vital feature of the golf course, the feature that more than any other conveys character and personality.

Since they were using the same fescue blend at Pacific as had been used at Bandon (though they did use a slightly different creeping strain of turf on the tees), Tom could fashion similar kinds of shots in, on, and around the greens. For a lover of links golf, these shots embody the subtle fascination of the game, testing a golfer's touch, feel, and imagination. Tom reveled in the opportunity to create these shots, but the contours of the greens and their surrounds were, inevitably, a topic of conversation with Mike.

Mike considered himself a "leveler of greens," an attitude that made perfect sense on a resort course exposed to heavy ocean winds. The rule of thumb in golf design is that a private course, where members have years to learn and overcome difficulties, is the place for severe, quirky greens; on a resort course, where players are seeing the greens for the first time, the greens are usually more straightforward. Nobody—not the developer, not the architect, and not the player—likes a course where 4- and 5-putt greens are commonplace.

Mike wanted manageable greens, and Tom at first complied—even though his own penchant was to build undulating greens, and even though he wanted the greens at Pacific to be different from the large and relatively flat greens of Bandon Dunes. The first greens built on Pacific—the 5th, 6th, upper 9th, 10th, and 11th—were smaller than those next door, and Jim decided to take matters into his own hands. "Jim and I agreed that we would start building greens with relatively subtle internal contours, and then work more into the later greens as we gained Mike's confidence. Jim knows that the final decisions are mine, so he doesn't argue directly, but he will try various forms of reverse psychology to get me to do things his way. Our discussions aren't so much about strategy as about shape, but of course shape affects the strategy, so Jim's primary way of making his point is to go out and shape something the way he thinks it ought to be done. None of the first greens have a lot of internal movement, but when we got to the 7th green, Jim decided it was time for something more radical. Before I got there to work on it, he shaped a green on that site himself. It was laughably wild. I thought for a minute he'd lost his mind. The finished green is nothing like that one, but it has a lot more contour than those early greens did, and it might be the coolest green on the entire course. And Jim takes credit for that, for getting me to start being more like my wild-green self."

Mike never abandoned his position on greens, but he did trust his architect, especially when he saw how utterly focused Tom was on making sure that the greens worked, on tying in the various slopes and planes and angles of the green surrounds, and on building a golf course that captured the complexity of the site. As a lover of "throwback courses," of links courses and courses that didn't follow the rules, Mike was happy with what he was seeing. With its sand blowouts, fringed bunkers, and its small and increasingly wild greens, Pacific Dunes, in the spring of 2000, was emerging as an altogether different critter, just as the architect had hoped.

"DAVID KIDD WAS a restorationist," Mike has written, making a distinction between two modes of construction; he describes Tom as "a preservationist." David had cleared the site of Bandon Dunes of gorse and shore pines, and returned the land to something like the condition it had been in when the Coquille and Coos tribes "managed the estate." On the other hand, Tom had sought to preserve the much more "irregular, vertical, windblown, heaving peaks and valleys of his site as he created Pacific Dunes."

What this meant in practical terms was that, wherever possible, and wherever the fire hadn't scorched the earth, Tom left the natural vegetation untouched. He was deliberately working with a natural palette of shore pines, beach grass, and gorse (even though the fire had destroyed much of it, some stands were left and, being naturally invasive, the gorse came back wherever it had an opening). Add the beige tones of sand in the ragged blowouts and the hue and texture of smooth green fescue, and the course took on a particular kind of aesthetic—a look of an enchanted Celtic landscape, a shaggy place full of hidden corners and crevices, a jumbled-up, tumbled-up, otherworldly kind of place where leprechauns might hide and frolic, a place where surprising vistas and intricate beauty seemed to lurk at every turn.

The design of Pacific Dunes preserved the wild qualities of the site through its attention to the existing colors, shapes, and textures, and its efforts to blend them into the golf holes. A more geological form of preservation is evident at the 16th hole, where the fairway tumbles and rolls in ways that Mother Nature and Father Time sculpted over many millennia. Tom did not want to disturb these natural forms, and he and Jim decided to use the lightest equipment when working on the 16th, not only to make sure that the shapes remained, but also to prevent any compaction of the playing surface. Heavy equipment was kept off several other sections of the course, and even drainage cuts were kept to an absolute minimum; in many places, the sandy soil drained quickly and completely on its own.

This was the minimalist ethos in full practice (though there were a few holes where small mountains of sand had to be moved), with all efforts directed toward a single goal: to build a magnificent golf course. Though he was in love, and though the work was going swimmingly, Tom Doak was under pressure at Pacific Dunes; *good* wasn't going to cut it. He was working next door to a course that had already attained the status of an instant classic, and his site was, he believed, "one of the twenty or thirty" best properties ever made available for a golf course.

But no site is foolproof. Golf architects cringe when they hear, as they regularly do, that a great site guarantees a great course. The landscape of golf is dotted with great sites that were either botched or that simply defied the best efforts of a talented architect. The New Course at Ballybunion, for instance, is on a stunning piece of linksland immediately adjacent to the Old Course; but the original Robert Trent Jones layout was by general agreement well-nigh unplayable (it has since been renovated). When he built the New Course, Jones was at the top of his profession, an established figure more or less immune to criticism. Tom Doak was in a completely different position, a brash young man who'd been knocking at the door for years. If he didn't step through now, when would he ever get to make his entrance?

Tom knew that Pacific Dunes was his shot at building a course that would take its place at the top of every list. It was his chance to create something that could stand alongside the work of MacKenzie and Macdonald and the other greats. For him, the design challenge wasn't just to come up with eye-popping holes along the ocean. One of the great virtues of the site, he realized, was that "the inland parts of our property had such great sand dune topography. Anyone could see that we would build great holes along the cliffs, but I felt that holes like 2, 7, and 16 were the ones that would really put the course in another class."

He was determined to make those inland holes as beautiful and interesting as he possibly could. The 6th and 16th at Pacific Dunes are both inland holes, and both are devilish little masterpieces. "I didn't give many courses a perfect 10 in the *Confidential Guide,* and when I asked myself what was the difference between those courses and ones who got a lower score, the answer was usually short par 4s. Everybody has a chance on a short par 4. For the average player, there's a chance to make par, and the better player has a chance for a birdie. I knew I wanted to have a couple of them on this course."

The first construction push lasted from January until early June. When the Renaissance crew knocked off for the summer, they had completed eleven holes. When they returned in August, they had seven holes to go—Nos. 3, 4, 12, 13, 14, 15, and 18. Despite the active topography of the site, not every hole was lying there waiting to be discovered, and Tom had to tinker with a few of them to get them right. Like A. W. Tillinghast, the Golden Age architect who liked to call himself the "Creator" of Baltusrol and Winged Foot, Tom approached the problem with patience and cunning. "Often," Tillinghast wrote, in another passage quoted in *Anatomy,* "it is necessary to get from one section to another over ground which is not suited to easy construction, but that troublesome hole must be made to stand right up with the others. If it has nothing about it that might make it respectable, it has to have quality knocked into it until it can hold its head up in polite society."

Tom's usual process was "to save the short holes to bridge the gaps," but at Pacific, the short holes—the 5th, 10th, and 11th—were among the first to be identified and built. So he reversed the process and used the par 5s as the connective tissue for the course, and the three par 5s on the back nine—the 12th, 15th, and 18th—needed to be massaged. Mike was concerned that the 12th and 15th, both relatively flat from tee to green, weren't as interesting as the rest of the holes; he wasn't satisfied until the shaping and bunkering added movement and complexity to the design.

Indeed, the second phase of construction was altogether more problematic than the first. The easier holes had been built first, and the Renaissance crew was a little like the kid who eats dessert first—and then has to confront the less tasty vegetables. Added to this was the fact that several members of the spring crew hadn't returned in the fall; even though Brian Slawnik and Tony Russell were still on board, Tom and Jim were worried about maintaining the same look and the same attention to detail. Since they were working to meet an opening date in the summer of 2001, the crew was under the gun, and any kind of delay was enough to put a damper on Jim Urbina's mood— when, on top of everything else, he was laid low for a couple of weeks with back problems. There were plenty of days when the planets seemed to fall out of alignment.

And then there was the clubhouse. The clubhouse, of course, was outside the bailiwick of Renaissance Golf Design, although the golf course architect and the clubhouse architect usually confer with each other about where the clubhouse should be located and how it can best be integrated with the course. For the Pacific Dunes clubhouse, Mike and Howard had selected not Bill Church, who designed the lodge at Bandon, but an architect who shall remain nameless. He came up with an appealing design and then proceeded to resist every suggestion of his clients. "Mike only puts up with people so long," Howard said, "and he reached his limit pretty quickly." Since there was no time to hire another clubhouse architect, Mike got something he had talked about for years: a clubhouse that was a double-wide trailer, with a clock tower.

There is only one other building on the golf course, a concession stand and restroom that is built like a bunker—a military bunker, not a golf course bunker—in the side of a sand ridge between the 4th and 13th tees. It was important to Mike that it should be as hidden from sight as possible; he didn't want any building to mar the unspoiled landscape of the golf course. The little building also had a pair of urinals *al fresco*. Of this open-air men's room, Mike says, with an irony that is difficult to gauge, "This is one of my favorite places on the course."

By that fall the golf course was being called Pacific Dunes, and it had a blue and gold logo showing a pair of harbor seals—another sea creature, a mate for the tufted puffin. The logo had been easier to hit upon than the name. During much of the construction period, Mike had favored "Sand Valley," a name that suggested a pedigree combining Sand Hills and Pine Valley, but he hadn't been able to win much support. He kept a long list of possible names, none of which had the right ring. (The list now sounds preposterous, as discarded names always do: Looming Dunes. Lost Dunes. Lazy Dunes. Lucky Dunes. Liberty Dunes. Lingering Dunes. Loony Dunes. Lordy Dunes. Lynx Hollow. Lucifer's Links.) In his usual fashion, he solicited ideas for a name from his friends, and one man he asked for suggestions was Rick Summers, who'd initially put him together with Gleneagles Golf Developments. They were having lunch together in the lodge, and Mike ran the list of names by him. "Most of the names had Dunes in them," Rick recalled, "and some of them were pretty wild. We were sitting in the restaurant, and I said, Mike, look out the window. There's a big ocean out there. Why not call it Pacific Dunes?"

Sometimes the most obvious things are the hardest to see, but once seen, they are impossible to forget. From that day forward, the golf course was Pacific Dunes.

THE OFFICIAL OPENING of Pacific Dunes was on July 1, 2001. Tom had been on-site more than 50 days, but Jim Urbina had put in 168 days, and Brian Slawnik about the same number. They pushed hard right to the end. Troy Russell's lasting image, as he was trying to get seeds down, was of Brian Slawnik using a rake to make sure that the final contours were right, finishing up one second before the seed hit the ground. In the opinion of several veteran Doak observers, one of the differences between Pacific Dunes and his other courses is precisely this sense of finish—in terms of design, Pacific Dunes is absolutely polished, and Brian Slawnik gets a share of the credit.

Starting in May, resort guests had been able to play a loop of holes, and the long drum roll of praise began to build. Pacific Dunes not only measured up to its sister course, Bandon Dunes, but it seemed to have lived up to the high expectations of its designer. Was it Cypress Point? Perhaps no golf course will ever attain the same kind of supernal beauty as Cypress, but Tom Doak had certainly fashioned a course worthy of comparison. At Pacific Dunes, he had answered every question about his talent and imagination. "Pacific Dunes," said Bill Shean, who had watched his career for so many years, "was his coming-out party."

One of the first and most important reviews came from Ron Whitten, writing in *Golf World,* the companion publication to *Golf Digest,* in October 2001. He described Pacific Dunes as "an astonishing layout, a mix of old-fashioned bump-and-run and drive-and-pitch golf holes snuggled within sand dunes atop an ocean bluff," and his words carried weight. George Peper, writing in *Links* magazine, came up with the idea of a "match" between Pacific Dunes and Pebble Beach, comparing them hole by hole. The winner: Pacific Dunes.

The acid test would come in the ratings by the different golf publications. Words are one thing, but numbers are another; whether or not the methodology of the rankings was fair, the numbers tended to assign a golf course its place in the public perception. Most magazines have a waiting period before they rank a course, to allow the novelty to wear off and to permit a sufficient number of raters to visit and make their judgment.

When the ratings did appear, they removed all vestiges of doubt about just how highly golfers regarded Pacific Dunes. In every ranking, Pacific Dunes made its debut close to the top of the list, and ahead of Bandon Dunes. In *Golf Digest*'s 2003 rankings, the august list that starts out with courses like Pine Valley and St. Andrews, Pacific Dunes placed 47th. *Golf Magazine*'s 2003 rankings, again including all courses on all continents from all eras, put Pacific Dunes in the 19th slot (the only modern course with a higher ranking was Sand Hills, ranked 11th). *Golfweek* magazine published its 2004 rankings of America's Best Courses in two lists, Classical Courses and Modern Courses, with the cutoff date at 1960.

The No. 1 modern course on the list was Sand Hills, and the No. 3 course was Bandon Dunes.

Pacific Dunes was No. 2.

When the votes were tallied, Tom Doak could no longer be called the boy wonder of golf course architecture. No one would speak again about his promise or his potential. Tom had arrived in a big way, and the ratings only certified it. He had won his place, the place he had always coveted, alongside the best who had ever designed a golf course.

He sent Mike Keiser a photograph of the 13th hole at Pacific, and inscribed it, "Thanks for the opportunity of a lifetime."

18 | Tom at Pacific Dunes

Around our office, fair is the F-word.

—Tom Doak

After the opening of Pacific Dunes, Tom Doak wasn't an easy man to pin down. New commissions came his way more quickly than ever before in his career, and many were on properties that were in their own way as dramatic as the Pacific Dunes property. By the time I caught up with Tom in March 2004, Renaissance Golf Design had completed several new projects, and the company was scheduled to open three courses that year in the Southern Hemisphere: Barnbougle Dunes and St. Andrews Bay in Australia, and Cape Kidnappers in New Zealand. An impressive trifecta, but even more startling was the news that Tom Doak and Jack Nicklaus would be collaborating on the design of a golf course on Long Island, next door to National Golf Links and Shinnecock Hills. Maybe oil and water really could mix.

Tom was clearly the man of the hour, and in an update to his website, he announced with some bravado that Renaissance had found its legs: "We've established ourselves as one of the leading firms to consider if you have a great site, and certainly that is our favorite role. Since Pacific Dunes we have seen seven sites which we thought had the potential to become one of the great courses in the world, and with luck, we will get to see what we can accomplish on six of them. We will never stop hungering for those opportunities."

Tom was in Oregon with the entire Renaissance team for a couple of days of golf and company planning, as well as to meet with potential clients for a project in Ireland. He was busy, and everyone knew the moment he entered the lobby of the lodge, or the pub, or the restaurant; he has a clear, even voice that carries easily over the usual babble of the 19th hole. Among the ordinary guests at the resort, there was a celebrity buzz with Tom on the property. A lot of people—not just the golf architecture freaks, the ones Jim Urbina calls "the martians," the guys who study his courses the way grad students parse the work of Shakespeare—recognize him these days. Davis Love III was probably more famous, but it was Tom that the golf magazines wanted to run feature articles about, and he was very much in the golf design spotlight.

Except for Brian Slawnik, who was finishing a course in Australia, all of Tom's design associates were there: Bruce Hepner, Jim Urbina, Brian Schneider, Eric Iverson, and Don Placek. In the evening, when they were cleaned up and quaffing a beer, they didn't look particularly like a group of guys who spent their time astride heavy machines on construction sites; tall and tanned, neatly dressed and coiffed, they could have passed for a group of young surgeons, or lawyers, or investment analysts. (Jim Urbina is the exception who proves the rule; he does look like what he is, an ex–football player from a tough town.) These Renaissance associates were riding high, and they knew it. Their boss was where Pete Dye had been in the early 1980s, and they expected to be building great golf courses for years to come.

They also felt that minimalism had won the day, though Tom was more guarded and also more cynical. "I don't think minimalism is anything new. We're just doing things differently than most guys were doing ten or twenty years ago. I'm not sure if it's a movement or not. The success of a handful of courses has meant that a lot of architects refer to minimalism now, but the architects who were successful before haven't changed their styles at all. They just sell it differently."

Tom readily acknowledges that he is one of the leading advocates of minimalism, but he identifies Ben Crenshaw as the leader, the one who blazed the trail. From the time he got to know Ben, at age twenty, he felt that they were "blood brothers," and on his busy trip to Oregon he was going to fit in a visit to the third course, Bandon Trails, which was then under construction. The architects for the project were Ben Crenshaw and Bill Coore.

We caught Pacific Dunes on a balmy day. The whole Renaissance group was playing that day, and they showed up at the course after what had been a ritual meeting at Ken Nice's office, where they finally erased Don Placek's drawing of the moons in alignment. That drawing had been on the whiteboard for four years, and it was time to close a chapter—well, almost. These guys are designers, after all, and they can't stop fiddling with their courses. At Pacific Dunes, they were discussing ways to solve some maintenance issues—the blowout bunkers always needed a lot of TLC—and considering how the course would handle a tournament. The USGA had announced its intention to bring a couple of events to Bandon, the 2006 Curtis Cup and the 2007 Mid-Amateur Championship, and there hadn't been a final determination of what courses would be used for what events.

So Tom was preoccupied when we teed off. He was wearing his usual outfit of khakis, a turtleneck, and lightweight, ankle-high work boots that didn't look like anything made by FootJoy. He carried his own bag. I'd been told by Grant Rogers that Tom still played with a few persimmon woods, but his clubs were reasonably up to date, all of them except his battered putter, a replica of the George Low model that Jack Nicklaus had used to win most of his championships. If the driver was the favorite club in David Kidd's bag, the putter was probably Tom's.

As we left the clubhouse, we had a short walk to the first tee through a tunnel of shore pines. This small passage nevertheless sets the tone of the experience, and it announces that you are entering another kind of place—a maze, a labyrinth, a world of surprising twists and turns where nothing is as obvious or straightforward as you expect. If you want to take a few last putts, the practice green is tucked like a secret chamber behind a wall of pines. You almost want to look for the hidden staircase or the trapdoor. You're about to play a round of golf, but it feels as though you're tumbling down the rabbit hole toward Wonderland.

Hole No 1. Par 4, 370 yards.

Standing on the first tee, I felt like asking Tom, "OK, now where's the hole?" There's a sliver of fairway rising to a crest about 200 yards out, but the remainder of the hole, with all its vitals—the green, the bunkers, and the places that a drive might finish—are on the far side of the crest, hidden from sight. This hole is clearly the work of an architect who is perfectly willing to ratchet up a golfer's usual first-tee jitters.

"If you hit a good drive," Tom said, "this hole is ridiculously easy." He took one practice swing, stepped up, and knocked his own tee shot straight over the crest. He has a controlled, balanced swing with a simple, secure turn, the kind of dependable swing intended to get the ball in play. "It's a short hole, but it's usually into the wind, and there are all kinds of problems if you let the tee shot drift out to the right."

He wasn't kidding. The right side of the hole is gnarly with sand and gorse and pines; the left side of the fairway opens up far more invitingly than appears from the tee. The green is small and rejects all but truly struck approach shots.

Judging by our foursome, it was just as easy to double bogey this little opener as to birdie it.

Hole No. 2. Par 4, 368 yards.

There's a walk from the first green up to the elevated tee of the second hole, a twisting, turning, follow-the-faint-path-through-the-fescue walk that takes you from the small valley of the first green up and over a sand ridge. Pacific Dunes is full of these transitions, and this one leads to a stunning view—the first sweeping view of the course, with all its elements, from the active dune to the right, to the ocean far in the distance, with the middle ground occupied by gorse, beach grass, shore pines, fringed bunkers, heaving fairway, all of it so charged with movement that it is hard at first to take in all the requirements of the golf hole.

"From day one," Tom said, "I've loved this hole. I have pictures of it in my office, and I use them to show people what I want to create in a golf hole.

There's a great view from the tee, and a lot of different places to hit the tee shot, and a lot of ways to come in to the green."

The ideal shot is over the Shoe bunker in the center of the left-sloping fairway, but against the wind it takes a good lick to carry the Shoe. (The Shoe bunker takes its name from its builder—Bob Gaspar, or Shoe, who responded to the invitation to contribute to the course by spending days out there with a shovel.) A drive to the left side opens up the approach to the green—but too far left, and the ball doesn't stop rolling until it's in one of the deepest bunkers in Christendom. The right side is the safe side, but the approach is then blind—and I won't even go into the contours of the green environment, except to say that Tom was back to his "wild-green" self when he built this one.

There is so much happening on this hole, so many slopes and textures and contours, that even on a calm day it looks as though a breeze is rippling through, keeping everything in continuous motion.

Tom is usually straight-faced and serious, but he had a smile on his face when he talked about No. 2. Why not? It is a hole with a true sense of humor.

No. 3. Par 5, 499 yards.

From the elevated tee we were looking at fairway that led to a perched green and the blue Pacific. This is the point on the course where the ocean suddenly fills the horizon and you see more fully what you are in for. It's no accident that so many tees give you these expansive views; Tom and Jim wanted to provide tantalizing glimpses from the tee. On most holes, the golfer then drops down into a sort of valley, and plays along in an enclosed realm. It was a design principle to make each hole a world unto itself; while there are places where a golfer catches a glimpse of a neighboring fairway, this hole-by-hole isolation is a part of the experience at Pacific Dunes.

The third fairway looks to be a mile wide, and Tom pointed out that the gorse on the right is cut way, way back. "There's plenty of room over there," he said, and grinned again. "Jim's a slicer, and he didn't want to lose a ball here."

This is another hole that plays into the prevailing wind, and on most days it is a three-shotter even for long hitters. Noting how the deep bunker in front of the green gnaws into the putting surface, and the wicked little slopes all around the green, Tom said with satisfaction, "This was a hole that evolved nicely as we worked on it."

No. 4. Par 4, 463 yards.

This tee is at ground level, but the ground is at the edge of a cliff and the view is straight to Hawaii. "If I don't have you by the time you get to this tee," Tom said, "I won't get you. At this point in the round you've had a complete preview of the course. These first holes show what the course is about—the short par 4s, the strategy, the blowouts, all the elements that go into the course. The routing is important for emotional reasons, not just golf reasons. When you get to this tee, you should be well into the round."

This long par 4 usually plays downwind, with the ocean on the right. The cliff edge is clean and bare, and Tom contemplated building another tee *below* the cliff edge, a tee that would have jutted out like a platform and required a drive up and over the cliff. The construction, however, presented many problems, and the existing tee is sufficiently challenging for most golfers. The ideal tee shot gets as close as possible to the drop-off. The green is nestled between the cliff and a sand ridge. The front of the green is open, and Tom ended up with a third shot from about 20 yards; he played it with his putter, and the ball took a huge, wheeling turn as it scooted along the tilted green. It was not a break you could see with the unaided eye, but the architect knows where he has hidden these things.

No. 5. Par 3, 199 yards.

"This was the first hole we built," Tom said. "It wasn't on any of the routing plans, but we found this natural valley after we'd done the routing and we decided to go ahead and build it. It didn't take much to rough it in. We figured that if Mike objected, we could just erase it and do something else here."

Mike, obviously, did not object. Tom played his approach on this hole well to the left; the ball kicked right, disappeared behind a knob, then reappeared as it trickled onto the green. Every links course worth its salt has a couple of these peek-a-boo shots.

No. 6. Par 4, 316 yards.

Another inland hole that is a stunner, another short par 4 that makes a lasting impression. There's an enormous fairway and a tiny, narrow green atop a sand ridge; it sits there like a bare scalp. Unless you come into this green from the far right of the fairway, with a shot that can travel down the center line, it is very difficult to hit and hold, even with a little lofted wedge. Many balls trickle off the green and roll well down the slope to the right that then must be negotiated with some kind of links shot, either a putt—the best option—or a crisp, low-running chip. A golfer with the skills of Phil Mickelson might play a wedge shot. This can be a birdie hole, but anyone down in the swale is hoping to get a par.

Tom: "I knew from the start I wanted to build this hole. This ridge was the natural terminus for a par 4. The problem was that the left side was too steep, and Mike thought it was unfair for anyone who got into the bunkers down there at the bottom. I said you could get out of those bunkers, and I went down there with my wedge and a couple of balls. No problem—I hit my first shot onto the putting surface. That persuaded him. I don't know what this hole would look like if I hadn't hit that shot."

No. 7. Par 4, 464 yards.

This long par 4 is the No. 1 handicap hole at Pacific Dunes. The landing area for the tee shot is generous, but the long approach is as hard as it gets. A row of natural blowout bunkers, the seven sisters, guard the left side of the green, and a gnarly sand ridge flanks the right. Out in front of the heavily contoured green is a weird series of shapes that look like burial mounds, or like a bunch of turf-covered junk cars. Downwind, the average player can think of getting home in two, but this is the kind of hole that is often called a par 4½, and it illustrates Tom's conviction that not every par 4 has to be reachable. "Why should everyone be able to get home in 2 on a par 4? I like to build some long par 4s, and I agree with Pete Dye that 400 yards is the wrong length for a par 4. That's too short for the good player and too long for

The 5th green under construction, all twenty thousand square feet of it. Photo by Wood Sabold.

Completed, the 5th green looks as large as the deck of an aircraft carrier. The greens at Old Mac cover 6.3 acres in aggregate, making them even larger than the greens at St. Andrews.
Photo by Wood Sabold.

The advisory panel, from left to right: Bradley Klein, George Bahto, and Karl Olson.
Photo by Wood Sabold.

Playing dirt golf, Mike Keiser drives over the ridge on the 3rd hole, with the "ghost tree" showing the line to the green.   Photo by Wood Sabold.

Key members of the Old Macdonald design team, from left to right:
Bradley Klein, Tom Doak, Jim Urbina, Ken Nice, and Mike Keiser.
Photo by Wood Sabold.

The Hell Bunker on the 6th hole, faced with railroad ties,
looms like a shark's jaw.   Photo by Wood Sabold.

The view from Hell.   Photo by Wood Sabold.

Thanks to a discussion about the turnstand,
Mike Keiser put the 7th green "up in the air."
Photo by Wood Sabold.

The 15th hole, Westward Ho!, is an "original"—
one of the few holes on Old Mac that has no specific
classical model. It is also the start of the tough
finishing stretch.   Photo by Wood Sabold.

The 17th hole is another long par 5 with alternate routes to the green, a veritable garden of forking paths. Photo by Wood Sabold.

Rainbow over the 5th hole at Old Macdonald.
Photo by Wood Sabold.

the weaker player. I'd rather have a hole 450 yards long. The smart way to play this hole might be driver/9-iron/9-iron. I can guarantee you that the person who plays it that way is going to have a good chance to beat the guy who plays it driver/3-wood. It's a narrow place to land the 3-wood up there."

He played the hole cautiously, and had a 20-footer for par. He left it way wide, reading twice as much break as there was. Every now and then, an architect can fake himself out.

No. 8. Par 4, 400 yards.

Another wide fairway for a hole into the wind. Shore pines line either side wide of the fairway and once covered the entire site. The interest of the hole centers on the Ross-like crowned green and the slopes to the right of the hole. "This hole is a dogleg right, and I wanted to make it possible to come in from the right. I don't worry about getting an exact balance of holes, so that half the time the best approach is from the right and half the time from the left, but a lot of holes at Pacific naturally bend right, and this seemed like a chance to open up the right side. But what's the best way to do that when the hole is a little bit of a dogleg right? The only hole I could think of where that happened was the 3rd hole at Woking, and I tried to do something similar. This right side is shaped so that you can draw the approach shot and play it off the slope."

Another curiosity of this hole: The back tee looks in both directions, north and south, and it stands on the line between Pacific Dunes and Bandon Dunes. It can be used to play either the 8th hole at Pacific, or the 8th at Bandon.

No. 9. Par 4, 406 yards.

You will wonder, when you stand on this tee, where in the world to hit the ball. There's no fairway—or rather, there is a sliver of fairway visible atop the bluff that slants diagonally away from you. To make matters even more confusing, there are two greens on the hole, an upper and a lower, and the line for the tee shot will vary according to which green is in use.

Back to the tee. The landscape that lies before you is such a jumble of hazards that you have to will yourself into believing that there is a safe place out there. Some golf courses set up so that you feel that you are cruising ahead on broad boulevards; Pacific Dunes, especially on holes like the 9th, is a more rugged, cross-country experience.

You have to trust the yardage book, your caddy, or the architect to give you the best line for the drive. As for the two greens, Tom said, "The lower was added at little cost. We were going to have to run the irrigation through there anyway, and it also gave us a way to get to the back tees for No. 10. We had the tees near the upper green, but I wanted a way to lengthen the hole."

No. 10. Par 3, 205 yards.

From that back tee, into the north wind, this par 3 is a full-blooded wood shot. The green sits in a natural bowl, a site that Tom always intended to use for exactly this purpose. We played it from the upper tee, in a light breeze, at a distance of about 160 yards. With the hole so much lower than the tee, and the by-now familiar ridges and dunes pressing hard on the right and the ocean visible just behind the green, the matter of club selection was tricky. Tom pulled out his 7-iron and hit his best shot of the day, one of those approaches that never veers from its line straight toward the flag.

When his birdie putt missed by a wide margin, he looked stumped.

No. 11. Par 3, 148 yards.

Possibly the most photogenic hole on the course, this short par 3 looks perfectly natural—but it's not. The blowout bunkers, fringed with beach grass, are there courtesy of Renaissance Golf Design. The green is the smallest on the golf course. A shot that is yanked, really yanked, will come down on a very different section of the planet—on the beach far, far below. I mentioned that Grant Rogers liked to play this hole, the only par 3 that will not accept the bunt driver, with a high, wide slice, preferably hit with a fairway wood, a shot that flies way out over the beach and then, just before the point of no return, flutters against the wind, takes a boomerang turn, and rides softly down onto the green.

Tom, who has played a few rounds with Grant, said, "He would."

No. 12. Par 5, 529 yards.

"This is one of the easiest holes out here," Tom said. "Mike was worried that it didn't have enough of a "Wow" factor, but I was able to persuade him that it didn't need to be jazzed up. With 13 coming, and then with the finish, this was the last chance for a breather."

Maybe it is easy, but it plays dead into the prevailing wind, and there's a significant fairway bunker to carry, the "Career" bunker, so called because Tony Russell spent so long working on it, prompting comments such as, "Do you plan to spend the rest of your career in there?"

There is also an innocent-looking bunker on the right side of the fairway at about the place where a hacker's second shot might finish. The fairway is enormously wide, and it appears that a) there is plenty of room out there, and b) the bunker can easily be carried even if the ball does drift right.

I won't note the number of balls that I have seen fly into that bunker. Moral: There are no innocent hazards on Pacific Dunes.

No. 13. Par 4, 444 yards.

One of the few holes in golf where the Pacific Ocean, which borders the left side of the fairway, is overshadowed by the hazard on the other side—a mammoth sandhill that looks like something from the kind of golf cartoon with the caption "World's Most Incredible Hazard!" It can't be real, but of course it is. There is sand along the entire right side of the wide fairway, and Tom pointed out the shape of a couple of original blowouts. They have gotten larger with every passing year.

The hole is one of the most exposed on the golf course, and the green is consequently one of the deepest. "I always knew this hole was here, with that big dune, and I built this green myself. Jim was having problems with his back, so I just got on the bulldozer and built it." The green is slightly elevated, and most golfers walk to its northern edge, where Pacific Dunes seems to vanish into thin air. The natural exit from the green is to the north, but in that direction there is nowhere to go. There is only the view of the ocean and of a rocky point in the distance—Five Mile Point, which belongs to Mike and to Phil Friedmann, Mike's partner at Recycled Paper Greetings.

To leave the 13th, you must double back and walk along the flank of that mammoth sandhill, dodge through another narrow passage, and climb a few steps to reach the 14th tee. The routing lets you know that you are now heading home.

No 14. Par 3, 145 yards.

A short hole, but this is no rest stop on the homeward journey. Tom: "This is a tough little hole, and you won't hold the green with anything but a well-struck shot. If you miss the green, you have one of the most difficult up-and-downs out here."

If you miss left and hit anything but a perfectly calibrated chip, the ball will run over the green and tumble into a severe bunker. Don't ask me how I know this.

Up on the green, Tom pointed out the faint sediment line inside the cup, showing how the present green surface has risen above the original surface. "That's just normal buildup from sand blowing out of the bunkers."

No. 15. Par 5, 539 yards.

The fairway is bordered by gorse, but it is plenty wide. The strategy of the hole, Tom pointed out, is determined by a knob on the right side of the green. Basically, you have to protect against getting on the right side on that knob, because it's impossible to get up and down. This is one of only two holes on the golf course (the other is the 10th) without a greenside bunker, and it doesn't need a bunker, not with that knob.

"That was another hole where Mike worried about the "Wow" factor. The day we were finishing up, Mike was here, saying the hole needed a little more. So we put in the bunker 60 yards in front of the green and we were done."

No 16. Par 4, 338 yards.

It's a cliché to say that a fairway heaves like the sea, but that's exactly what this fairway does: It heaves. It looks like the waves have been stopped in mid-swell. These aren't big rolling waves, either, but confused, choppy, tumbling waves. Wherever you place your tee shot in this fairway, you will almost surely be tested by an awkward lie.

Assuming that the ball is on the fairway, the next shot is a pitch to a narrow green perched into the side of a sandhill. That's narrow as in thin-as-a-knife-blade. The yardage guide says innocently, "Holding this putting surface will be a challenge." The fact is that, even from a perfect position, the second shot demands pinpoint precision—even if, à la Grant Rogers, you decide to play the shot with your putter.

This hole drives people nuts, and Tom knows it. They stand on the tee, thinking they can drive the green, and the next thing they know they've staggered away with a 7. The hole reminds Tom of the 9th at Cypress Point; the humped-up fairway looks as inviting as the back of an alligator."

After watching my shot bumble its way toward the green, following the slope ever farther downward into a hollow where many a divot had been repaired, Tom admitted, "It's a tough shot into that green. In the summer, when it gets really hard and fast, I admit that it's borderline unfair."

That was almost a comforting remark. It was Tom being diplomatic, though the Renaissance men often say, "Around our office, fair is the F-word."

No. 17. Par 3, 208 yards.

Here we caught up with the foursome ahead of us, and we were just in time to watch Tom's associates play their shots into this version of a Redan hole. The afternoon light was streaming down, and the entire hole was ringed in the canary yellow of gorse in full bloom. Few Redans have, as the 17th does, an elevated tee, but they all call for a green shaped so that the slopes will bring in a tee shot from the right. That was exactly the shot that Don Placek hit from the back tees, a solid 4-iron that landed a step or two in the right fringe and then made a horseshoe curl toward the hole.

That was the high road. Tom took the low road, and hit a skanky shot into the cavernous bunker guarding the left of the green. Actually, his ball landed on the slope short of the green and took the same violent horseshoe turn, heading toward the bunker like the proverbial homesick gopher. But he played a beautiful long explosion shot and missed a tiddler for his par. "This is not my best putting day," he said mildly, the only hint of complaint on a day when the putter had really let him down.

No. 18, Par 5, 591 yards.

There'd been another delay, and since we were the last group on the course, the Renaissance men joined up to play this hole together, two foursomes playing from the back tee high up on the side of the ridge. It was a long carry out to the fairway, and another long carry to get clear of the huge bunker on the left. The hole was in shadow, and the chill of the evening put a bite in the air. All three shots have to be hit with power and accuracy to reach this green in regulation, and only a couple of the Renaissance men were up to the task.

Tom wasn't one of them, but didn't seem to care; he was having too much fun watching his pals try to come up with the shots required for this hole, the home hole. There was plenty of good-natured needling. There's an old saying that you can tell a lot about a group of golfers by the way they sound, and these guys, laughing and talking, with Tom's clear voice piping louder than any of the others, sounded as if they were on top of the world.

19 | The Old-Fashioned Way

I can't compete with nature, and it would only showcase my futility
if I tried. So I try to cooperate. —BILL COORE

IT'S FEBRUARY, AND a cold rain is falling here in Oregon. Bill Coore and Mike Keiser look like a pair of slick, wet crows in their black raingear, but they aren't about to let the weather discourage them. Mike has just flown out from Chicago to see what progress Bill and his crew have made on the third course, and they're all trudging through heavy sand toward the first tee.

Mike mentions a recent article in *Sports Illustrated,* an article that clearly stuck in Bill's craw. The dismissive tone of the article was established in a headline: "No. 3 Tries Harder." The magazine ran a picture of Bill and his partner, Ben Crenshaw, over the caption: "Magic Touch? Crenshaw and Coore making the most of a lesser site."

Bill whisks his hand along the bill of his cap, a black cap that reads "Coore & Crenshaw & Russell" (stay tuned for more about that cap), using his finger like a windshield wiper to flick away the water. He is not pleased, but he and Mike both know that this new course is going to attract close scrutiny. Here in the place already billed as the Holy Grail, building a third course is like trying to write the third work of an epic trilogy. What do you do after *Star Wars* and *The Empire Strikes Back*? What do you do after Bandon Dunes and Pacific Dunes?

"We have a new name," Mike says in his deep voice, "Bandon Trails." This name is actually the most recent in a series of names, nearly all of which toyed with the word "dunes." Dunes Valley. Ancient Dunes. Hidden Dunes. Now

Mike is thinking that it might be a good idea to try something different, a name that will help establish a separate identity for this new course.

Bandon Trails. The name seems to fit the rambling layout, and it does distinguish this third course from its sisters. Bandon Dunes and Pacific Dunes are both links courses, built side by side on the clifftops above the ocean. Bandon Trails is not going to be a links course, and there isn't a single oceanside hole. From the first tee, even on this dreary day, the view is exhilarating as it sweeps down to the sea stacks at Bandon; but only the first two holes, and the finishing hole, are in dunes, and they're at least half a mile from the surf.

At the third hole, the golf course turns inland and moves into the "meadow," an open landscape textured with plants like huckleberry, manzanita, madrone, and knickaknick. At the seventh hole, the course skirts the flank of Back Ridge and enters into a dense forest of spruce, pine, cedar, and rhododendron. Seven holes in the middle of the course, holes No. 7 through 13, are to be carved out of this monsoon forest, and then—spectacularly—the routing takes the golfer out of the woods and over the ridge to the high, dramatic 14th tee. The finishing holes return to the meadow, and there's one last change of key for the 18th, which rolls and tumbles homeward through the dunes.

That's three distinct environments: dunes, meadow, forest. On his wet walk, Mike Keiser can see enough of the holes roughed out in the dunes and the meadow to be confident that golfers are going to be completely smitten by them, but he worries that Bandon Trails might be "schizophrenic," like Spyglass Hill. He says, "Everybody loves those five opening holes at Spyglass, the ones going down to the ocean, but then it's an anticlimax to go back up into the pines."

Mike wants the holes in the forest to "sing" just as vibrantly as the holes in the dunes and the meadow. Because of the construction schedule, however, the forest holes are going to be the last ones built; and now, in February, the clearing isn't even completed. Bill Coore acknowledges that he isn't quite sure about some of the forest holes.

Yet there is no sense of alarm or urgency. The owner does not insist that the architect present him with a definite plan or a set of drawings. In Bill Coore and Ben Crenshaw, Mike has allied himself with a pair of artists, and he has complete faith in them. Ever since he'd seen Sand Hills, he'd wanted to work with them. Their lay-of-the-land design philosophy had inspired him, just as it had Tom Doak. And it certainly wasn't lost on Mike that with the addition of a Coore-Crenshaw course, Bandon Dunes would be a showcase for minimalist architecture.

Those holes in the woods are known as the "mystery holes."

JUST AS THE SCHEDULE to build Pacific Dunes was accelerated by the success of Bandon Dunes, so the timing of a third course was advanced by the success of Pacific Dunes. In fact, although he had originally conceived of only two courses back when he hired Gleneagles Golf Developments, Mike had steadily acquired property adjacent to the initial tract, and his vision for the resort had expanded proportionately. In 2004, he owned close to 2,500 acres of land, a stretch that extended for miles along the ocean and included a 500-acre chunk co-owned with his RPG partner, Phil Freidmann. Variously referred to as Five Mile Point, Area 51, and the Sheep Ranch, this property was a peninsula north of Whiskey Creek and had previously been the site of a Pacific Power and Light windmill installation. Rumors swirled constantly about the "secret" golf holes up there. The *Sports Illustrated* article devoted less space to Bandon Trails than to the Sheep Ranch, as though some sort of golfing Shangri-La was hidden away from the public.

The truth was much less juicy. Tom Doak had indeed roughed out a few greens at the Sheep Ranch, including one immense green on the very tip of the peninsula where his "wild-green self" emerged in full glory. Phil Friedmann kept a basic maintenance operation going, but he hardly treated the golf holes on the Sheep Ranch as a personal plaything, as reported; golfers who wanted to play there could arrange to do so by plunking down $50. Flyers advertising the Sheep Ranch were taped up in several Bandon shops; it wasn't much of a secret. And except for the Doak greens, the land remained unshaped and without features; the thirteen holes were as flat and homely as the holes of an airport muni. Phil and Mike owned the land on a 50-50 basis, and there had been tension about the Sheep Ranch, but not enough to disrupt the operations of RPG or dislodge either one of them from their comfortable, cluttered office back in Chicago.

Yet, given the mystique that had grown up around Bandon Dunes, the hoopla about the Sheep Ranch was understandable. Out here in Oregon, far away from the known world for most golfers, Mike Keiser seemed to be able to build one miraculous course after another. Who was to say that he wouldn't build a secret course, a course with beauties never before seen or imagined, a course so dazzling and so cosmic that he'd decide to keep it to himself? To many in golf, Mike was seen as someone with the special powers of Merlin, the wizard who had all the magic, and people were watching to see how the next course would add to the reputation—the legend—of Bandon Dunes.

"The golf writers were in love with us," Mike says matter-of-factly. Down on the bottom floor of the Bandon Lodge, in the hallway outside the Bunker Bar, the walls were crowded with the rave reviews from every golf magazine on the planet. The writers seemed to vie with one another to come up with the most superlative superlatives: "Inspiration by the sea . . . a religious experience." "Found: America's Missing Links . . . the Sublime Chaos of Scottish Golf in Oregon." "Most significant new course in 50 years." "Most stunning course in the world." "Calls for an entirely new vocabulary." "Bandon has arguably surpassed St. Andrews and Monterey as home of the best tandem of courses in the world."

Even allowing for the hype and puffery that seeps into golf travel writing, the writers of these reviews were clearly trying to come to terms with the Bandon phenomenon. With a single course, Bandon Dunes had to be regarded as a bit of a curiosity, in the same way that a triumph by an unknown player in a major championship is a curiosity. But when Pacific Dunes was unveiled, it was clear that what was happening in that faraway part of America was no fluke. To have two such courses side by side, two superb links courses that were nevertheless entirely different from one another, each with its own character, flavor, and quiddity—this put Bandon in a special category.

The combination of the beauty, the wildness, the mood-altering sea air, the winds, the brilliance of the design—somehow or other, Bandon had found the magic formula. The place seemed to tap directly into the collective psyche of American golf. It had the mojo, and the resort's slogan—"Golf As It Was Meant To Be"—seemed to many visitors nothing more than a straightforward expression of the truth. Golfers kept coming to Bandon in growing numbers. In 1999, the total of rounds played was just over twenty-two thousand. By 2004, with two courses on line, the tee sheets were booked solid from May through September, and the number of rounds topped eighty thousand.

By then, the resort had added a whole new set of accommodations, and still people had to be turned away. Hank Hickox, an Oregonian and a veteran of the hotel industry, had become the general manager; he needed all his experience, poise, and managerial skill to keep up with the resort's growth. The whole operation remained under the management of Kemper Sports, and the goal was to manage growth so that the resort never seemed big and bustling, but instead retained its intimacy, and its tone of friendly, unfussy, sincere hospitality. For Hank, this meant finding and training a staff of 450 people, a tall order in Coos County, Oregon.

The success of the resort could be measured in several ways. One was its 2005 rating by *Golf Digest* as the No. 2 golf resort in America, second only to venerable Pebble Beach—and second only by the slimmest of margins. Another measurement was the bottom line. To use the business cliché, Bandon Dunes wasn't just a home run—it was a bottom-of-the-ninth grand slam. Total revenues in 2004 were about $25 million.

One further measure of Bandon's success was the flourishing caddy program. Indeed, for many who make the pilgrimage to Bandon, the golf comes with a face, a pair of white coveralls, a catchy name like Crazy or Pinky or Dr. B, and an experience of one of golf's oldest traditions—in a word, it comes with a caddy. Since those early days when Shoe rounded up a few friends to loop for the writers who flew in, the Bandon caddy program has grown to become the largest in the world, by a significant margin. More than three hundred caddies work at Bandon over the course of a season, and collectively they do about forty thousand loops—about twice as many as caddies log at St. Andrews.

Many of the caddies are professionals, and the resort has a policy of assigning a caddy to a golfer for the duration of his stay (when the pairing doesn't work, a golfer can request a different caddy—but such requests are rare). For the golfer who plays four or five rounds, that adds up to many hours of contact, and it makes for a very particular kind of camaraderie. The caddy is an essential part of the Bandon experience, and a part of the Bandon spectacle, too. From any high point at the resort, any place where the view takes in several holes, the scene includes groups of golfers and caddies walking abreast as they move along the fairways—a scene that has more in common with the old sepia-tinted photographs of St. Andrews than it does with images of modern American resorts. No carts. No cart paths. Just men and women walking along side by side, playing an ancient game by the sea, making a little journey together.

"Take away the caddies," says Ken Brooke, the director of the caddy program, "and Bandon would be like any other resort. The walking, the caddies, are what give this place its character."

WHEN THEY DECIDED to build Bandon Trails, Mike and his colleagues from Kemper Sports revisited the policy of walking-only. The site for Bandon Trails was more spread out and rugged than the sites for the other courses, and they worried that the new course might be too difficult to walk. In the end, though, they just couldn't imagine guests arriving at the resort and seeing, from the entrance road, golf carts rolling all over the landscape. Bandon Trails would be, like its siblings, a walking course.

All the holes in the meadow—the area that was once known as "the circus"—would be visible from the entrance road. Mike and Howard hadn't intended to build the third course there; they had imagined that the third course would be a "forest" course lying to the east, on the inland side of Back Ridge. On their first visits to Bandon, Bill and Ben had wandered around mostly in the monsoon forest, but they were drawn to the open land in the meadow and the dunes. They looked around, trying to discover natural holes, and Bill initiated a negotiation with Howard. "The land we wanted was along the road, but Howard wouldn't give me the topo maps. I'd say, 'Howard, I know you have those maps,' and he'd go off and come back with a map that covered another little section, and it kept going like that. We had a tug-of-war over those maps."

At one point, Bill and Ben were considering a course that lay entirely west of Back Ridge, but they couldn't find enough holes. When all was said and done, and Howard had handed over all the maps, they decided that the best routing was one that would meander from one environment to another, from dunes to meadow to rain forest and back again. They'd also staked a claim to a huge chunk of property; Bill estimates that the course sprawls over as many as 350 to 400 acres, or about the same acreage as Bandon Dunes and Pacific Dunes combined. A piece of land of this size, with this much beauty and variety, would in most cases be regarded as a fabulous site for a golf course; only here, in proximity to a pair of superb links course, could anyone question its merits. "If you'd offered us this site and a site on the ocean," Bill said, with a faint touch of defensiveness, "we might have chosen the ocean. Those cliffs and the big dunes are gorgeous, but this property is in no way inferior. It's certainly no less interesting. It shows off a lot of different features of the Pacific Northwest. It's just a fascinating blend of elements."

In Mike Keiser's estimation, the routing contained one of the most exhilarating views in the world. The 14th tee was to be situated high on Back Ridge, overlooking the meadow and dunes, taking in the sweep of the ocean from Bandon all the way up to Five Mile Point and including, of course, Bandon Dunes and Pacific Dunes.

This spot is almost exactly where he had stood on the day he first visited the property and decided to buy it.

• • •

WITH THE ANNOUNCEMENT that Bill Coore and Ben Crenshaw were building the third course at Bandon—an announcement made on the now-standard card—Mike was checking a few more items off his master To Do list. He was also changing the story line, sending a message that Bandon Dunes had come of age. David Kidd had been an unknown, untested architect when he came to Oregon; Tom Doak had been the young genius with brilliant, unfulfilled potential. Bill Coore and Ben Crenshaw were veterans, and ever since the unveiling of Sand Hills, they had been at the top of their profession.

And they did it the old-fashioned way: They earned it. In a line of work often perceived as glamorous, Bill and Ben were unapologetic grinders. Tell Bill that he and Ben are touted as the "hottest" architects going, and his face takes on a wry expression, half-grin and half-grimace. He's not interested in adding to the mystique that seems to surround golf course designers. "Most people just don't understand what a golf course architect does," Bill says. "Somehow they have the idea that nothing gets done until the great man arrives, and *presto!*, he waves his arms around, and the magic happens. An army of machines rolls out at his command. Everything just falls into place exactly the way he wants it. But that is *not* the way it works."

How it works for Bill and Ben is this: They get out on the site and start walking. Their entire design process depends on coming to know a site, every last inch of it. Their crew members sometimes move around a site on vehicles, but Bill and Ben have an unspoken rule that they will walk everywhere. They don't want to miss a single thing. They walk and look, pause, mull over some detail, discuss it, and start walking again. When Mike was in Oregon, he walked with them, and it wasn't easy to keep up with him and Bill and Ben. Neither rain nor sleet nor cold nor mud kept them from walking Bandon Trails from one end to the other, and I came to realize that this is what happens *every day*. They walk and look. They talk a little. They walk and look some more.

If that sounds repetitive, well, it is meant to. Bill Coore and Ben Crenshaw have become one of the most respected partnerships in the profession of golf course design because of their willingness to take infinite pains. Ben, of course, is the better-known member of the team, a man who has had one of the most extraordinary careers in golf. Blond, blue-eyed, handsome, and gentlemanly, he was hailed as "the next Nicklaus" when he turned pro, known for his sometimes unreliable ball striking and his brilliant putting. In 1995, when he seemed to be washed up, he won his second Masters championship in a tournament that gave goose bumps to golf fans all over the world. Earlier in Masters week, Ben's lifelong teacher Harvey Penick had died, and Ben had served as a pallbearer at his funeral. His inspired play during the tournament stands as a golf miracle, and a few years later Ben took part in another miracle, one that he prophetically announced. As the captain of the 1999 Ryder Cup team, he found himself looking at what appeared to be an insurmountable 10 to 6 deficit at the end of Saturday's play. "I have a feeling," he said, wagging his finger at the press. "Just remember that tomorrow." And the Americans went out the next day and staged the biggest comeback in Ryder Cup history.

Compared to other professional golfers, who tend to be guarded, factual, bland, and boring in their public utterances, Ben had always worn his heart on his sleeve. He could be unabashedly sentimental, but he was also a scholar of the game. There was no one on the PGA Tour who embraced golf—its history, its traditions, its legends—more ardently than Ben Crenshaw. As a young player, he had soaked up the atmosphere of the great courses at home and abroad; when he went over to play the British Open, he made time to explore the lesser-known courses as well as the great ones on the Open rota. Like Tom Doak, Ben Crenshaw knew hundreds of links courses and classic American courses pretty much by heart, and he had, in his quiet and gentle way, gone about fashioning courses that kept alive a style of design that captured the classic spirit.

Bill, the lesser-known member of the team, could be Ben's brown-eyed older brother. He is a mild-mannered, soft-spoken, courtly North Carolinian, and he is quite content to have Ben out there in the spotlight. Not that Bill doesn't have things to say; he has ideas about just about everything under the sun. He went to Wake Forest on an academic scholarship and became a classics major. ("It was by accident, really. I was in a hurry to get to the golf course but I had to sign up to take a language. I was going to take Spanish, but the line was way too long. Then I thought about taking Russian, but there were people in that line, too. The only place with no line was classics, so I signed up and went off to play.") As one of the few classics students, he found himself in tiny classes with brilliant professors whose interests ran in all directions, and it made a deep impression on him. His idea of a career was something that would combine golf and a professorship.

He has come close to succeeding. While he doesn't hold a chair anywhere, he is very much a mentor to the young men who come to work for Coore-Crenshaw. As the one who puts in the most time on the ground—with daughters at home, and with his playing commitments, Ben inevitably spends fewer days on-site—Bill has an unusual rapport with the shapers, most of whom have worked for him for years. Bill and Ben talk daily by phone, and they are as attuned to each other as a pair of twins, at least when it comes to design. They don't finish each other's sentences, but they do speak naturally in the first person plural—not a royal we, but a collective we that extends to their crew and has its basis in a deeply shared idea of what a golf course should be.

That idea, in is simplest form, is to take what the land offers. Bill and Ben don't impose their conception on a site; they let the site speak to them. And speak it does. It's almost comical to listen to Bill as he communicates with his crew in a flow of personifications. He refers to topographical features of the course as though they are living creatures with a mind of their own. "This green wants to slide a little farther to the left," he'll say. Or, speaking of a mound, "That guy is crowding in too much on the green. He needs to back off a little before he gets too big for his britches."

The point of all their looking is to "discover" golf holes. This is a notion to which most golf course architects pay lip service, but the standard practice for many modern architects is to visit a site for a day or two, then retire to their office to study the topo maps and lay out a routing. Soon there are drawings, and eventually the land will be made to conform to the drawings. The designer in the office inevitably starts to look for certain kinds of familiar shapes and configurations, places where he can design a certain type of hole, and before long his courses begin to resemble one another. His "signature" is all over the place.

Coore and Crenshaw reverse this process. They never work from drawings. ("I can't draw worth a hoot," Bill says. "Ben and I both work by feel.") They try to avoid a signature, looking to design holes that are so "natural" that the matter of a signature never rears its head. In the Coore-Crenshaw theology, the cardinal sin of golf course architecture is anything that appears to be forced or contrived or "thought-out." The hand of the architect should be invisible—and this takes much labor and patience and discipline. "We don't want our holes to look like golf holes," Bill says. "They should look like landscapes which just happen to include a golf hole."

Easier said than done. In the age of the bulldozer, it's more difficult to build holes in which the architect's contribution is concealed than to build holes that are stamped with a style. A bulldozer can mold any piece of land into the forms the architect desires—but, as Bill Coore will quickly tell you, these forms are never as varied, striking, bold, intricate, random, and intriguing as the shapes created by Mother Nature. "I can't compete with nature, and it would only showcase my futility if I tried. So I try to cooperate."

MARCH. IT'S RAINING again, and the mud is well-nigh impassable back here in the woods. To follow Bill and Mike, I had to borrow a pair of waterproof boots from Dave Axland, known simply as Ax, a burly, deep-voiced, ex–football player who has been Bill's right-hand man for some years. Ax is a golf course designer in his own right (his credits include the much-praised Wild Horse), and he and Bill seem to be amused by my questions about the routing of the course. They don't know how long it will be, and they're not completely sure of the par. "I guess we're building another par 71," Bill says, and Dave has a sheet of notepaper on which he's estimated the yardage for each hole, but things do keep changing.

For instance, the par-5 9th hole got longer by about 50 yards when they found a better green site. The 10th hole veered to the left when Tony Russell went off course as he cleared a center line. The 11th is probably going to be a long par 4, but on this drizzly day Bill and Ax spend a long time talking to Mike about where to locate an irrigation lake, a necessary feature that has both budget and design implications (Bill had said earlier, "We don't do water holes," but this will be an exception). At the par-3 12th hole—that is, at a place where some preliminary clearing has been done, and fresh, soaked, fragrant spruce logs lie every which way—Bill says, "This can be your hole, Dave. This is the real underdog hole, but you can knock some sense into it."

Dave says in his gruff voice, pretending to need sympathy, "I was wondering if he was ever going to let me do something creative again. Something besides drainage."

This kind of banter is the currency of exchange among the crew, and Bill's cap—the Coore & Crenshaw & Russell cap—is one of the running jokes on the site. Tony Russell, the ex–dairy farmer who worked for David Kidd and blossomed as a bunker-shaper for Tom Doak, was hired to cut paths and center lines for this third course.

"What happened," Bill says, "is that Tony went off course, and I said, 'Tony, if you're going to put the holes where you want to put 'em, not where we said we want 'em, then I'm going to make you a design associate. You're going to have to share the blame.'"

Bill gets tickled when he tells the story, and he points out one of the red-barked madrone trees that Tony has left standing. He is a protector of madrones, but this particular tree looks pathetic and scraggly, and someone on the crew has put up a hand-lettered sign and a crude alms box, taking up a collection to help Save Tony's Madrones.

Like Tom Doak and Jim Urbina, however, Bill Coore recognizes talent when he sees it, and Tony had a definite feel for the kinds of shapes Bill wanted to create. Before long, Tony became a full-fledged member of the crew, responsible for many bunkers, greens, and fairways. Often, when the time comes to put on the finishing touches, Bill calls on Tony. "I like to get him out there with his knuckle bucket, listening to music. I don't want him to think about what he's doing, or try to create any kind of shape or pattern. I want him to put dings and dents wherever the spirit moves him. He can do things out there that I couldn't possibly tell him to do. It just has to *happen*."

AS BANDON TRAILS took shape, certain themes began to develop. One issue had always been how to blend all the different environments together, and two answers were gradually presenting themselves. (*Gradually* is how everything happens on a Coore-Crenshaw site. If there are trees to clear, they come down one at a time, and then Bill and Ben look, and talk it over, and let it percolate, and then decide that maybe, just maybe, they can take down a few more.) Privately, Bill and Ben were worried more than they ever let on about the problems of tying together a site with such significant differences, but they had just completed a course on Long Island, Friar's Head, that presented similar challenges. There they had to blend potato fields with dunes, and they were able to pull it off. They were going to need some of the same strokes of imagination here.

One unifying element was to be the bunkers. The style of bunkering that seemed to fit the course was lacy edged, like the bunkers of the Australian Sandbelt. That was a look that Mike liked, and had advocated, though he can't remember who first looked at the configurations and the native plants and said, "Aha! This cries out for bunkers like those Down Under!" Like Mike, Bill and Ben had recently been to Australia, where they had taken a careful look at the bunkers designed by Alister MacKenzie for his remarkable Kingston Heath course outside Melbourne, bunkers noted for their many twists and tongues curling into the sand. The crew was passing around a book with photographs of MacKenzie bunkers, and it hardly mattered who came up with the idea; the fact is that it was *simpatico* with the site.

Another way to help blend the different environments was to emphasize the plants that grew on the site. True, the dunes environment was radically different from the rain forest, but the madrones, manzanita, and huckleberry that thrived in the meadow tickled the edges of the other environments.

Troy Russell and his gang did some transplanting, with the aim of providing a few familiar reminders to golfers making their way around the course.

But the true, deep consistency and character of the course came from the slow, laborious process itself. At the 17th hole, for instance, a par 3 in the meadow, shaper Jim Craig looked like he had to be miserable in the March rains as he worked on the green and its surrounds. Over the course of three days, he went back and forth, back and forth, back and forth, occasionally stepping down from his small dozer to squint at the work from a different perspective. Bill calls Jim a "playful puppy," but Jim is from Fort Worth, Texas, and he is cut from the same cloth as Captain Call in *Lonesome Dove*, the silent and stoic Texas Ranger who will not rest until the job is done. This particular green has a beautiful setting, and a ridge in front, and bunkers on both sides fringed by native plants that Jim was trying to save as he pulled all the various contours into one harmonious entity. He was wet to the bone and shivering. Every now and then Bill checked in to see how the task was going, but it was Jim's eye that made the final adjustments. Asked why he didn't have a covered cabin on the dozer, a cabin to get him out of the weather, Jim shrugged. "I feel like I can't see what I'm doing if I'm in a cabin."

Jim is a glutton for punishment—or perfection, if such a thing can be said to exist in golf course architecture. The members of this crew aren't so different from surfers who roam the globe in search of the perfect wave. They are obsessive, driven, nomadic creatures—like young Dave Zinkand, a Cornell grad who took an extended trip to study the golf courses of Great Britain before coming to work for Coore-Crenshaw. Zink, as he's called, spent days on the short par-4 14th hole, shaping the contours of the pedestal green, feathering a bunker into its flank.

From the height of the 14th tee, Bill Coore watched Zink and Ben confer, back off, look at the green from several angles. Even at a distance they appeared to be deep in thought, lost in concentration. I wouldn't have been surprised if someone had whispered, "Shhh! Do not disturb!"—but another member of the crew, Jeff Bradley, strolled up, and the needling began. "Jeff's the Leonardo of bunkers," Bill said by way of introducing Jeff, and in the world of golf course aficionados, Jeff is indeed a star. He has his own website, bunkerguru.com. He's come a long way since joining the Coore-Crenshaw team as a long-haired member of a rock band.

From this top-of-the-world tee, Bill was wondering whether a bunker should be placed at the edge of the trees on the right side of the landing area. The location for the potential bunker was at least 270 yards away, and he mused about how a bunker might snuggle into the "native" (the existing plants) and how it would affect big hitters on the tee.

To my ear, his musings sounded inconclusive, and when he set off down the hill, I asked Jeff if Bill was going to mark the bunker for him with flags or spray paint.

"He just marked it," Jeff said.

Telepathy.

BY JUNE, THE GRASS was beginning to grow on several holes at Bandon Trails, and Mike Keiser was feeling cautiously jubilant. He wasn't prepared to offer his own judgment; he left the superlatives to a group of friends from Chicago who'd flown out for a few days and were walking the first holes with him and Bill Coore.

The tour started on the first tee, that elevated platform that will surely take its place as one of the most magnificent first tees in all of golf. With the fairway glistening green in the sunshine, and the beach grass stirring in the salty breeze, and the ocean sparkling in the distance—well, it was no wonder that the visitors kept saying "Wow!"

Mike nodded, and he and Bill talked business as they moved along—design business, that is. Over the long process of construction, the two of them had found their own companionable groove, and at the second hole they reviewed—for the nth time—the matter of where to locate the walkoff for the tees and green. At the third and fourth holes, they looked hard at the bunkering and the way that the native plantings were worked into the scheme of the design. At the fifth hole, they reprised an old debate about a tree and a green.

The fifth hole is a lovely little par 3 that plays across a small valley of manzanita to a green fronted by bunkers and framed by fir tees. The shot required brings to mind some of the difficulties faced by Romeo as he considered climbing into Juliet's window. The green, with a tremendous swale in the middle, is a natural Biarritz green; even Bill Coore, who is superstitious about claiming too much, acknowledges that this green "has the potential" to be one that people remember and talk about. Mike, in his role as leveler of greens, worried about its severity, but Bill and Ben held out for thrills and excitement. In the effort to get it just right, this green became perhaps the most discussed, massaged, trimmed, and tweaked feature on the entire course. The edges of the green were drawn at least three times, and Jim Craig worked on its slopes and contours, endlessly shaving away a millimeter here, adding a millimeter there, until all concerned were prepared to give it their blessing.

The fir tree guarding the left side of the green has also been much debated. Mike has been in favor of taking it down, but Bill took a wait-and-see position. They've talked about this tree so often that Bill has taken to calling it Mike's Tree—or, as he said that day, "We've gotten to know that tree so well that we've shortened the name. Now we just call it Mike." (The tree remains, though a compromise was eventually reached: Ken Nice, who moved from Pacific Dunes to become the superintendent at Bandon Trails, climbed up the fir tree and took off the top with a handsaw, making it easier for a golfer to loft a shot over it.)

After the fifth hole, Mike's Chicago friends sloped off to play a round of golf, leaving Mike and Bill to continue their working walk. Bandon Trails, I had come to realize, was the sum of these discussions and decisions, and I tried not to interrupt—tried not to gush incoherently—as we moved through the mystery holes. These holes were still very much in progress, but even so, it was hard to imagine that anyone could fail to respond to their scale and beauty. With its three environments—dunes, meadow, forest—Bandon Trails was a rich microcosm of this coastal property. The course was going to be different—"stunningly different," as Mike would later tell a reporter— from its sisters, and it was going to be majestic.

The opening of Bandon Trails was still a year away, but the first articles would begin to appear before the opening. There was simply no precedent for what was happening at Bandon. The first course, Bandon Dunes, had been a sensation; the second, Pacific Dunes, made it a compound sensation; and if the resort were to add a third course of the same caliber—a third course by different architects, and built on different terrain, yet inspiring the same kind of exaltation—what would that be called? Sensation cubed? For a golf resort at the end of the earth to have three courses that leapt immediately to places in the Top 100—what were the odds on that?

On this June day, however, such thoughts were far from his head. He was reveling in the more immediate pleasure of a new course on a glorious summer day, and enjoying the give-and-take of the conversations that kept developing—with Jim Craig, with Ax, with the irrigation guys and the crew leveling the tees. Mike Keiser, the businessman from Chicago, had most definitely diversified himself. As a golf developer, he'd found a role that led to a full development of his talents along the lines of excellence, and that, as the ancients say, is a definition of happiness.

Mike and Bill spent a good while at the 13th hole, one of their favorites, and a hole that required moving a mountain of sand; the green is nestled into Back Ridge, and it is surrounded by shaggy Port Orford cedars. The trail from the 13th green is one of the longest walks on the course, leading up and over the ridge, through the dark forest with its tapestry of spruce and fir and madrone and rhododendron.

The trail brought us out to the 14th tee, the place where Mike was standing years ago when he had his *Eureka!* moment and decided to buy the property. High on the west side of the ridge, its view is even more encompassing than the view from the first tee. The Pacific Ocean still glitters in the distance, of course, but the foreground is filled with golf. In the meadow, and off to the north where Bandon Dunes is visible, the golf holes seem to extend as far as the eye can see.

In the years since Mike first stood here, this land has been transformed. It is still wild and beautiful, but wild in a way that creates the ideal conditions for play, and beautiful in a way that speaks directly to the dreams of golfers. The place could be described, to quote the words Mike wrote years earlier, as "nature perfected." On the map of golf, there are not many holy places; from this height, it is easy to understand why Bandon has so swiftly claimed its place among them.

Mike, however, is not quite ready to declare the venture a success. Surveying his realm, he asks a question that is directed to no one in particular, the same question that he has been asking for years. This time it seems to be put to the air itself, perhaps to the golf gods.

"Do we like it?"

Part Four

OLD MACDONALD

20 | The Peekaboo

*As it happened, Macdonald ran right into the panic of 1907 the very
year his great work [National Golf Links] was to take shape. That never
bothered him at all; nearly all his seventy founders came across with
their subscriptions and he gaily went into his own pocket for the rest.*
— H. J. WHIGHAM, *COUNTRY LIFE* MAGAZINE, SEPTEMBER 1939

IN THE CABIN of the private jet winging westward, Mike Keiser grinned as
he checked out a pair of caps. They were emblazoned with the dueling logos
for Old Macdonald, the fourth golf course at Bandon Dunes.

Old Macdonald. It was an unusual name, but the course was conceived as
a tribute to Charles Blair Macdonald, inducted into the World Golf Hall of
Fame as "the Father of American Golf." Especially as a golf course architect,
Macdonald had put his large, lasting imprint on the game. Insisting that
American courses could rival those of Great Britain, Macdonald built the
National Golf Links of America, the "ideal" course that served as a call to
arms for American designers of the classic era.

Now, a century later, Mike Keiser was looking to tap into that same source
of inspiration. Selecting a name for the other Bandon courses had been a
drawn-out process, but this name — Old Macdonald — had immediately
sprung to mind, thanks to the children's song with the funny barnyard
noises. A more grandiose name might have given the impression that the
course was a museum piece, a dull lesson in the history of golf architecture.
But Old Macdonald was playful and irreverent. It sprinkled a dash of irony
on the idea of a tribute, doing away with any whiff of solemnity or dreariness.

Old Macdonald — it was a name that could make a golfer curious, and that was exactly what Mike was hoping for.

The name had taken care of itself, but the logo had proven tricky. The designs on the caps that Josh Lesnik, the president of KemperSports, handed out to the other passengers on the plane were as different as a rose from a rooster. Actually, one was a rooster, its outline like that of a weathervane rooster, proud and brash, flaunting its fantail. The other, more traditional design consisted of a round *O* encircling an *M* whose diagonal lines were golf clubs. Mike put on a cap with the rooster and stood in the aisle of the plane while the others tried on their caps, staging a cheerful impromptu debate. A friend of Mike's, Larry Booth, said that no self-respecting truck driver would wear a hat with the OM logo — it looked too highfalutin. Mike reported that the advisory panel for Old Mac preferred the rooster, all except Brad Klein, who thought it was silly. He thought it looked as though you ought to be able to push the rooster to play the song.

Mike enjoyed the banter, but he was listening attentively. His antennae were out. He always wanted to know what people liked and why they liked it. Having spent decades in the greeting card business, he knew how important it was to hook people with the first impression. With Old Macdonald, he was trying to figure out how to present a new golf course, one that was different enough, and exciting enough, to make golfers feel they absolutely had to see it and play it. Mike wanted people to buy into the story of Old Macdonald, and the name and the logo were key elements of its identity. They had to convey at a glance or in a couple of syllables something of the essence of the course. They had to be just right. Mike had a lot riding on it.

The date was November 5, 2008, the day after the presidential election, and the economy was in a meltdown. The banking system teetered at the edge of the abyss. On the first half of this flight, Mike sat in the front of the plane, going over the balance sheets with Josh and other top people from KemperSports. The numbers weren't pretty. Just a couple of years ago, Bandon Dunes had been operating at capacity, even turning people away. At the time, it had made good business sense to expand the resort, adding new accommodations and a fourth course.

That was then, and now was different — scary different. Advance bookings were down by 40 percent at Bandon Dunes, and still they were doing better than many other golf resorts. The conversation between Mike and his business colleagues kept straying to reports about old-line resorts like Sea Island and the Greenbrier that were in trouble, either bankrupt or on the verge. Even the venerable Pebble Beach — Pebble Beach, for crying out loud! — was running specials. As for new golf course construction, it was basically dead. Everyone on the plane could add to the list of projects that had been canceled, postponed, or abandoned altogether. Back in the boom years, golf courses were opening at the rate of one a day; now, as Mike had heard from a well-placed source, only six courses were scheduled to open in 2010. Six.

But Mike didn't seem worried as he listened to the logo debate. Changing seats to sit with his Chicago friends in the rear of the plane, he was ready to put business aside to talk about the Peekaboo, the 10-hole preview round on Old Macdonald that was scheduled during this trip to Bandon. There was certainly no hint that he'd spent the last few weeks deciding whether he should halt work on the course. "If I'd listened only to the guys with the green eyeshades," he said later, "I would have stopped the project in October." But Mike had made up his mind, and that was that. He is not one to spend time second-guessing himself. In the words of his wife, Lindy, Mike has one gear: forward.

His golfing partners on this trip were Wayne Andersen, a federal judge, and Larry Booth, the architect who designed the small, cottagelike clubhouse at the Dunes Club, the 9-holer that was Mike's first golf venture. Larry had also prepared a design for the original Lodge at Bandon Dunes, but it got nixed. Lately he'd been working on a design for a clubhouse at Old Macdonald, and he'd brought along a model to show Mike. The building was long, low, and elegant, with two separate sections, a pro shop, and a restaurant; high windows overlooked the first tee and last green, and people entering the building, Larry said, would see the course suddenly, in much the same way that someone entering a baseball stadium sees that first slash of green.

Mike and Larry have the same quick, sharp wit, and the conversation was full of friendly thrust-and-parry. "You're determined to get a foothold here, aren't you?" Mike asked, inspecting the meticulously crafted model. There was a needle in that remark, but it was gentle in comparison to Mike's comment when Larry estimated the cost of the building at $4.5 million. Mike cocked his head to the side, a gesture that he often uses to mark an emphasis, and said to anyone listening, "Larry likes to spend money. Other peoples' money."

BY TEN A.M., Mike was standing on the first tee of Old Macdonald, holding an umbrella to protect him from the rain, a cold, steady, heavy-duty coastal drizzle. Jim Urbina didn't seem to notice. Jim had been Tom Doak's right-hand man during the building of Pacific Dunes; here at Old Macdonald, his role was much the same, but his billing was different. At Mike's request, both Tom and Jim were listed as codesigners of Old Macdonald — or Old Mac, as everyone seemed to call it, going with the inevitable nickname.

With Tom scheduled to arrive later in the day, Jim was conducting this walk-around. Drops of water beaded on his black jacket and dripped from the bill of his black cap, but Jim was too absorbed in his task to care. In Mike's description, Jim is "one of those dirt guys who can do anything — and he's also a natural showman and storyteller." Dark-eyed, olive-skinned, and animated, Jim is passionate in his beliefs about golf course design, and he was into Old Mac all the way, blood, guts, and feathers. His voice brimmed with excitement as he explained the strategies of the opening hole, a short par 4 called Double Plateau.

The features of the hole had been roughed in so that its major shapes — the fairway, bunker, and green — emerged clearly from the sandy, soggy ground. Jim started his remarks with a few thoughts about opening holes and the desirability of getting the golfer off to a smooth start, which he followed with a glancing reference to the first hole at National Golf Links and a rhetorical question: "Do you see how wide that fairway is? If you can't hit that fairway, you should think about taking up another sport. Right away, we wanted to show the golfer a wide fairway, because that's what this course is about — width. That's what they're going to see. We're not saying you have to hit it here or hit it there. We're saying, look at this huge fairway and *you* choose where *you* want to hit. Macdonald never told anyone where they had to hit the ball."

"Width is good," Mike said. "We like width." But he did have plenty of questions. How far away was that fairway bunker on the right? A tour player might blast it right over that bunker, but could he? Would it catch his drive? Could he get out of it? Was it too severe for an opening hole?

And so it went as the group moved down the fairway. These walk-arounds had a well-established pattern of question and response, as Jim knew from his previous experience of working with Mike. The dialogue was between the two of them, though the group that morning numbered about a dozen, including Mike's friends from Chicago; Ken Nice, the head superintendent at the resort; the three members of the Old Mac advisory panel, George Bahto, Brad Klein, and Karl Olson; a small KemperSports contingent; and a couple of media folk. Mike hovered near the fairway bunker for a while, looking back at the tee and forward to the green, and said in an aside, "I'm not sure Tom is worried about what the retail golfer thinks."

Mike, however, regards himself as the voice of the retail golfer — the golfer who pays the freight at Bandon. When everyone reached the green, dominated by a pair of mounds that formed the Double Plateau, Jim talked about how fond Macdonald was of this green configuration and how often he and his associate, Seth Raynor, had employed it. Nearly every course they built, he said, had a double plateau. Still, Mike wasn't convinced about these humps that were the size and shape of elephant burial grounds. He had another barrage of questions: How high were those mounds? Weren't they higher than the mounds on the Double Plateau at National? They looked higher. Were they flat enough to hold an approach shot? Not just a wedge shot, but the kind of approach he might hit? If he was on the wrong plateau, could he two-putt? What if his approach hit the side of a plateau — would it bounce off the green altogether? How far off would it run?

Jim's eyes sparkled. He was prepared for these questions. Almost every answer contained a quote or reference to Macdonald, whose views on golf architecture Jim seemed to know by heart. If any project was going to get Jim's creative juices flowing in full flood, it was Old Mac. The first classical course that he'd ever made a special trip to study was National Golf Links, the course on Long Island that stands as Macdonald's most definitive statement on golf design. And the first golf architecture book that he ever read was Macdonald's book, *Scotland's Gift — Golf.* Out here in Oregon, he carried his well-worn copy in the cab of his truck. "The red book," he called it, and it was his Bible.

The discussion of the Double Plateau ended with an agreement to reconsider the height of the mounds. "I am a leveler of greens," Mike muttered as the group trudged toward the nearby 17th hole, a par 5 that was just beginning to take shape. Jim was eager to show Mike a new tee site, though it was difficult to see immediately just how the hole would play. A small marsh encroached on the right side, a hill on the left, and in the middle of what seemed to be the fairway there was a ditch, a gash about eight feet wide and six feet deep.

"That's our burn," Jim announced, sweeping his arm like a magician making a revelation.

In classic design, the burn — the Scottish term for a small stream — has a pedigree that goes back to the Swilcan Burn at St. Andrews. At various points in the design process at Old Macdonald, there'd been talk of incorporating a burn, but the right opportunity hadn't presented itself. Now Jim thought he'd found just the place. This 17th hole called for alternate fairways divided by a hazard of some sort. Why not a burn? As he described the tee shot and the way the burn would wind through the fairway, Jim seemed to see it already, filled with clear water flowing between green banks.

Mike was still seeing a muddy gash. In general, he was partial to the idea of a burn, and he liked the way the burns influenced play at St. Andrews and Turnberry, but the idea of a burn on this hole caught him off guard. Jim had sprung a surprise, a tactic he often used in his work with Tom. When he wanted to make a strong suggestion, Jim would sometimes go ahead and rough in a feature so that Tom could actually see it, an approach that was more dramatic than simply describing what he had in mind.

In this case, Jim hadn't gone to the trouble and expense of digging a big ditch just to make a suggestion. The ditch had been cut to accommodate the main stem of the drainage pipe that would run through the course. When he laid eyes on it, Jim couldn't stop imagining it as a burn.

"I think it would be bold," Jim said. "And we want bold. Macdonald took chances. That's one of the great things about National — it's full of surprises. And this would be a surprise. A golfer comes off the green at 16 and walks through the saddle, and *bam!* What does he see? A burn. It's something he's not expecting."

For the next half hour, the group mulled over the burn and milled about, looking at potential tee sites and landing areas, trying to gauge what effect the burn would have on the playing of the 17th hole and on the overall experience of the golf course. Some were intrigued, some bemused, some turned off. Mike didn't seem smitten, but he said diplomatically that he'd wait to hear what Tom had to say.

Then he and his buddies hustled off to get in a wet round of golf before dark.

THAT NIGHT, AT A LONG TABLE in the rear of the Gallery, the main restaurant in the Lodge at Bandon Dunes Resort, Mike hosted a dinner for the design team of Old Macdonald, and all the main players were present: Jim, the members of the advisory panel, and Tom, who'd arrived on schedule and spent the afternoon at Old Mac, getting briefed on the walk-around he'd missed and taking a hard look at the burn.

Before the first course was served, Mike rose to make a toast. He was dressed casually in shirt and sweater, but he sounded dead formal when he lifted his glass. As he saluted the talents and contributions of the course designers, there was a sense of we're-in-this-together, an attitude of damn-the-torpedoes, full-speed-ahead. "To the success of Old Macdonald," he said in his ringing baritone.

Then Jim got to his feet. He began his remarks by thanking Mike for the opportunity to work on such a great project. He paused as he shifted gears, moving into more philosophical territory. "A golf hole is a complex, beautiful thing. Once you start to build it, it becomes a living thing, not just a pile of dirt to push around. It starts to evolve, and as you get to know it, as you watch it take shape, you have to listen to what it's trying to say. Sometimes the best ideas come from paying attention to what a hole seems to want. Sometimes a hole starts to give you clues and makes you think about it in new ways — "

Tom interrupted him. "Are you still talking about No. 17 and the burn?"

"Yes, I am," Jim said, and he turned to Mike, pressing his hands together in a prayerful, imploring gesture. "I'm ready to get down on my knees and beg for that burn."

"You're that passionate about it?" Mike asked, smiling at Jim's melodramatic plea.

"I am," said Jim.

In a clear, firm voice, Tom said, "I thought we settled it this afternoon." Actually, Tom thought it had been settled even before then; in conversations with Jim before the ditch was dug, he'd indicated that he didn't think a burn would work on the 17th.

Jim laughed nervously, skipping a beat before answering "I guess it's settled. You said you'd fire me if I built it."

Tom said flatly, "It doesn't work."

Changing tactics, Jim tried to offer a practical rationale for the burn. "We already have the ditch and it's not that wide. The fairway is huge and the burn would only be about 8 percent of the area — 8 percent. That's not much. The other 92 percent would be grass."

Brad Klein chimed in. "That's a specious argument. The 8 percent would be all that a golfer on the tee could see."

Jim still wasn't ready to back away. "A burn wouldn't be just a hazard. It would be aesthetically pleasing — we could make it look great. It would be something that would make that hole completely memorable, and it would be a surprise."

Brad shook his head. "It would just look odd. There's nothing on the course that foreshadows it. There's no water anywhere, no hint that there's a burn out there and that it's going to be the major feature on one of the finishing holes. There's a difference between surprise and stupidity."

That remark carried a sting, but it drew laughter, even from Jim. Brad, an editor of *Golfweek* and a prolific writer, was the member of the advisory panel who could be counted on to deliver the acid comment. Jim took his seat, but the discussion banged on. It wasn't exactly music to Mike's ears, but it was evidence of healthy conflict. There were sharp opinions pro and con, and the discussion didn't end until Tom agreed to sleep on a final decision about the burn.

IN THE DAYS FOLLOWING THE ELECTION, the economic news was the same as it had been pre-election: grisly. The Dow Jones fell more than four hundred points on Wednesday, and four hundred more on Thursday. As he watched cable news that evening, Mike didn't try to disguise his frustration. He had always been a firm believer in free markets, and the behavior of those at the center of the financial crisis — the bankers and hedge fund bigwigs, as well as the crew in Washington trying to orchestrate the various bailouts — seemed panicky and ineffective. "I'm an old-school, small-town capitalist," he said. "I'm not a speculator, and that's what these guys are. I think that if you're in business, you're accountable. None of these guys want to be accountable. I hope they get thrown in jail."

Mike had spent the day making his rounds at Bandon Dunes, seeing first-hand how the resort was feeling the downturn. Some effects were starkly visible — empty parking lots, vacant tables in the restaurants, gaps between groups on the golf courses. There were groups of die-hard golfers, mostly Oregonians who'd driven to Bandon to play some adventure golf at the special local rates, but business was definitely off.

The resort had grown by leaps and bounds since the opening of the third course, Bandon Trails, in 2005. The Gallery restaurant had doubled in size, and there were two new full-service restaurants, one in the Bandon Trails clubhouse, the other in the new clubhouse at Pacific Dunes. Mike had finally replaced the old clubhouse, a double-wide trailer with a clock tower, with a dramatic new glass and concrete building. The accommodations capacity had also taken a quantum leap with the addition of the Grove, a cluster of sixteen luxurious cottages designed for foursomes, and the Inn, a shingle-style building with thirty-nine guest rooms. Yet another major addition, not visible to guests of the resort, was the village for staff housing, intended for the use of employees who couldn't find affordable housing elsewhere.

Expanded facilities, fewer guests — this was not the equation Mike had been looking for. The only good news was that the resort was still going to show a profit for the year. Josh Lesnik and Hank Hickox, the general manager of Bandon Dunes, had spent more time than ever working on marketing and publicity, and they'd been doing the painful budget slashing to keep the resort in the black. There were contingency plans to close one or two of the four restaurants, at least for the season. Updates to the carpets and lighting in the Lodge would have to wait. But the biggest, most painful cuts were in the payroll. Bandon Dunes had become the largest employer in Coos County, employing over five hundred people in peak season; that number had been cut in half. Some of the layoffs were seasonal, but others cut into the core staff. Some longtime employees had to be let go, and others had their jobs reconfigured. Bob Gaspar, aka "Shoe," the first person hired at Bandon Dunes and a fixture at the greeter's stand, the man who had a bunker named for him on all of the Bandon courses, was a Bandon institution; but now he filled in where most needed, sometimes working as a course marshal or driving a shuttle.

Plans for a pair of residential developments on the property had come to a standstill with the death of Howard McKee, Mike's friend and partner. First diagnosed with cancer in 1996, Howard had died in December 2007; but he was a whirlwind in the last years of his life as he sought to bring his plans for Bandon Dunes to fruition. An architect and land planner, Howard was also an environmentalist, and his vision of the resort had always been as a community where the genius of the place was expressed and nurtured.

Howard had also trained his replacement, Don Stastny, a Portland-based architect who shared his architectural tastes and environmental concerns. While continuing his practice in Portland, Don had taken over Howard's role as the overseer of the nongolf operations at Bandon Dunes — the buildings, the infrastructure, the landscaping, the system of trails. It fell to Don to show Mike a new trail that had been built near Chrome Lake, leading to a spot where a circular opening was cut in the towering trees.

This was the site proposed for a labyrinth that would be built in Howard's memory. Labyrinths, constructed to provide in microcosm a spiritual journey, had always held a special fascination for Howard. The stones of the labyrinth hadn't yet been installed, but Mike gave his blessing to the site. The labyrinth would be a private place, but for miles in every direction there was public evidence of the legacy Howard had helped create for others on their own journeys.

THE PEEKABOO ROUND at Old Mac took place on a Friday morning. The skies had cleared, and five foursomes gathered at the tee. Jim Urbina, bad knee and all, cranked out the first drive, and Mike hit the second. He probably hadn't taken a practice swing in ten years, and he didn't take one now; he just stepped right up and piped the ball down the middle.

The Peekaboo was played over 10 holes. They were all grassed, of course, but the fairways and greens were still a bit tender and shaggy. No holes were cut in the greens; the flags were just spiked in. Not all the regular tees were open, and the rough was crisscrossed with tire tracks and the ruts left by heavy machines.

Nevertheless, this unveiling left no doubt as to the character of Old Mac. First, the greens are vast. The Short hole has a green of twenty thousand square feet, and the Biarritz green is even larger. Second, Mike wasn't kidding when he said, "We like width." Some fairways are more than a hundred yards wide, reminiscent of the great, sweeping, crumpled fairways of St. Andrews.

A refrain starts running through your mind: *Elysian Fields, Elysian Fields, Elysian Fields.* Third, Mike got the boldness he wanted. The cross-bunker on the Long hole is the Old Mac version of the Hell Bunker, but it is made of railroad ties and projects up into the air. To anxious golfers wondering whether they can carry the bunker, those ties look like the teeth of a giant shark that wants to devour your ball, and you along with it. Fourth, the course is nothing like its neighbor, Pacific Dunes, though built by the same folks. The scale, the greens, the bunkering — everything is different, so different that the two courses hardly seem to have a family resemblance. With its holes framed by shore pines, craggy sandhills, dense thickets of gorse, and the immensity of the ocean, Pacific Dunes is a shimmering, dazzling beauty. In terms of eye candy, Old Mac can't compete.

This is not to say that Old Mac lacks visual appeal. What commands attention at Old Mac is not the scenery but the golf itself. The features of the course are arresting, to say the least. A half-acre green with a trough running through it? A tee shot over a tsunami of sand? A green perched on an ocean ridge so that, in the wind, it's like trying to land a ball on a magic carpet as it sails by? Even the well-traveled players in my group at the Peekaboo smiled and shook their heads as they tried to wrap their minds around the golf shots that Old Macdonald required.

The course was by turns sly, imposing, dainty, mischievous, and outrageous, but the common denominator was that every hole tempted you to play a more difficult shot than you were comfortable playing.

The punch line on Old Macdonald: the golf course is serious fun.

TOM SPENT A GOOD CHUNK of the morning doing an interview with a camera crew from a golf magazine, but he showed up behind the 5th green to watch the groups play through. The grass was still thin and the greens weren't rolling fast, but he took careful note of where the approach shots landed and how players managed their putts. Months of deliberation and fine-tuning had gone into the shaping of the massive green in an effort to tie together the planes and contours, and if the early returns from the

Peekaboo were reliable, the effort had been a success. For the golfer who hit a precise approach, this par 3 played as a birdie hole; but the golfer who left himself a long putt had his work cut out to avoid a bogey. In fact, the cross-country putts were so tempting that many players, after finishing the hole, walked to the far corners of the green and putted toward the flag just to watch the ball ride the undulations.

When Tom is focused on a problem, he wears the architect's version of a game face, and he can stare right past someone who asks a question. On this day, though he was still working, he was relaxed and communicative. The problems at the 1st hole and the 17th had been resolved. As promised, he'd slept on the decision about the burn, but after another hard look, he just didn't think that it belonged there. "It had to start from nowhere," he said, "and then it would dump into a ravine that was much lower, and there was no way a shallow burn would end like that. Plus, I've tried to build a burn on three different courses, and it was never a satisfactory solution. I got rid of the big hill on the left side of the 17th fairway and replaced the burn with a nest of bunkers. I guess that's all I got to yesterday."

The burn was history.

And there was one more casualty. After his first loop at Old Mac, Mike played a second round with his buddies. A $2 wager was on the line. Mike and Larry were bearing down hard, but they wrangled back and forth about Larry's plans for a different, smaller clubhouse. Sometime over the last two days, Mike had come to a decision about the $4.5 million clubhouse: no, not now, not in this economic climate. Not easily discouraged, Larry had sketched out a more modest building that he claimed could be built for only $250,000. "You can't set up a double-wide trailer for less than that," he said, "not after you've poured a slab and run the plumbing. But I know you — you just like double-wides."

"I do like double-wides," Mike said. "I miss that old clubhouse at Pacific. It served the purpose."

"This would serve the purpose, but serve it better. There was nothing to eat at Pacific."

"There was a grill."

"Yeah, but nothing on the menu. Burgers, that was it. You can do better than that. Why not tacos? You order tacos for lunch every day."

"So, a taco stand for $250,000. I get a decent lunch and you've cut the budget by 95 percent. We're moving in the right direction."

21 | Granddaddy Throwback

The impression of the true old game of golf is indescribable. It was like the dawn or the twilight of a brilliant day. It can only be felt. The charm, the fascination of it all, cannot be conveyed in words. Would that I could hand on unimpaired the great game as it was my good fortune to know it! — CHARLES BLAIR MACDONALD

OUT OF THE BLUE, George Bahto got a phone call from someone who wanted to congratulate him on his book, *The Evangelist of Golf: The Story of Charles Blair Macdonald*. The caller identified himself as Mike Keiser, but the name didn't really register. He told George that he was particularly fascinated by the story of the Lido, the Macdonald course that had once been hailed as the equal of National Golf Links but had fallen on hard times in the 1930s and simply vanished. Did George think it would be possible to re-create the Lido? George was on high alert now, and he said, Yes, he thought so. Could he do it himself? It so happened that Mike had a piece of land in Oregon, and he'd been wondering what to do with it. He'd like to see if the property might be suitable for the Lido. Could George come out and take a look at it?

Resurrect the Lido? As far as George was concerned, the Lido was one of the lost wonders of the world, and the idea that he would have a hand in bringing it back to life . . . He was jubilant, shocked, dumbfounded. By the time the conversation ended, he was packing his bags and his life had changed.

Or changed yet again. The first change had also come about unexpectedly when the clubhouse at his home course, Knoll Country Club in New Jersey, burned to the ground. George wasn't a golf historian, but he volunteered to do some research to help with the plans to rebuild the clubhouse. In terms of education, he hadn't gone past high school and had never really been much of student, but how hard could it be to investigate the history of a golf club? He didn't know a thing about Charles Banks, the designer of the course, but soon discovered that "Steamshovel" Banks had been lured into golf course construction by Seth Raynor, who in turn had been drawn into the profession by C. B. Macdonald. And the more he studied, the more George realized that with Macdonald he was dealing with the prime mover, the man who set the wheels in motion. Macdonald had written his own book, but the book was like the man himself, an odd mixture of self-aggrandizement, name-dropping, lyricism, sentimentality, contentiousness, soul-searching, and brilliance.

And so George decided to write a book that would, among other things, restore Macdonald to his rightful place in the pantheon of American golf. Macdonald's reputation had lagged behind while other architects of America's classic era, like Donald Ross, A. W. Tillinghast, and Alister Mackenzie, were rediscovered and lionized. The explanation was simple enough: Macdonald built fewer courses than the others, and his courses, unlike theirs, didn't regularly host high-profile tournaments. In George's mind, this was a historical injustice, since Macdonald was the pioneer who'd cleared the way for the others. And Macdonald had been more than an architect: he'd played a key role in setting American golf on a course that would keep it true to the Scottish origins of the royal and ancient game.

There was a social irony in George Bahto's ambition. Macdonald was an overbearing blue blood and a charter member of America's ruling establishment; born to wealth and privilege, he had learned the game as a student at St. Andrews. George had never been to Scotland. He ran the family dry cleaning business, and he was the opposite of overbearing, a man who wore his heart on his sleeve and never missed an opportunity to mention his daughters and grandchildren. In the normal scheme of things, it would be hard to find any connection at all between the two men . . . but golf arranges some unusual pairings. George Bahto made himself Macdonald's spokesman and advocate. He even began, as any reader of the book quickly realizes, to think of Macdonald as a friend. He takes his side in disputes and sees things through his eyes. Fondly, he calls him "Charlie."

THE EVANGELIST OF GOLF is not the kind of biography that chronicles the life and times of its subject, though it does follow Charlie's tumultuous dealings with other golfers and golf associations. Most of its pages, however, are devoted to a meticulous account of the ideas and methods that C. B. Macdonald used to design and build his courses. For Mike, who was already an admirer of Macdonald's and ranked National Golf Links as one of his favorite courses, the book had touched exactly the right nerve. As a bred-in-the-bone entrepreneur, Mike always thought in the future tense. He was always on the lookout for new ideas.

For years, he'd been wondering about the fourth course at Bandon. He knew the valley behind Pacific Dunes provided a wonderful site, and he'd talked to several people about building a course there. Some young designers had lobbied for the opportunity, hoping that Bandon Dunes could be their breakthrough, just as it had been for Tom Doak and David Kidd. Much as Mike admired the talents of these young architects, he found that he was waiting for something different, something big and daring and exciting.

When he read about the Lido, he thought he might have found it. Of course, Mike already knew the story of the Lido, the most famous of America's lost courses. What he'd learned from the book, and his conversation with George, was that there might be enough information to rebuild it in all its vanished glory. What could be more exciting that the reconstruction of a lost treasure?

Over the next few months, Mike regularly asked his golfing companions what they thought of the idea. He was conducting his own consumer survey, and his tone was neutral and conversational. He didn't let on that he'd already taken the first steps by inviting George Bahto to Oregon, where George had produced a routing for a new Lido. To his surprise, most people weren't as fired up as he was. Wouldn't the Lido be just a novelty or curiosity? Why should they care about it? Wouldn't it be a replica? There were plenty of replica courses, but the best of them were generally regarded as novelties and the worst were plain cheesy. (It's one thing to play the 1st hole at St. Andrews in the shadow of the Royal and Ancient clubhouse, with the wind from the North Sea stinging your cheeks; it's quite another to play a replica hole set in a landscape of loblolly pines and to go tooling over the Swilcan Burn in an air-conditioned golf cart.) As replicas go, the Lido would be in a special category, since there was no longer an original to which a new golf course could be compared. Nevertheless, it would be a replica, and a copy is a copy is a copy.

"The responses I got to the Lido idea," Mike said, "convinced me that, at best, we'd get a ho-hum reaction to the course. Oh, that's interesting, or that's neat. But that wasn't the reaction I was looking for. I wanted people to be excited about a fourth course."

Mike ran the idea past Tom Doak. Though Pacific Dunes was finished, they were partners in another project — Barnbougle Dunes, in Tasmania. Tom had steered Mike toward the project with a kind of challenge; when the two of them were standing on the site of the 13th green at Pacific, Mike had declared, "This has to be one of the best sites in the world for a golf course."

Tom replied, "I've seen one that's just as good."

Before long, Mike had a made a trip to Tasmania, fallen in love with the site, invested in the project, and advised the developers of Barnbougle to go ahead and let Tom do whatever he wanted. They did, and the course Tom built is now ranked as the No. 1 resort course in Australia.

Tom wasn't keen on the Lido idea, but he had a different take. "I told [Mike] I loved the idea of building a real replica of that course, but if it didn't fit the site he had, I wouldn't do it. Plus, I didn't really believe George or anyone else had good enough information on the Lido to build it just like it had been."

Tom and Mike kept talking about it, though, and the idea started to morph. What about a course that re-created some of Macdonald's best holes — not fastidiously detailed replicas of those holes, but contemporary versions that employed the design concepts and principles that Macdonald had articulated so fiercely and used throughout his career? This was a looser concept, but it was actually much riskier and more demanding. To build a course that captured the strategies and genius of a pioneering designer — and to make it work as a contemporary course — took some nerve. Indeed, as Tom pointed out, it took the kind of nerve that Macdonald himself had shown when he built the National. CBM, as Tom calls him, had decided that he didn't have to build slavishly exact duplicates of the most revered holes in Great Britain. To make them work on a different site, those celebrated holes would have to be adapted.

So now they were talking about doing what Macdonald had done at National and building some of the iconic Macdonald holes — a Redan, an Alps, an Eden — at Bandon. The new concept was to do a tribute course, and it wasn't so far removed from what Mike had done in his first course, the Dunes Club, which is a tribute to Pine Valley. "Essentially," Mike said, "Tom stole the idea and made it his. He was interested in doing the Macdonald course, and I wanted him to do it, but not by himself." There was already a Doak course at Bandon Dunes, and he didn't want Old Mac to be regarded as a second Doak course. This wasn't an issue with Tom. "What I suggested to Mike originally was that he should bill it as a Macdonald design built by Jim and myself. Not codesigned, but built, which I still think of as a noble title — I generally talk about how many courses we have built, not how many I have designed. I understood Mike's desire not to hire me to do a second course at the resort; we never had to talk about that."

Mike preferred the "codesigner" billing for Tom and Jim, and he had a last condition. To give the course credibility and to make a clear distinction between it and the others at the resort, Mike wanted a panel of consultants to be involved. "What I imagined," Mike said, "was that Tom would be the CEO of the project and Jim would be the COO, with the panelists functioning as members of the board."

Tom agreed, and he and Mike came up with a group of panelists who were uniquely qualified. George Bahto knew more about Macdonald than anyone on the planet. Brad Klein had for years written with authority about classical courses and architects. Karl Olson, whom Tom suggested, had been the super at National Golf Links for almost two decades, guiding the effort to restore the course to the dimensions and playing conditions that Macdonald had intended.

By the late summer of 2006, the team was in place. Their first meeting would take place on Long Island that fall, where they would walk National Golf Links to soak up the spirit of Charles Blair Macdonald.

CHARLES BLAIR MACDONALD was not only present at the creation of American golf but was a leading actor in the story. In 1892, he laid out the first golf course outside Chicago (also one of the first in the country) and personally supplied the clubs and balls for those who wanted to have a go. In 1895, he won the first Amateur Championship sanctioned by the United States Golf Association. One year earlier, he had been runner-up in a tournament billed as the first national championship, but he was such a sore loser and howled so loudly about what he perceived as an unfair ruling that the result of the tournament was declared null and void. When the tournament was replayed a month later, he again finished as runner-up and launched into another tirade, this time protesting that the host club, Saint Andrew's in Yonkers, New York, lacked the authority to conduct a national championship. Macdonald made such a stink that representatives from leading clubs got together to form a governing body that would soon go by the name of the United States Golf Association. Macdonald, of course, was present at the first meetings of the USGA, becoming one of its founders and officers.

Charlie was a piece of work. Having attended college at St. Andrews in Scotland, where he played matches with young Tom Morris and other greats, he behaved as if he were the supreme authority on all matters pertaining to golf — its rules, competitions, and traditions. He was a crusader for golf, and when he spoke of the "best interests of the game," he had no doubt that he, above all others, knew precisely what those best interests were. If there was a single theme that ran strongly through all his efforts to promote and advance the cause of golf, it was that the American version of the game had to remain faithful to the Scottish model.

Today, it seems self-evident that this was the wise choice, but in Macdonald's day, there were vocal advocates for an American version of the game. They saw no reason to adhere to the rules and practices that prevailed in Scotland, and Macdonald made it his "battle" to "keep the game clean in America and prevent it from being controlled by a mob." At one contentious USGA meeting, he gave a speech with these rousing words: "To my mind, for the United States Golf Association to break away from St. Andrews would be as great a calamity as schism from any great church. We have played the game of golf for some twenty years, and if I may be permitted to state this without offense, I do not think the golfers in this country are imbued with the highest spirit of the game as yet."

It was with the same lofty sense of purpose that he decided to undertake the building of a "classical golf course in America, one which would eventually compare favorably with the championship links abroad and serve as an incentive to the elevation of the game in America." Macdonald could already lay claim to building the first 18-hole course in the country, but he envisioned a course that would surpass Chicago Golf Club and perhaps even the classic links of Scotland.

The concept for his course had taken shape in 1901 when he read an article in Britain's *Golf Illustrated* that posed the question: "Which Are the Most Difficult Holes in the World?" The writer was Horace Hutchinson, two-time winner of the British Amateur, and he invited other experts to respond to his query by identifying and describing the "best and most difficult" one-shot, two-shot, and three-shot holes (in present terms, these would be par 3s, par 4s, and par 5s, but the concept of "par" hadn't yet been established).

Macdonald was fascinated by the discussion that filled the pages of the magazine for several weeks. There seemed to be agreement among the top players about the holes that belonged on the list, and many were selected from St. Andrews — the Road hole, the Eden, the Long hole. The Redan at

North Berwick and the Alps at Prestwick were also deemed to be exemplary. If these great holes could be so readily identified, Macdonald reasoned, why couldn't they serve as the basis for an ideal course? Why not build an American course made of golf holes modeled after those that embodied the spirit and genius of the links? And while he was at it, why not build a course that consisted of 18 ideal holes?

Macdonald had no doubt that it could be done, and, by Jove, he was just the man for the job. He went abroad in 1902, and again in 1906, to gather material, making sketches and acquiring survey maps of famous holes. Not surprisingly, his plan for an ideal course stirred up controversy and indignation. To some Britons, who regarded the game as their invention and their rightful property, the concept wasn't just ambitious but absurd. It made no difference to them that Macdonald was paying homage to their courses by basing his ideal holes on British models; the very thought that these holes could be transported to the United States seemed blasphemous. Macdonald even had the gall to suggest that in the process of relocating these great holes, he could actually improve them by getting rid of their "blemishes." And to compound the insult, Macdonald had to note that "although they had eighteen holes on each course, there were never more than four or five holes that a player who was devoted to the game in its best expression might regard as a shrine to which he might kneel." The remainder of the holes, in other words, were ordinary — and on Macdonald's ideal course, there would be no such thing as an ordinary hole.

Nothing about the endeavor was modest, including this later claim: "I believe this was the first effort at establishing golfing architecture." Macdonald was putting himself way out there, but give the man his due: he made good on his promises. As he studied the classic holes, he was able to make a distinction between the defining topographical features and the underlying strategy of the hole. He realized that the Alps, for instance, wasn't a great hole because it had a towering sandhill. What mattered was not the sandhill itself but where it stood and how it affected a golfer's strategy as he played the hole. To build the National, he wouldn't need a sandhill identical to the one at Prestwick, or the exact topography of the other holes he planned to build. He would need only a site that enabled him to present a similar set of strategic challenges.

Underlying his approach was another radical idea — namely, that golf holes could be "built." The classic links were regarded as having been shaped by the hand of God, not the hand of man. Of course, some bunkers, like the Road hole bunker, had been worked and reworked, but the links themselves had been sculpted over the centuries by natural forces of wind and tides, not to mention the scrapings and leavings of sheep. When the earliest Scottish "designers," like Old Tom Morris, were asked to lay out a new course, that's what they did — they laid it out. Since it was virtually impossible to change the existing contours of the land, they sought to employ the features of the terrain to best advantage, but they were discovering golf holes, not building them.

Macdonald acknowledged the vital importance of the site and its soils in determining the character of a golf course. He would always rail against "artificiality" on golf courses, insisting that the designs of nature were superior to man-made features. Nevertheless, he was ready to lend Nature a helping hand and to build golf holes, and he was quite prepared to "adapt" features of great holes to his own designs. When he made his own sketches of holes to emulate, he didn't try to record their every detail but rather "the outstanding features which I thought made the hole interesting, and which might be adapted to a hole of different length." Some of the holes might become "composite" holes, and they might be built, but they would be as natural as possible in appearance — and they would all incorporate classic, time-honored strategies.

At the National, Macdonald adapted, combined, rearranged, and sometimes invented features to suit his purpose of building an ideal links. The construction of the course began in 1907, and it was ready for limited play by 1910 (Old Macdonald would open exactly one hundred years later, a nice symmetry). Because of Macdonald's prominence and the long roll-out, the National attracted a great deal of publicity throughout its planning and development and even more when it opened officially. Above all, Macdonald wanted the approval of leading figures in British golf, and he got it from people like Horace Hutchinson and Bernard Darwin. The eloquent Darwin, writing in the London *Times,* went into raptures about the course:

> How good a course it is I hardly dare trust myself to say on a short acquain-
> tance; there is too much to learn about it and the temptation to frantic enthu-
> siasm is so great, but this much I can say: Those who think it is the greatest golf
> course in the world may be right or wrong, but are certainly not to be accused
> of any intemperance of judgment.

National Golf Links was Macdonald's pride and joy. He built a few other courses, but he never accepted a fee and never really attempted to fashion a career as a golf architect. He took commissions that were of special interest — like the Lido — but he passed along most opportunities to his protégé, Seth Raynor, a surveyor who'd helped during the building of the National. Not a golfer himself, Raynor was a skilled and shrewd engineer, and he stuck with Macdonald's program, employing the same strategies and the same model holes. At course after course, Raynor built a Redan, an Eden, a Biarritz, a Double Plateau. Each of the Raynor versions of these holes was different, and they were all a little softer around the edges than Macdonald's versions. The courses themselves were different, too, but as Tom Doak points out, Raynor's success pretty much showed how well Macdonald's program worked. Today, two of his finest courses, Fishers Island (built with Charles Banks) and the revised Chicago Golf Club (built with CBM looking over his shoulder), are ranked as high as the National.

IT'S IMPOSSIBLE NOT to notice the parallels between the careers of C. B. Macdonald and Tom Doak. Like Macdonald, Tom spent a big chunk of time at St. Andrews (though as a caddy, not a student), and the experience shaped his perception of golf. While there as a caddy and in subsequent visits, he made an extensive study of the classic courses of Great Britain (though not with the objective of using specific holes as models). Before setting up practice as an architect, he ruffled many feathers by writing critically about

American golf course design, charging that it suffered by ignoring the lessons to be learned from the classics. The way to build good, sound courses, Tom declared, was to look to the classic courses for guidance and inspiration. Though he never went so far as to announce that he wished to elevate the standard of American golf by building an ideal golf course, he did name his firm Renaissance Golf Design and took a strong stance with a brief mission statement: *Dedicated to the rebirth of great golf architecture.*

Many established architects took umbrage at Tom's criticism, but there were others, particularly Pete Dye and Ben Crenshaw, who shared and encouraged his point of view. But unlike Macdonald, who called on friends and reached into his own pocket to pay for his courses, Tom also found owners — like Mike Keiser — who believed in his philosophy and his talent. At Pacific Dunes, Tom felt that Mike had given him a once-in-a-lifetime opportunity. In addition to having a marvelous seaside site, Mike wanted a course that was based on classic principles of design, recast in a contemporary context.

At Old Macdonald, the same classic principles would apply, and a tribute course would obviously have to include many of the holes that Macdonald used so repeatedly. With Mike's encouragement, Tom took the concept a step farther, venturing even more deeply into the past; he went back to the source to revisit the holes that had inspired Macdonald. Traveling with George Bahto, who had never been to Scotland, he went to Prestwick, North Berwick, Leven, Scotscraig, and St. Andrews, where the two of them spent several days. Tom wasn't trying to "channel" Macdonald (the word is too hokey and New Age for his taste), but he didn't want to work only from Macdonald's versions of classic holes. He wanted fresh impressions of the originals.

When he built the first course at Bandon Dunes, Mike Keiser often described his wish to build a "throwback" course. Now it was clear that Old Macdonald, with roots reaching back through National Golf Links to the courses that had inspired CBM himself, was going to be something like a throwback squared. And if CBM was a throwback in his day, and Tom Doak was a contemporary throwback . . . Old Mac was shaping up as the granddaddy of all throwbacks.

22 | Plans in the Dirt, the Dew, and the Sky

Why don't we put the green up here?

— MIKE KEISER

WHEN THE ENTIRE DESIGN TEAM for Old Macdonald gathered for the first time in late October 2006, the meeting had the air of a reunion. The codesigners and the three members of the advisory panel all had lengthy relationships with Mike, and in many cases with each other. Karl Olson, having served so long as superintendent at National Golf Links, had been George Bahto's field guide at the course when George was researching his Macdonald book. Years earlier, when Tom Doak and Jim Urbina were just settling into their design careers, Karl had also initiated them into the mysteries of the National. Brad Klein had known Tom and Jim for years, and he'd recently gotten a long, close look at them when he wrote about the building of Sebonack Golf Club, a course designed in collaboration with Jack Nicklaus.

The meeting took place at Sebonack, literally next door to the National. Also present were the associate designers from Renaissance Golf; whenever possible, Tom included the associates to build a sense of team solidarity and to get different perspectives into the mix. On their first afternoon, the whole group set out after lunch to walk around the National, but they moved so slowly that darkness fell before they covered all 18 holes.

The main impressions, Jim Urbina recalls, were the boldness of the features and the sheer scale of the course — the width of the fairways, the size of the greens, the bulk of the hazards and landforms. Karl Olson was in his familiar role as tour leader, pointing out places where the fairways had narrowed over the years, reducing angles of play and eliminating some strategic options. Similarly, he was able to show the group how some greens had contracted with time. By his reckoning, the average size of the original greens at National had been about twelve thousand square feet — roughly twice the size of the average green on courses used by the PGA Tour. During the walk, and later that evening over dinner at Sebonack, these impressions were distilled into a more specific set of points that Brad Klein wrote up in a memo. He stated several key design considerations:

- Old Macdonald Course should be an attempt to showcase the vision, grandeur, and boldness of CBM's design vision . . . The commitment should be to playing up to the edginess and depth of CBM's vision rather than soft-balling design for the sake of the supposed lower tolerance of resort or public-play golfers . . .
- This is . . . an effort to evoke the (volatile) personality of CBM . . . That means a firm commitment to the spirit of golf as a vigorous outdoor adventure, and to the importance of chance, (mis)fortune, and the outrageous as part of a normal round.
- What's particularly striking about the National is the massive width of the tee shot landing areas, and the fact that with all the undulation of the fairways, CBM often shaped out a dead flat landing area of as little as 400 square feet in the middle of it or on one side.
- The complexity of angles and shapes at the National ensures its endless fascination.
- Interesting greens are paramount.

Brad's memo ended on a stern note, admonishing the group to limit comments and public disclosures to "general statements and agreed-upon plans rather than divulge internal disagreements or individual contributions and ideas." As a writer and editor, and especially in his role as the overseer of

Golfweek's course ratings system, Brad was mindful of the dangers of too much early buzz. The group agreed to put a lid on communication — but the word was already out among the subset of golfers who follow developments in golf course architecture. In their world, this combination of elements — Mike Keiser teaming up with Tom Doak and Jim Urbina to build a tribute to Charles Blair Macdonald at Bandon Dunes — amounted to a perfect storm. There was no stopping the blogs, the chat room posts on Golf Club Atlas, the notices and stories in the golf magazines. Like it or not, Old Mac was going to be the subject of lively discussion and speculation. It was too big a story to keep under wraps.

EVEN BEFORE THE SEBONACK MEETING, Tom had started working on a routing for Old Macdonald. Right away, he came up against the familiar Bandon obstacle — gorse. The prickly stuff was so thick that much of the site was impenetrable and topo maps were unreliable. Nevertheless, the general outlines of his challenge were clear enough. Since he had a securely fixed starting point (the clubhouse site had been established years earlier by Howard McKee as part of a planned residential complex that never got off the drawing board), he knew where Old Mac would begin and end. The first holes and the finishing stretch would occupy a flattish stretch of ground east of Back Ridge, the sandy ridge that is the spine of the Bandon Dunes property. The other holes would lie in the valley west of the ridge. So the first problem he had to solve was how to cross the ridge twice, once going out and once coming home.

As he walked and studied the property, Tom found that he was operating with a different mind-set. Instead of looking at the landforms to see what sort of holes they might suggest, he was actively searching for contours that would lend themselves to holes in the Macdonald repertory. Like Macdonald at National, he was hoping to discover a "natural" Alps, a "natural" Redan, and so on. Before long, he found a "perfect spot" for a Sahara, a hole that calls for a blind shot over an expanse of sand. This Sahara, No. 3 at Old Mac, would confront the golfer with a wall of sand. The tee shot would cross the Back Ridge diagonally, a terrifying poke that had to pass close to a dead cedar, a spiky skeleton that seemed to scrape the sky.

This was a dramatic solution to the problem of the first crossing of the ridge, and it had the extra benefit of giving golfers, as they crested the ridge, a panoramic view of the golf course (and part of Pacific Dunes, too) with the ocean as the background. The next three holes — a long par 4, a par 3, and a par 5 — fell easily into place. After that, though, the routing got sticky. It felt squeezed, even though several holes fit their sites nicely. Tom had identified locations for a Redan, now No. 12, and No. 13, a short par 4 called Leven. He was happy with No. 10 — "the fairway contours and raised green site for No. 10 suggested the Bottle to me as soon as I walked it"— but no one on the design team was completely satisfied with the whole sequence.

Tom was open to suggestions. He'd already penciled in a 7th hole, with the green situated at the foot of the ridge along the ocean. Mike wanted to locate a turnstand up there so that golfers, at this point in the round, could fortify themselves with a full-body view of the Pacific. The seventh hole isn't the traditional spot for a turnstand, but this wasn't going to be a course with two 9-hole loops or an out-and-back course like St. Andrews or National. It was an asymmetrical course. In broad metaphorical terms, it could be likened to a giant Celtic knot, a little loop within a pair of larger loops. This 7th hole, in any case, was one of the places where the course bumped up against the ocean ridge, and Mike wanted golfers to have a look at the ocean.

When he and Tom climbed the ridge to check out the feasibility of a turnstand, Mike asked, "Why don't we put the green up here?"

It was a classic Mike question, seemingly innocent but sharply pointed, and it cut through all kinds of whopping objections, such as how much dirt would have to be moved and how much that would cost. Tom understood that a huge new possibility had just opened up, and it wasn't just a matter of relocating the 7th green. In Tom's mind, where the pieces of the routing were still being arranged, moving the 7th green would have a ripple effect, starting with the 8th tee. The moment he looked down from the ridge, wondering how it would work as an elevated tee, he realized that he could break the logjam. "The one Macdonald hole I was apprehensive about building was the Biarritz . . . I have never been a big fan of how symmetrical that hole is, and the whole time we were working on the routing, I felt like I was trying to fit a square peg into a round hole. That was really the miracle of the change on No. 7 and No. 8 . . . because as soon as Mike and I were up there on No. 7, we picked out a green site for No. 8, and when I went down there it looked perfect for the front half of a Biarritz, with those great natural shoulders to both sides. We were just very lucky there."

In less than a half hour, the two new greens were marked, and the change locked in the next sequence of holes. Moving the Biarritz also cleared the way for another change. Tom had first drawn a Biarritz east of Back Ridge, where, as it turned out, there were wetlands issues. Then Jim had come up with a plan to relocate it west of the ridge, but still near a natural saddle, or defile, which seemed like the obvious place to get golfers across the ridge for the home stretch. With the Biarritz now moved to the interior of the course, the holes around the saddle — the Alps was one of them — could be reconfigured.

But there was a hitch. The land north of the course had been set aside for possible residential use, and it was off limits to golf. Here the economic downturn worked in Old Mac's favor. Mike had never been completely sold on the idea of adding a residential component to the resort, and once it became clear that Old Mac would benefit by expanding northward, he was willing to push back the boundary. Glad to, as a matter of fact, since a new routing for No. 15 put another green on the ocean ridge, affording a last ocean panorama.

The golf gods apparently liked this decision to go north, for — lo and behold! — a timely fire cleared the area of gorse. A similar fire had opened up the site of Pacific Dunes, a coincidence that seemed providential. At any rate, Old Mac now assumed its final shape, with a new No. 15, a whale of a par 5, and a redrawn Alps hole that had plenty of brawn and bravura.

The preliminary scorecard read as follows:

Hole	Par	Name	Yards
1	4	Double Plateau	340
2	3	Eden	190
3	4	Sahara	335
4	4	Hog's Back	510
5	3	Short	160
6	5	Long	590
7	4	Ocean	377
8	3	Biarritz	210
9	4	Cape	415
Out	34		3,127
10	4	Bottle	470
11	4	Road	460
12	3	Redan	210
13	4	Leven	325
14	4	Maiden	370
15	5	Westward Ho!	580
16	4	Alps	465
17	5	Littlestone	595
18	4	Punchbowl	490
In	37		3,965
Total	71		7,092

When Jim first showed me the card, he saw my reaction to the asymmetry. Pacific Dunes is also a par 71, with a pair of wildly different nines. "Yep," he laughed, "we've done it again."

A STORMY WINTER disrupted construction plans. The work was supposed to begin in January 2007, but it got off to a slow start and instead of building the opening and closing holes, the crew began with holes 3, 4, and 5, which lay in the more protected valley. Much of the major shaping was done by members of the Renaissance crew, and the grunt work — the rake-and-shovel work, the endless fine clearing to remove all traces of the infernal gorse — was carried out by a crew of groundskeepers who'd signed on for it. Ken Nice, the superintendent of Old Mac in addition to his duties as director of agronomy for the resort, figured that involving the crew from the get-go would give them a sense of ownership.

Jim and Tom followed their usual pattern, the one that had worked at Pacific Dunes: Tom would fly in at regular intervals, often when Mike and the panelists were on-site, and Jim more or less took up residence in Bandon. He handled the administrative tasks, and he was the on-site overseer of the daily work. As a guy who'd come up through the ranks and knew something about the business end of a rake, he could speak the crew's language. "He joked around with us," says C. J. Keurscher, a crew member who is now the superintendent-designate. "Fun isn't a word I'd put with what we had to do, but Jim tried to make it interesting. He let us make suggestions and try out our ideas when we were edging bunkers or tying in the greens and the sur-rounds." For C. J., the opportunity to influence the final look of the course went a long way toward taking the curse off the toil. He had started out as a golf pro at the resort but then gone over to the "dark side," the dirt side. His experience had opened his eyes to golf design, and he'd volunteered for the Old Mac crew to be in on what he saw as history in the making. "The way Jim ran things, it was way more creative than working in the pro shop."

Tony Russell, the local tap-dancing bulldozer operator who'd shown his flair for shaping at Pacific Dunes, did most of the large-scale earth moving at Old Mac, but he didn't do any of the shaping. Jim and Tom had not revised their opinion of Tony's abilities, but Renaissance was starting to feel the ef-fects of the economic slowdown. Projects that Tom had lined up were being postponed, and his associates needed work. The new design commissions just weren't coming through — so Bruce Hepner climbed up on a bulldozer and carved out the dizzying contours of the 3rd green and its surrounds, with a deep hollow on the left and a nest of gnarly bunkers on the right. Brian

Slawnik seemed to be everywhere, either riding a machine or wielding a rake, and he would end up doing the lion's share of shaping.

But the scarcity of projects and uncertainty about the future took their toll, and the "codesigner" designation seemed to make Jim first among equals. The shared euphoria of Pacific Dunes — the giddy sense that the planets were in alignment — didn't transfer to Old Mac. The members of the Renaissance team had believed they were doing something special at Pacific Dunes, something that, once revealed, would vault them straight to the heights. And they were right. Since 2001, Renaissance Golf had been on an amazing run. They had built high-profile courses from Tasmania to Scotland. Barnbougle Dunes, Cape Kidnappers, St. Andrews Beach, Sebonack, Ballyneal, the Renaissance Club at Archerfield — it almost seemed that you couldn't pick up a golf magazine without a picture of a Renaissance course on the cover.

Now the boom was over, the weather was rotten, and morale had taken a hit. Even so, there was no compromise in the work on Old Macdonald. They weren't starry-eyed kids anymore; they were old hands, tough-minded pros who knew how to build a golf course. When the situation called for it, Bruce Hepner climbed down from the seat of the dozer and put the finishing touches on his work with a rake. Jim Urbina took more than a few rides on a Sand Pro, the machine used for fine grading, and Ken Nice hadn't forgotten how to use a broadcast seed spreader. Pacific Dunes had been the product of collective excitement, but Old Mac was turning out to be the result of discipline and deep-seated professional pride. The work was being executed with an almost fanatical attention to detail.

The evolution of the Hell bunker at No. 6, the biggest and boldest bunker on the course, is a case study in perfectionism and the lengths to which the builders were willing to go. When Tom decided that the bunker should rise above ground level, he also decided to face it with railroad ties, or sleepers. The ties would not only stabilize it but make it make it appear more daunting and fortresslike. When Hell was built with new railroad ties, however, the effect was of new construction, and that didn't seem right on a course like Old Mac. So Ken Nice went out and located some discarded sleepers, already weathered, with moss and lichen clinging to them. It had taken weeks to set the original ties, but they were ripped out and replaced, and the crew worked to place the old sleepers in patterns that have the precision of a cabinetmaker's inlay, finishing the whole with plantings that blend the edges with the turf. The Hell bunker looks as though it's been there forever.

Hole by hole, feature by feature, Old Mac was emerging like a giant that had been slumbering in the earth.

THE PANELISTS VISITED the site every three or four months. Each of them had three holes in which they were especially involved; they had bid for their holes in a process that Brad Klein describes as a "sort of NFL draft." One of the holes he'd selected was No. 3, Sahara, and he'd had the thrill of playing dirt golf at the tee site, hitting some of the first drives over the wall of sand, up toward the ghost tree.

But the real thrill for Brad was taking part in what he considered a high-level seminar in golf architecture: "It was like a group of Nobel physicists getting together to focus on a problem." The analogy came readily for Brad, who left a promising career in academia, specializing in national security matters, to write about golf. He just couldn't get golf out of his system. He caddied for a few Tour players and did some freelancing while working toward a professorial appointment. The turning point came when he had to decide between an academic conference and the Masters. Though he talked it over with his wife, it was really no contest — he went to Augusta and never looked back. As the architecture editor of *Golfweek,* he'd played an important role in sparking a renewal of interest in classic architecture. His book *Discovering Donald Ross* was the definitive work on the most prolific golf designer of the Golden Age. *Rough Meditations,* a collection of his essays, showed him as one of the most engaging and incisive writers on the game.

Though Brad often describes himself as "jaded," he'd always been an enthusiastic admirer of Bandon Dunes. The first time he visited the place, he knew that he was looking at something remarkable, and *Golfweek*'s rating of the first course at the resort, a few weeks before it officially opened, helped to establish Bandon Dunes as a must-play destination. It was also the beginning of Brad's relationship with Mike Keiser, and a few years later, in 2006, Brad was back in Bandon for the annual gathering of raters. He'd had an unusual premonition: "I just had a feeling that I was going to be involved with Mike on a project," he admits, somewhat sheepishly for a man with such a sharply analytical bent. After Brad's presentation to the raters, Mike took the podium — and announced that he wanted Brad to play a role in Old Macdonald. The jaded critic admits that he had a lump in his throat.

The conversations, or seminars, between the panelists, the codesigners, and Mike were free-flowing. Sometimes they took place at the site of a green or bunker, but since the Renaissance way was to design in the field, there weren't always plans or drawings to mark up. Once, Jim Urbina recalls, he sketched in the dew on the panel of a truck. And Jim did try to give a loose structure to the discussion, one that was true to Macdonald's method: "When we discussed each hole," he said, "we'd list all the features that we thought were important to the strategy and go from there, deciding which ones we wanted to keep, which ones to change, which ones to emphasize."

The discussions weren't always conclusive, as Brad noted in an article he wrote for *Golfweek*, "The Bandon Charrette" (the term refers to a meeting at which design plans are reviewed and refined). The group was looking at the site of the 5th green when Jim drew a diagram in the dirt.

> There began a discussion that an architecture junkie lives for, 45 minutes worth, of the 11th hole at St. Andrews, the sixth at National Golf Links and the third at Yeamans Hall. It was detailed talk, about the depth of the little depression and the falloff at the rear, as well as the way in which the green would look big but play like a series of small targets if properly tied together. We sat there, variously drawing with sticks and fingers and boots. Satisfied that we had made some progress, Urbina, with a single sweep of his foot, erased a graduate seminar's worth of work and simply said, "Next hole."

That "charrette" took place in April 2007, and not all the work was erased. One of the group's tasks was to mark the site of tees and greens with white PVC pipe. "When we got to the site of the mid-length, par-3 Redan," Brad wrote, "we all turned to Bahto to establish the marker. As he did, someone noticed a tear on Bahto's face and observed how apt the emotion was. 'Something got in my eye,' Bahto said, gruffly dismissing any emotionalism . . . Next hole."

Old Mac had a knack for stirring up sentiments.

MEANWHILE, THE OCEAN RIDGE was being sculpted to make a place for the green at No. 7, the oceanside green, Mike's green in the sky. Though its contours make it appear wind-shaped, this is yet another place where the skill of the Renaissance crew came into play. Macdonald had always insisted on making the features of a golf course appear as natural as possible: "The human mind," he wrote, "could not devise undulations superior to those of nature." Tom Doak shared this conviction, and he and his crew had worked hard to learn how to mimic natural contours and features.

What's especially notable about the green (though I didn't see it until Tom pointed it out) is that it is actually a huge rectangle draped on the ridge, set at an angle to the line of play. Many Macdonald greens have geometric shapes that, in some cases, seem to run counter to his preference for natural forms. Nature simply doesn't produce many right angles or neat ovals. But Tom was crafty enough to produce geometric shapes that didn't call attention to themselves. "Our focus was on the construction details. I reckoned that Jim and my crew are a much more experienced and polished construction team than Macdonald ever had, and that we should not give up everything we have learned about natural-looking construction over the past one hundred years . . . Many of the greens at Old Mac are geometric, but instead of reinforcing the square corners we tried very hard to blur the edges and lines so that you don't notice it too much. Most of them are big, blocky greens where you have a hard time finding the corners."

Every time Mike goes up to that 7th green and feels the wind coming off the ocean, he drinks in the view. He mentions, with satisfaction, that the approach to this elevated green might be the most difficult on the whole course. "I got just what I wanted," he says. "I got this green up into the air."

23 | The Power Spots

*Courses that are shaped by the land, with features created by hand,
letting each golfer play his own game — this is what golf used to be, and
what it's going to be again. This is the future of golf course design,
right here.* —Ian Andrew, golf course architect

THE SCENE IN THE BAR of the Lodge at Bandon Dunes was something
else. Instead of the usual crowd of golfers savoring their drinks and exam-
ining scorecards in a glow of post-round contentment, the bar was filled
with people who didn't look much like golfers. Most of them were young,
sporting beards or stubble, wearing scruffy jeans and talking fast. Ions of
crazy energy were popping all over the place. Holding court at the bar, a
good-looking guy with a gravelly voice was knocking back Guinness and
building brilliant word castles in an Irish — or was it Scottish? — accent.
A fellow in a white turban drifted through the room wearing a sphinxlike
smile. Every now and then, a tall, elegant woman appeared and surveyed
the room, wary as a heron. The dude in the red plaid blazer had a rabbit's
foot in his lapel, a big, furry rabbit's foot that looked as if it had belonged to
a rabbit until just a few moments earlier. A short, intense woman wearing
a wool cap and carrying a clipboard darted in and out; the words MIDGET
SMOOT were written on the front of her hoodie. Surveying it all from his
table in the corner, obviously relishing the whole scene, an older man with
his eyes full of happy mischief made occasional remarks. He said, "Another
day, another dharma."

The older man was Michael Murphy, author of *Golf in the Kingdom,* and he had come to Bandon to see how his classic book would be made into a movie.

The bar scene, admittedly, is a composite, but in late April 2009, the cast and crew of the film had pretty much taken over the resort, filling it with their own high-octane buzz. The guy knocking back the Guinness was Irish-born actor David O'Hara, who played the wild Irishman in *Braveheart* and a thug in *The Departed*. He was cast as Shivas Irons, the charismatic hero of the novel. And one of the young chaps, the one in the patchwork golf cap, was Mason Gamble, the actor who played Dennis the Menace; in *Golf in the Kingdom,* he would play the role of the young Michael Murphy. The tall, wary woman was director Susan Streitfeld, who collaborated with Murphy on the screenplay; the man in the turban was cinematographer Arturo Smith; and the Chief Smurf, the dynamo with the clipboard, was producer Mindy Affrime.

Among golf books, *Golf in the Kingdom* is surely the most revered. It has sunk its hooks into the golfing souls of its readers, and they tend to be people who read the book not once but over and over again, seeking to plumb its mystical, metaphysical depths. The novel is a celebration of golf— its joys and frustrations, its addictive appeal, its mysteries, its sharp glints of insight and fascination. Since its publication in 1972, *Golf in the Kingdom* has been translated into nineteen languages and sold over a million copies. It is the cosmic opposite of those best-selling golf books that deal with mechanics of the swing, promising to improve one's game. "Gowf is a way o' makin' a man naked," says Shivas Irons. That's not your usual swing thought.

The action of the novel is simple. The young Michael Murphy, a seeker after truth who is on his way to an Indian ashram, has an unexpectedly free day in Scotland when his flight is delayed. He decides to play a round at Burningbush, a legendary links. There he meets Shivas Irons, a golfing genius who has learned to use the game as his vehicle for understanding "true gravity," a phrase that translates loosely to the force that governs all being.

Not the usual stuff of which a movie is made, but Clint Eastwood held the film rights for years, and Sean Connery was reportedly eager to play Shivas

Irons. Their project never came to fruition, and when the rights reverted to Murphy, he teamed up with Streitfeld and Affrime to make a movie that would have the rich, haunting flavor of the book.

The setting would be crucial. The place had to have the right look and feel, the right karma. They weren't interested in filming great golf shots but in capturing, as the book does, the timeless magic of the game and the way it can transform an understanding of life. The images in the movie would have to evoke the awe and transcendence that golf can inspire.

As early as 2005, they began making trips to Bandon. They had a key ally, Howard McKee, whose relationship with Murphy dated back more than two decades. Howard wanted the movie to be shot at Bandon, and the filmmakers were more and more convinced that Bandon was the right place. Not only did the golf courses have the appearance of classic links, but the surrounding landscape, with the rolling surf of the Pacific, the high bluffs, and the fantastic shapes of the sea stacks, provided locations for nongolf scenes. The script called for a tavern scene, and that setting — since dharma was now in play — was ready and waiting. The scene could be shot only in McKee's Pub, the resort's cozy watering hole that was named after Howard.

Mike Keiser, however, didn't take immediately to the idea of the movie. Though he had always loved the book (his first golf investments were drawn on an account he named "Chivas Irons"), he feared that the filming could disrupt operations at the resort. In 2005 and 2006, the place was bursting at the seams. Where would the cast and crew stay? It wasn't until 2008, after Howard's death, that Mike gave his thumbs-up. With the economic slowdown, the resort could accommodate the movie crew in the new staff housing. Which, as it happened, was another of Howard's legacies.

These many ties and connections would have tickled Howard, who once gave a talk on serendipity to the Bandon Dunes staff. And, really, as filming started, the number of coincidences got to be ridiculous. It was almost a standing joke that "true gravity" had taken over. Even the notoriously changeable April weather in Oregon seemed to cooperate, and the most hard-core rationalist would have been shaken by the confluence of events.

For instance, Grant Rogers — the Bandon Dunes golf instructor who is often compared to Shivas Irons — used to play golf with Michael Murphy in California. When Murphy came to Bandon to scout locations, Grant was his guide. And when David O'Hara needed to get his swing ready for the camera, he went to Grant for lessons. Shivas Irons, meet Shivas Irons.

But the most powerful evidence of "true gravity" was captured on film. In one of the movie's pivotal moments, Mason Gamble and David O'Hara — Michael Murphy and Shivas Irons — are standing near a cliff's edge. Michael has been playing poorly and he is sulky and frustrated. Shivas says to him, "Ye think too much, Michael. Ye must let the nothingness into your shots."

At that precise moment, a flock of gulls rises from beneath the cliff and wings its way into the sky. A viewer can't help but feel the electricity running along his spine; it seems as though Michael's thoughts have suddenly taken flight. "That was an amazing moment," Gamble said, "and it just happened. We could have paid a bird wrangler thousands of dollars, and it wouldn't have come off like that. That moment was perfect." Reflecting for a moment, he added, "I don't know who's making this movie, but we're not. Something else is making this movie."

The excitement of the cast and crew, of course, was not an assurance that the movie would have the same magic as the book. Yet it seemed inevitable — yes, predestined — that this movie should be filmed at Bandon Dunes, and that the karma of the place should influence the shooting of the movie, and vice versa. The two would be linked forever on the silver screen, and the symbolism was hard to miss. The Kingdom had come to Bandon! The place was already known for its power to inspire, and now golfers everywhere will be able to see Bandon for themselves, at least on DVD. They might well be lifted to a "higher manifesting plane" when they see the shots of Shivas and Michael walking along over the crest of a fairway, their figures silhouetted against the horizon, looking as though they are leaving this earth and taking their golf game to heaven.

IN LATE APRIL 2009, Jim Urbina was at Bandon Dunes to oversee the last stages of the construction of Old Macdonald. The 10 holes that made up the Peekaboo round were now open to resort guests for preview loops, and the other 8 holes were in various stages of completion. No. 17, the long par 5 that had been the subject of so much discussion in November, was fully shaped and fine-tuned, its alternate fairways divided by a nest of bunkers and its green defended by yet another bold bunker faced with railroad ties.

On a cool spring morning, Jim and Ken Nice were watching the crew shoot the hydroseed onto the green and the green surrounds. Most of the 595-yard hole looked unnaturally smooth and shaven, like a giant patient being prepared for surgery. Where the hydroseed was being applied, the soil was a weird aquamarine color, a chemical color like a sterilizing disinfectant. This color would vanish in a couple of days, but it had the immediate benefit of showing exactly where the seed had been applied. The crew of a dozen moved slowly and carefully across the just-raked green, the heavy hose — the size of a fire hose — hoisted onto their shoulders. They didn't want that hose dragging across the soil, and they were trying not to leave any footprints.

Just off the green, Jim inspected the native plants, huckleberry and knickaknick, that had been tucked into the soil. "I want rough with soul," he said to Ken. "You've got to give the rough some character." These plants really wouldn't come into play for a golfer. For that matter, most of the rough at Old Macdonald was safely removed from the places where a golf ball would end up. But Jim kept going on about "rough with soul" as a way of providing texture and a touch of wildness to a course that was otherwise going to present an unbroken surface of fescue.

There was an obvious sense of camraderie between Jim and Ken. Their relationship had begun back in 2000 when Ken was at Pacific Dunes, overseeing the grow-in for that course; he later moved to Bandon Trails, moving up to become the chief superintendent of the whole resort in 2008. A tall, thoughtful man who played college basketball, Ken had always been a recreational golfer. The courses he grew up playing, though, were nothing like the courses that really sparked his imagination — the courses he saw on television when he watched the British Open. He couldn't explain why, but he loved those shaggy, rumpled, seaside courses. Watching the crazy rolls and bounces of the ball, the shots that players hit into the wind and along the ground, he decided that he wanted to work in golf, and specifically on a links golf course. In what seems like a meant-to-be career pattern, he ended up at Bandon Dunes.

He is now a leading member of "the fescue community" of superintendents who like to see their courses cloaked with fescue, not bent. Fescue, of course, is the natural grass of the links; it is a round-bladed grass. Bent is flat-bladed. In terms of their playing qualities, bent grass is like a plush carpet; fescue is like a hardwood floor. On a course like Old Macdonald, where the golfer would need a full array of low, running shots, bent simply wouldn't work.

In fact, Old Mac was being seeded with 100 percent fescue. On the other courses at Bandon Dunes, the seeding had been applied as a blend, with the amount of bent grass reduced for each successive course. At Pacific Dunes, the blend had been 90-10, and at Bandon Trails 95-5. At Old Mac, Ken was ready to eliminate the bent and go all-in with fescue. "Most places can't do that," he said, "but we have the right climate. Fescue works here. It's just better all around — it needs less water and practically no herbicides or fungicides. Our chemical budget on these courses is ridiculous, about 10 percent of what they spend at a course with conventional grasses and methods. "

From Jim's point of view, the fescue provides not only the right playing surface but also the seamless look he wanted. Most golf courses are anything but seamless. They are rippled with lines created by mowing patterns — fairway lines, rough cuts, intermediate cuts, collar cuts, trim cuts. There are lines everywhere, and the green sits there like a bull's eye in a target, with concentric circles all around it. Wasn't a seamless look going to seem radical to many golfers? "Radical isn't a word we use," Jim said, "but the fescue is different, that's for sure. We started doing this at Pacific, and we're taking it even farther here at Old Mac. We want the greens to blend in so completely that they almost disappear. The only way you'll know it's a green is because of the flag. The fescue is the only thing out here, and everything just flows into everything else. You don't see those lines and edges. The course isn't constantly giving you directions about where to hit the ball or what kind of shot you should play. It's all one playing field. Everything out here goes against the conventional wisdom."

By this point, we'd wandered over to the nearby 2nd tee. Jim and Ken were taking a walk-around to see how the grass was growing in, and Jim wanted to identify a few other places where he thought the rough could use more soul. The pace was deliberate, with Jim favoring the knee that was pretty much destroyed by an old football injury, and Ken looking carefully for the first reddish, almost microscopic shoots of fescue. "That's what a turf guy likes to see," he said, pointing out how evenly the specks were spread.

The 2nd hole is a par 3, an Eden hole, modeled after the Edens at St. Andrews and National. The green is perched high, but the most arresting feature of the hole is a sod-faced bunker — a revet, in Jim's lingo. "So, is that a bold bunker?" he asked, after reminding me that Macdonald prescribed six bold bunkers on a course. He talked about the variations of bunkering at Old Mac, where they'd used everything from natural blowouts to sleepered bunkers to grass-faced bunkers to revets. "We weren't really thinking we had to do something so different from Pacific, but one day Brian Slawnik shaped a bunker that had a grass face and we said, 'That looks neat.' So we went with it."

This revet on No. 2 was almost a command performance. The original Eden hole at St. Andrews is guarded by the Strath bunker, one of the most renowned bunkers in golf. With its steeply pitched green, the Eden River directly behind, and the Strath bunker in front, the hole has humbled many great players, including the young Bobby Jones; the Eden is where he famously tore up his scorecard and left the course in a fit of temper.

"It's not a very big bunker," Jim was saying, "and it's even smaller than it looks from here. If Ken was standing down there, if you had anything to give you perspective, you'd see how small it was. When you stand here on the tee, though, it's a scary bunker, and you're thinking you'd better avoid it. The Strath bunker." He drew out that *Strath,* enjoying the Scottish sound of it, relishing the thought that the bunker had a new incarnation here at Bandon.

En route to the 3rd tee, Jim told an anecdote about working with Jack Nicklaus at Sebonack. Nicklaus was staying next door at National Golf Links, and one morning Jim picked him up to drive him to work. As they drove out of National, Nicklaus asked him what he liked so much about the course. "I don't know how much Jack liked it," Jim said, "but he knew how I felt about it. I told him I loved National because it's so unpredictable. Every time I go there, there's something new to learn. I said, 'Jack, what I like about it is the mystery. It's a course you're never going to figure out.'"

Mystery. That seemed to be the right topic as we stood on the 3rd tee and looked at the dead cedar silhouetted against the sky. The ghost tree. I'd heard from Grant Rogers that Jim had once taken him around Pacific Dunes, pointing out the "power spots," so I asked him if this was one of the power spots on Old Mac. "I know it's a power spot," he said, laughing. "Absolutely. I almost got hit by lightning here. I felt the power."

Jim may be a "dirt guy," but it turns out that he has respect for intangible forces, too. He traces this back to his experience at Apache Stronghold, a course that Renaissance built in San Carlos, Arizona, near the Superstition Mountains. A medicine man, says Jim, initiated him into the mysteries and legends of the place, reputed to be a mystical haven where Apaches could walk invisible to their enemies. The medicine man also showed him where the spirits entered and exited the stronghold. Ever since, he had carried a string of mojo beads on all his jobs. The mojo beads and the Red Book, Macdonald's book, were his inspirations. "I don't talk about this much," Jim said, "but anyone who spends time on a site like this starts to have feelings about it. It's not all the same. Different spots out here have different vibes. I try to pay attention to them, that's all."

We circled through a set of interior holes, a Redan and the Leven hole, before climbing up a hill to pause for a while behind the 14th green. This is another high spot on the course, and we had views that spread for miles in all directions. To the north, we could see some of the holes on the Sheep Ranch, with tiny yellow flags marking the greens. Straight in front of us, groups were playing along the fairways and through the sandhills at Pacific Dunes. Altogether, the golf filled about four miles of coastline that had once been an impassable thicket of gorse. Jim Urbina had been instrumental in making many of these golf holes. "When I look around now," he said, "I almost don't believe it. I think, Wow. We did all that. Tom, and Ken, the whole crew — we did that. We changed this place."

Ken nodded, watching a foursome hit their approach shots onto the green. When one ball landed near the flag, he said, "I just love that *thunk* the ball makes when it hits a firm green."

There were still a couple of holes to check out. We walked down to the 15th tee and back up to the green with another ocean view, but Jim and Ken weren't looking at the Pacific. They were laughing at the fist-size rocks that had appeared in the bunker behind the green. "Brian [Slawnik] was up here for a week, working on this bunker, and the last time I looked it was perfect. Pure sand. Now look at it." It was almost as if he'd planned this demonstration to show me that the land has a will of its own. Ken said that an old haul road ran through this area, and shrugged. "It's just the kind of situation you work with. You can't see the road now, but it's under there, somewhere, and it's gonna show up now and then."

On to No. 16, the Alps hole, where the major hazard — the big hill that serves as the eponymous Alps — was surmounted by a small, glistening orb. It looked like a cosmic talisman but proved on closer inspection to be a bowling ball impaled on a stake. "We've got to get rid of that," Jim said, pointing out how the hole would play. The approach to the green would be blind, but a less-than-perfect shot over the left side of the Alps had a chance of running down close to the green. A weak approach to the right would finish in another sleepered bunker. The player who didn't want a blind shot and could smack a long drive down the far right side of the fairway would get a glimpse of the green. "Look at that green," Jim said. "When we came out here after the gorse fire, it was just sitting there waiting for us, a sweet little private bowl, with these hills surrounding it — how could we not use that?"

Another power spot? I asked.

His dark eyes gleamed and he just nodded.

JIM URBINA WAS A BUSY MAN. When he wasn't on the golf course, he was on the set of *Golf in the Kingdom,* where he had a cameo as a grumpy starter (keep the day job, Jim). Or he was conducting tours of Old Mac for the caddies who would loop there, educating them about the historical precedents and offering suggestions about how the course might best be played. Or he was meeting with a group of architects who'd stopped at Bandon Dunes on the way to the annual American Society of Golf Course Architects convention in Seattle. Many of the architects were old pals, but neither Tom nor Jim is a member of the ASGCA. If any group represented the establishment, and hewed to the conventional wisdom that Renaissance Golf Design had always challenged, it was the ASGCA.

Nevertheless, the architects — the group numbered an even dozen — were more than just curious about Bandon Dunes. For many of them, this visit was their first, and they openly envied the architects who'd had a chance to work here. "There's no one here who wouldn't have loved to have had a site like this," said Bob Cupp, the designer of many highly regarded courses, including Pumpkin Ridge, farther up the Oregon coast. "Watching this place develop makes me think of what it must have been like to see Pinehurst evolve. It's changing the way we think about golf — not just resort golf, but *golf.*"

Inevitably, there was also much conversation about the discouraging state of the economy. Everyone present had stories about projects that had been put on hold or gone belly-up. Even the big firms were letting people go. There just wasn't any work, not in the United States. The only bright spot was Asia. Tom Clark, a partner in a firm located in Maryland, had been in the profession for forty years and had never been without new work — until now. He did have some consulting and restoration projects, but he looked at me and wagged a warning finger. "You writers better watch out. There's going to be a lot of books by architects pretty soon. All of us are writing our memoirs now that we're sitting around with nothing else to do."

There seemed to be two distinct schools of thought among the architects, with the division marked by age. The older architects leaned toward the views of Robert Trent Jones, the designer who'd been such a commanding figure when they were learning their trade. Jones believed that the correct line for the playing of each hole should be obvious from the tee (a concept that is now usually expressed as "it's all right there in front of you"). They also had a staunch belief in fairness, and when they played the Bandon Dunes courses, they kept noting features they could never have designed. For example, Eric Larsen, the executive VP of Arnold Palmer Golf Design and a good stick, was baffled by the the 14th hole at Bandon Trails (this is the most controversial hole on the property, having been described in *Golf Digest* as "Crenshaw's Folly"). "You can't build a hole like this," he said. "Hit two good shots and you're still not on the green. You're off the back of the green, or off to the side, and you make double or worse — and that's after you hit the shot you're supposed to hit."

Jeff Brauer, the Texas designer, expressed his differences in broader terms, objecting to what he saw as a philosophy of defending par at the green. "To me, the courses are penal. There's no reward for the player who takes risks from tee to green because the greens and green complexes are so random. You hit the green but you still haven't hit it, if you see what I mean. Miss by just a little and the ball takes off and keeps running. There's no way most golfers are going to get up and down from the situations around these greens. He's already made bogey — why put him in a bunker, too?"

The remark that generated the most discussion was made by a senior architect who, after playing Pacific Dunes, was heard to say, "There's no strategy out there."

"None that he can see," said Ian Andrew, a young Canadian architect who spoke for the opposing camp. Ian is a close student of historic courses, especially those of Stanley Thompson, the great figure in Canadian golf design, and he has just gone into partnership with Canada's best golfer, Mike Weir. An unabashed admirer of the courses of Tom Doak and Coore-Crenshaw, Ian is the kind of guy who loves to go out at sunset with a few clubs in his hand for some adventure golf. I talked to him just after he'd finished a 7-hole loop at Bandon Trails, playing with five clubs and putting with his hybrid.

"There's a real difference between the older and younger members of the ASGCA," he said. "Some of the older guys have been doing things a different way all their lives, and they have their own way of looking at golf holes. At Pacific Dunes, there's strategy all over the place, but they don't see it. They're used to a more defined strategy — the fairway bunker tells you where to hit the ball, the green is designed for a certain kind of approach, the green complex tells you where you can miss and where you can't.

"But you can't read Tom's courses that way. He doesn't think you're entitled to a level lie if you hit the fairway, and he puts bunkers right in the fairway where you want to hit. There are all kinds of shots you can play into the greens and around the greens. The decisions are up to you, and they're not automatic. You rarely think, OK, I'm here, this is the shot I have to play. It's more like, I'm here, what shot do I want to play? The difference is that the older guys think of a hole as having a clear-cut strategy that the architect has devised, but on these courses each player has to come up with his own strategy — and that's what makes it fun. That's what turns golf into more than a matter of executing certain shots. It puts imagination and creativity into the game.

"I don't know any young architects who want to design with a strategy that's rigidly defined. I know I don't. I want to build holes like the ones I just played. It might be a while before people really start to notice, but there's a major change taking place in design. It's not just a change in fashion, it's a change in the philosophy. Courses that are shaped by the land, with features created by hand, letting each golfer play his own game — this is what golf used to be, and what it's going to be again. This is the future of golf course design, right here."

AGAINST THE BACKGROUND of a global recession, those words — the future of golf course design — rang with optimism. While no one could know how severe the recession would be, or how long it would stifle golf course construction, Ian's enthusiasm did underscore what Bandon Dunes had come to represent for an up-and-coming generation of golf architects. With its classically influenced, lay-of-the-land courses, the place was a source of inspiration and a treasure trove of ideas. Mike Keiser hadn't set out to build an "ideal" course, as Macdonald had at National Golf Links; but collectively the four courses at Bandon Dunes did provide an ideal. They showcased a vision of the way that tradition and originality could be combined to produce dynamic golf holes.

For Ian Andrew and other aspiring golf architects, the designers who'd built the courses at Bandon Dunes were role models. They'd blazed a path for others to follow. And in retrospect, even though Bandon Dunes had initially seemed like such a risky venture, it was increasingly clear that several historical developments had been working in their favor. When Mike first decided to take the plunge and build a throwback course on the Oregon coast, many people, including Mike himself, wondered if he had embarked on a huge folly. But he had the courage of his convictions. His years in the greeting card business had at the very least convinced him that the American public didn't want an endless diet of same old, same old. Recycled Paper Greetings had succeeded because it broke with the conventional formula for greeting cards. At Bandon Dunes, he was willing to take the risk that other golfers were as turned off as he was by formulaic courses, and what they wanted was something more exciting — specifically, links golf, not a watered-down imitation but the real thing, seaside links golf on hard, fast-running turf, the same kind of golf that had been played for centuries in Scotland.

As it turned out, his timing was excellent. Bandon Dunes tapped into three major developments and, in a golfing feedback loop, added to their momentum.

The first was the shifting of the axis of American golf from east to west.

With few exceptions, the most famous and highly ranked courses had always been east of the Mississippi, clustered around the cities that were hubs of power and influence. Starting in the 1970s, though, the new and dramatic courses — the game changers, the ones that made their way into the Top 100 — started to appear in wide-open spaces of the West. At facilities like Desert Mountain in Arizona and PGA West in California, designers like Jack Nicklaus and Pete Dye built layouts that seem to defy the dry, rocky landscape; designer Jim Engh came to prominence by building mountain courses like the the Sanctuary, in Colorado, and the Club at Black Rock, in Idaho, with holes hanging from the cliffs or tucked away in canyons at the foot of a waterfall; Bill Coore and Ben Crenshaw made their mark at Sand Hills, on the high, lonesome prairie of Nebraska. At first, to eastern eyes, these courses looked downright strange. They were certainly wilder, more spacious, and more rugged looking than the typical eastern course — a groomed, tree-lined, parkland course fit snugly into a green suburb. There wasn't a single western "look," but the challenge of designing in expansive landscapes seemed to unleash the creative energies of many architects.

Most important, these eye-popping western courses brought a heightened sense of adventure into the game. At Bandon Dunes, golfers were as far west as they could go, both literally and figuratively, and the journey to get there only reinforced the sense that they had left the familiar world far behind. Out there at the edge of the continent, they were face-to-face with a kind of golf that was bracingly, thrillingly different.

Second, Bandon Dunes became the poster child for the revival of classic architecture. In 2004, *Golf Magazine* ranked the great moments in golf over the last forty-five years. On the same list as Jack Nicklaus winning the 1986 Masters and the Tiger Slam of 2000–2001, Bandon Dunes earned a place for becoming "America's newest golf mecca" and inspiring a "classic-design revival."

The groundwork for a classic revival had been put in place earlier, with the excitement generated by the playing of the U.S. Open at historic courses like Shinnecock Hills and the Country Club. For any golfer who read articles by writers like Brad Klein and Ron Whitten, there was a real sense of rediscovering the classics. At the same time, the societies devoted to researching and preserving the work of classic architects were formed, and the vigorous, ongoing debate got started about the best way to restore — or renovate? — classic courses.

At Bandon Dunes, the discussion went to a different level. On the gorse-covered bluffs along the Pacific, there was nothing to preserve or restore. The task was not to make a classic course relevant but to create vital new courses using classic principles and strategies. In effect, this was a leap from the domain of the historian into the imaginative realm of the artist. The setting called for links golf, and the architects whom Mike selected — David Kidd, Tom Doak, Bill Coore and Ben Crenshaw — all drew on different classical models, but they showed how time-honored ideas could yield courses that were vibrant, muscular, and original.

Third, minimalism had gone mainstream, at least in theory. The days when architects boasted about how many cubic yards of earth they'd moved, as if the volume was a measure of creativity, were over. The pendulum had swung sharply in the opposite direction, and — to Tom Doak's annoyance — architects now bragged about how little earth they'd moved. Tom had been the most forceful advocate of minimalism, and he was still skeptical about the claims of designers who'd embraced minimalism so readily. "Minimalism is fundamentally about finding the best places to put all the holes," he said. "There are some architects who are trying to be minimalists as far as moving dirt, but they're not getting the routing right, and in that case the product is a mess."

Most golfers didn't give a flying fig about how much dirt was moved to build a course, but they most assuredly cared about the product. The acid test for minimalism was the same as for classically inspired design: Did the theory produce exciting golf? The golfers who came to Bandon Dunes quickly realized that the answer to that question was a stunning yes!

The beautiful, playable courses were of a piece, and at peace, with the land on which they were built. For golfers of all skill levels, they were rife with the kinds of challenges, thrills, and frustrations that are at the heart of golf's enduring appeal. They illustrated what minimalism, in practice, had come to mean; namely, that designers do not impose their will on the land (do not "rape-and-shape" it) and, equally important, do not impose their will on the strategic elements of the course.

Instead, the minimalist designer starts with the knowledge that golfers don't all take the same path from tee to green. From this perspective, a golf hole looks like a slope after skiers have carved it up; instead of the usual schematic of a golf hole, showing an ideal route from point A to point B, the whole thing appears crisscrossed with tracks indicating a multitude of routes.

The challenge is to give all golfers, no matter what route they take, something interesting to do with each and every shot. For these designers, a course with good "shot values" isn't the one that requires the longest, straightest drive or the highest, quickest-stopping approach shots. The goal is to design a course that calls for the greatest variety of shots — and for the greatest variety of players.

That might not fit within the strict definition of minimalism, but it's consistent with the aim Tom Doak announced years earlier in *The Anatomy of a Golf Course*: "The highest aspiration of a golf course architect should be to design holes that give the greatest scope for a shotmaker's skills." And it is exactly what Charles Blair Macdonald had in mind decades earlier when he wrote, "Variety is not only the 'spice of life' but it is the very foundation of golfing architecture."

ALL SUCCESSFUL VENTURES acquire an air of inevitability. They settle so deeply in our awareness, changing our perceptions of what is possible, that it seems impossible to imagine a world without them. In May 2009, Bandon Dunes marked its tenth anniversary — the blink of an eye in golf time — but it was already a landmark, a fixture on the map of golf. A power spot, as Jim Urbina might say. The place had beauty, it had character, it had soul, and it had three courses in the Top 100 — the only resort in the world that could make that claim. And with Old Macdonald getting ready to open, and already being touted by some visitors as the best course on the property, it looked as though it would soon have four courses in the Top 100.

Without doubt, Bandon Dunes had made everyone who cared about golf think a little differently about the game. For Mike Keiser, the change could be summed up simply: "Americans love links golf. Fifteen years ago, who knew? We'd been playing target golf for decades. Unless you were able to get over to Scotland or Ireland, you didn't have a chance to play classic links golf. So the plan was to build links courses here, throwback courses that were like the great old courses where the game started."

The plan worked on a scale that surprised everyone, including Mike, and the influence of Bandon Dunes has spread far and wide. Young architects, as we have seen, have mined the Bandon courses for ideas to use in their own designs. Tom Doak and David Kidd, whose careers took a quantum leap after working at Bandon Dunes, have gone on to build remarkable courses on several different continents. Bill Coore and Ben Crenshaw were already established figures, but the Bandon experience keeps leading to new undertakings, and they are now designing the Lost Farm, a course at Barnbougle Dunes, in Tasmania, that has driven Mike to uncharacteristic hyperbole; he says it could be "the best course since Augusta National." Speaking of Barnbougle Dunes, developer Richard Sattler says flatly that it "wouldn't exist without Mike Keiser," and other developers — Bob Lang of Erin Hills, Paul Schock of the Prairie Club — cite their debt to Mike's advice and example.

At turf level, most golfers have probably noticed the way that fescue has begun to creep onto their courses, showing up in the areas of rough or in the fringes of bunkers. This could be called the Bandon look. As with architects, superintendents have paid close attention to Bandon Dunes, to bunker shapes and mowing patterns and, thankfully, to the exemplary environmental practices. In course restoration, the emphasis on getting rid of trees can't be traced directly to Bandon — but one can safely say that Bandon Dunes enhanced the appreciation of treeless links golf and helped remind everyone that most classic American courses began on treeless sites. Likewise, it would be hard to argue that the current vogue for short par 4s got started at Bandon, but it has caught on because of the renewed interest in classic design.

The example of Bandon Dunes has motivated many clubs and individuals to take a sympathetic look at the past and to recapture, if they can, the time-tested appeal of the game. "Mike Keiser is a modern American connection to the earliest links golf," Bill Coore said recently, and that fundamental commitment has informed everything that has happened at Bandon Dunes. As golf writers have tried to assess the phenomenon of Bandon Dunes, they keep circling back to Mike Keiser. Yes, the individual courses were brilliant, but the whole was definitely greater than the sum of its parts. It was more and more apparent that Mike's vision was the basis of the consistency, integrity, and authenticity of Bandon Dunes. Every time there was a decision, David Kidd said, "golf won out." There were no houses, no carts, no cart paths, none of the usual clutter and distractions. Mike had never strayed from his goal of creating "dream golf. " He had never forgotten that dream golf had to stir both the senses and the soul, an idea expressed by another visionary, Charles Blair Macdonald, in words that seem to apply directly to Bandon Dunes: "To get the full exaltation of the game of golf one should when passing from green to green as he gazes over the horizon have an illimitable sense of eternity."

The owner isn't often the good guy, or even the most important guy, in a golf story. And even though Mike tried to stay in the background, letting the architects take the bows, the plot of Bandon Dunes always led back to him. The building of Old Macdonald, a course driven by a concept that he'd originated, nudged him to the forefront. True *Bandonistas* were on to him. They knew that Bandon Dunes was his creation. *Golf Digest* travel writer Matt Ginella — aka Mattie G — is a hard-core fan of Bandon Dunes and of its maker: "I say my prayers at night thanking God for Saint Mike Keiser, who brought us the greatest all-golf facility in the country. As long as I'm saying my prayers: *May every golf fan experience a four-man cottage at Bandon Dunes before they become one with the end.* Pardon the dose of spirituality, but Bandon brings it out of me."

24 | The Bandon Family

I think people see me as a kind of Johnny Appleseed, planting courses wherever I go. And that's all right with me. —MIKE KEISER

AS THE JUNE 2010 opening of Old Macdonald approached, the media buzz turned into a blitz. It was, as one writer said, the most highly anticipated course since . . . Bandon Trails. On the Internet, there were blog posts with videos and photographs of the most dramatic holes. In the early going, the Sahara hole seemed to be the most photographed, slightly ahead of No. 7, the hole with the green on the ocean ridge. In print, golf writers noted how Old Mac bolted down Bandon Dunes' connections with the classic courses both here and in Scotland. Writing in the *Wall Street Journal,* John Paul Newport began his report by declaring that National Golf Links was his favorite course but Old Mac "may be even more fun to play." And after his first look at Old Mac, Mattie G wrote: "My best guess: Old Macdonald will exceed all hype and expectations."

There was even a full-length documentary in the works. On a recent trip to Scotland, after watching Tom Watson make his gallant run at winning a sixth British Open, Mike Keiser spent a day at St. Andrews in front of the camera with Tom Doak. The filmmaker, Michael Robin, had already made several trips to Oregon, but he wanted to go all the way back to the source. To Mike, this was a necessary part of the story; he was pleased that so many people commented on the way that Old Mac suggested comparisons to St. Andrews just as surely as it echoed the National. One obvious point of comparison was the size of the greens; it came up so repeatedly that Ken Nice, Jim

Urbina, and Brad Klein did some research and measurement to find out just how large the greens were at St. Andrews. As it turned out, the total acreage of the greens at St. Andrews was 6.1 acres. According to their calculations, the greens at Old Mac were even larger, covering an aggregate of 6.3 acres. As far as anyone knew, these were the largest greens in the kingdom.

The preview rounds had been a thumping success. Knowing that people want to praise his courses, Mike doesn't believe everything he hears; but several people whose opinions he trusted had told him that Old Mac was the best course on the property. Mike briefly considered changing the sequence of the routing and starting with No. 6, where the preview rounds had started. This would mean moving the location of the clubhouse — whatever the clubhouse turned out to be — but that was another argument in favor of the change. "The spot overlooking the 5th green and the 6th tee is spectacular," Mike said before slipping back into his habitual questioning mode. "How many places can you sit and look out over a valley with 14 golf holes and the ocean on the horizon? That's the view from that hill, and that's what I want people to have as their first impression of Old Mac. When we bring people over for preview rounds and get to the top of that hill, you can see their jaws drop. That's the reaction we want."

As he grew more familiar with the course, however, playing all 18 holes in sequence, he decided that the rhythm of the routing worked so well with original 1st hole that he shouldn't tamper with it. The golf took precedence over the clubhouse view. And golfers would still get the jolt of the lift-off view when they crested the hill on the 3rd hole and saw the whole panorama of the course and ocean laid out before them. Then, they'd see it again from a different angle at the "champagne turnstand" on the 7th hole. "That name might not stick," he says. "Josh shakes his head every time I say 'champagne.'"

As he had from the beginning, Mike was still talking over every decision about the golf at Bandon Dunes with Josh Lesnik, no longer the untested young man who was the first GM of Bandon Dunes but a savvy and experienced executive, the president of KemperSports. The two men still communicated daily, often three or four times a day, still trying to decide how to present the course, looking at every decision from every angle, then setting it aside and looking at it again. The logo debate, for example, had gone on for months and had even surfaced in the Bandon Dunes pro shop, where customers were asked to take part in a survey. In the final count, the more traditional OM logo won out narrowly over the rooster.

And they were still concerned about making a distinction between a "replica" course and a tribute. In Mike's formula, replica holes were 98 percent the same as the original, but holes "inspired by" were in the range of 5–25 percent identical. "Holes that are 'inspired by' are sisters, brothers, cousins, and distant cousins," he told one writer. He and Josh knew that the architecture junkies would be locked and loaded when they came to Old Macdonald, "discussing our new take on the different holes and whether our Biarritz hole or Redan is a better model, or a sacrilege." But he also knew that the retail golfer would be a lot less interested in the pedigree of a hole than in the immediate experience on the course. As always, the goal was to make every hole exciting — to make them all "sing."

Mike was giving more time to the golf business now that he was a "non-employee" of Recycled Paper Greetings. In 2006, he and founding partner Phil Friedman sold RPG to a holding company that soon ran into difficulty managing its debt. Mike continued to select cards and work with artists, but RPG was then sold to American Greetings, and there is now a lawsuit hovering over the company. Mike, however, is merely an onlooker. He said years ago, "Companies don't last. Golf courses do."

He'd also said, half-jokingly, that it was time for him to start making a career transition — and now he'd made it. The golf business combined naturally with his other continuing interest, philanthropy. In November 2008, he stepped down after a two-year term as the board chair of the Rehabilitation Institute of Chicago, the top-rated rehabilitation center in the country, with thirty locations, thirteen hundred employees, and cutting-edge research scientists. As part of his contribution to RIC, Mike arranged red-carpet trips to Bandon Dunes for potential donors; each trip raised over $300,000 and brought new donors into the fold. Mike is on the board of the Field Museum, and he continues to be an active, engaged supporter of several educational initiatives, both in Chicago and in Oregon (every Bandon high school graduate who went on to college, Hank Hickox told me, received some form of assistance from Mike). His inclination to combine golf and philanthropy has produced one informal charity that Mike calls "the Nobel Laureate Support Group." His interest in economic theory has put him in touch with the high-powered economists on the faculty of the University of Chicago, who, he soon discovered, were frustrated golfers. Through his network of friends, Mike arranged for them to play at many of Chicago's top clubs.

According to his wife, Lindy, Mike is playing a little more golf these days, and spending a little more time with his family. His four children are grown-ups now. Michael Jr. works in commercial real estate in Chicago, but he's a passionate mountain climber who recently ascended the Matterhorn. Daughter Leigh, recently married, is an avid reader, former dancer and performer, and now a graduate student at Berkeley headed toward a career as a therapist. Daughter Dana has moved back to Chicago to pursue a PhD in early childhood development; recently engaged, she will be married at the Dunes Club (specifically, says Dad, on the 8th fairway). Youngest son Chris is a senior at Georgetown, weighing a future that might include business or a stint for Teach for America, or both.

It's not easy for all of them to get together, but when they do, the conversation cycles rapidly from one subject to another, from a discussion of Smart Cars to the problems of attracting and retaining science and math teachers in public schools to Kindle readers to computer-generated images and the broad effect of computers on our ways of thinking and doing business.

It's clear that all the Keisers enjoy these quick, crackling, open-ended conversations, and it's clear that they know what to expect from their father: questions and more questions, pushing them to think through their answers.

I GOT TO LISTEN in on that family conversation because I'd flown out to Chicago for a last interview with Mike. He'd set up a round of golf at

Chicago Golf Club the following morning, and we drove out to Wheaton in his new ride, a pre-owned Audi. On the way, he admitted that it had taken him a while to develop a liking for this golf course. "The site is very level," he said, "and the first time I saw it, with the features built up, it just looked like a bunch of big boxes out in a field." Once we got out onto the course, it was clear that he'd come to appreciate the style and subtlety of the course, the greens in particular. Throughout the round, he made sure that I noticed the weave and roll of the greens, and the variations in the Chicago Golf Club version of the Macdonald/Raynor iconic holes — the Punchbowl, the Cape, the Biarritz, the Double Plateau, the Redan, the Eden, the Road. He was a gracious tour guide, but he still played with his usual briskness, drove it straight, holed putts from everywhere with his long putter, and carded a tidy 81.

Afterward, we looked at the exhibits and documents in the clubhouse that was fashioned from a barn. The place is saturated with the history of American golf. Macdonald's drawing for the first 18-hole course in the country is on display, and there is a bronze statue of Macdonald between the pro shop and the locker room. In the grill room, we stopped in front of the portrait of Macdonald, the one in which he is wearing a military garrison cap. With his full mustache and fierce eyes, he looks like an officer about to go the front. Somehow, Mike had never noticed the portrait before. After studying it for a second, he said, "I've seen a lot of Macdonald."

His tone was neutral, but it seemed to mark a turning point in the conversation. At any rate, on the ride back into town, he didn't want to talk about Old Mac but the projects that were just over the horizon. His plans for Bandon Dunes aren't finished yet. He's already had Bill Coore and Ben Crenshaw design another course in the dunes just west of Bandon Trails. No one could figure out how to get a regulation 18-hole course into the dunes, so Mike asked Coore-Crenshaw just to make the most of it — and they came up with a 12-hole, par 3 course. Mike doesn't have the permits yet, but he's antsy to get started on yet another project that would unite golf and philanthropy. He wants to call it the Conservation Course ("I still have to persuade the brand-keepers to let me have that name") and charge $100 for a round. All the profits would go toward the South Coast conservation fund. "There's an area one hundred miles long and ten miles wide south of Bandon, extending down to Brookings, with a population of only ten thousand people. That's a thousand square miles that we might be able to preserve so that people could see what this coast was like when it was wild."

This prospect excites him, as does the thought of a new course designed by Gil Hanse, a former associate of Tom Doak's and a designer who's come into his own with courses like TPC Boston, Rustic Canyon, and Castle Stuart. On a site a few miles south of Bandon, a site that Mike believes has as much natural appeal as Pacific Dunes, he has asked Hanse to design a public course. "We'd operate it the way St. Andrews Links operates," he says. "Locals wouldn't pay much to play, but guests would pay a steep rate. That way the townspeople get great golf, and it's subsidized by the visitors."

Mike's not sure when the Hanse course will get started. Meanwhile, he's looking forward to the opening of another course in Tasmania, where Bill Coore is finishing up the Lost Farm. This is the sister course to the existing Doak layout at Barnbougle Dunes, and Mike thinks it's probably even better — which is saying something, since the Doak course is ranked No. 1 among resort courses in Australia. "The land is a lot like Bandon," he says. "The whole feel of the resort is like Bandon, too. It's not as big, though — it's Baby Bandon."

And then, moving about ten thousand miles in the opposite direction, there's Bandon East. That's Mike's way of referring to a project up in Nova Scotia, where Canadian architect Rod Whitman has been building a "rough draft" of a golf course, shaping the whole thing himself on a capped industrial site. The place is called Cabot Links, and all 18 holes have ocean views. "Can you name a course where every hole has an ocean view? And this one has twelve infinity greens, where the green sits right against the ocean. There's one place on the course where Rod's built four interconnected greens, a five-acre green complex sitting on the Gulf of St. Lawrence."

Surely that's all? Well, no. Moving another few thousand miles eastward, to the tiny island of South Uist, in the Outer Hebrides, fifty miles from the Scottish mainland, there's a perfect bit of linksland and a course called Askernish that was laid out by Old Tom Morris. Mike is thinking of getting involved. The greens are rough and tiny, hardly greens at all, but it wouldn't take much to fix that. "It's really in the middle of nowhere, and I have no idea who'd go there, but it would be a real gem. You wouldn't have to try to make it seem timeless and ancient. It already is."

As I listened to him describe these courses that spanned half the globe, it seemed that he was creating a small empire. In his mind, the lines seemed to radiate out from Bandon Dunes like the lines on those airline maps, showing the routes to magical, faraway places. It was hard to get my head around the places he was talking about. Tasmania? Nova Scotia? The Outer Hebrides? To Mike, though, they didn't seem that remote. Baby Bandon, Bandon East. With names like that, they sounded like members of a family, not the outposts of an empire. One of Mike's gifts is that he keeps everything on a human scale, a trait that has been central to his success. He just doesn't care about impressing people; he'd rather provide them with something — a greeting card or a golf course, a scholarship or a chance at rehabilitation — that might enrich their lives. Temperamentally, he isn't an empire builder, seeking to possess and control, arranging things so that they add to his importance. He is much more of an explorer, someone who keeps moving on, always looking for the next great venture.

But he does like to leave something behind. Reflecting on the role he's made for himself in the world of golf, he said, "I think people see me as a kind of Johnny Appleseed, planting courses wherever I go. And that's all right with me."

Acknowledgments

I HAVE TO BEGIN by acknowledging that the idea for this book was not my own. To this day, I am not exactly sure who decided that Bandon Dunes would be an ideal subject for a book, but I know that George Peper was the one to put forward my name as the writer.

As a consultant to Workman Publishing, Inc., George was helping to develop ideas for golf books. I was so flabbergasted when he called me to talk about Bandon Dunes that I thought I was going to run off the road. I'd never been out to Oregon, but I was a lover of links golf and I had followed the Bandon story closely. Very closely, for I happened to be a minor player in a golf course in Maryland in which Mike was a major investor. Though I'd never met Mike, I was intrigued by the tale of the man from Chicago who'd decided to build his dream course on a remote stretch of the Oregon coast.

I might not have come up with the idea, but I did know enough to recognize the sound of opportunity knocking. Thanks, George, for the vote of confidence and for knowing better than I did what I should be writing.

I also knew that if the book was going to be any good, Mike Keiser would have to be willing to sit for his portrait, and I was apprehensive about whether or not he would open himself to the kind of attention that a book can bring.

Mike dispelled that worry right away. He let me tag along when he played golf, when he conducted business meetings, when he met with golf course architects, when he visited inner-city schools in Chicago. He invited me to dinner with his son Chris and his wife, Lindy. He gave me a free run at the metal file cabinet in his office that contained all the material he had accumulated about Bandon Dunes. In short, he made it as easy as he possibly could for me to understand how his dream had taken shape and how it had been transformed into a reality at Bandon Dunes.

I'm grateful to Mike for his patience and his willingness to answer any and all questions. He was usually able to figure out and answer the question I was trying to ask, even if it was wasn't framed very clearly. And I am grateful to Lindy Keiser for her hospitality and the insights that she shared; she understands that her husband is incisive and purposeful when he is functioning in his entrepreneurial mode, and she helped bring into focus both Mike's playfulness and creativity, qualities that are part of the fabric of their family life.

Not long after I started working on the book, Mike put out the word to others connected with Bandon that he hoped they'd provide whatever I needed, and that is exactly what happened. His business associates and golfing friends—particularly "retail golfers" Bob Peele, Warren Gelman, and Alfred Hamilton—provided a valuable perspective on the evolution of Bandon Dunes. To Bill Shean, Rick Summers, and Dick Youngscap, a word of special thanks; all of them made important contributions to Bandon Dunes, and to this book. Similarly, Dick Nugent and Ron Whitten loom large as influences on Mike's thinking about golf course design, and they couldn't have been more forthcoming.

There's an unusual and appealing quality in the attitude of those who've been involved longest with Bandon Dunes; most of them seem a little bemused by the phenomenal success of the place, and even humbled by it. They still seem to be shaking their heads, trying to figure out how it all came together.

That is certainly true of Howard McKee, whose role in the development has been essential but largely invisible. For his ability to articulate large ideas, and for his patience in explaining the minutiae of the permitting process, I am most grateful—though not as grateful as I am for his sense of humor and his whooping laughter.

Shorty Dow is another whose stories were laced with wit and humor. He was and still is the one who best knows Bandon, the place, and has the most interesting things to say about its inhabitants, human and otherwise. Chuck and Jeannie Bruce showed me around the Cascade Ranch and filled in some blanks about the early chapters of Mike and Howard's experience in Oregon. Bob Johnson is not only a storyteller but a fisherman, and his tales of Bandon capture the perspective of a native Oregonian who watched the Bandon Dunes phenomenon gather force.

I came to have great respect for the way that the people at Kemper Sports have managed Bandon Dunes, and their role in the success of the resort is a part of the story that couldn't be fully told in this book. Their willingness to spend time with me added depth and dimension to my understanding both of Bandon Dunes and the golf industry. Steve Lesnik was candid about his relationship with Mike, even when that candor didn't always show him in the most flattering light. The same goes for Jim Seeley, who accepted his role as the naysayer in the Bandon Dunes experiment with grace, and without excuses.

As for Josh Lesnik, the first GM of the Bandon Dunes resort, he gives credit to everyone but himself. I always knew that I could go to Josh with my questions, and I always trusted his answers.

I wish that I'd been able to spend more time with Jimmy Kidd; I met him at Gleneagles and fell under his spell, as most people do. I spent many fascinating hours with David Kidd, who admitted that he'd been advised to hold back when talking to me but finally decided to be forthcoming; that is his nature, and a part of his considerable charm. I first met him and his sidekick, Jim Haley, in a bar in St. Andrews; they waltzed in late one summer evening, and it was instantly clear that the two of them loved to tell stories, and had a gift for it. Jim Haley has one of those memories that fixes events with dates, and David, for all that he is a performer, is a man of passions and vulnerabilities. I hope that his depth comes across as well as his impish humor.

Pete Sinnott was unfailingly helpful in providing the documentation for the construction of Bandon Dunes, and in clarifying some of the struggles that occurred. As a reliable and nonpartisan observer, Troy Russell was an invaluable source, as was his brother Tony, another early volunteer for work at Bandon.

For Tom Doak, I have a very particular thanks, since he has started writing his own book about Pacific Dunes, and has postponed it while I finished this one. I am grateful to him for more than his patience, too. He might easily have decided to withhold information, but he answered every question that I asked, and several that I didn't have the insight to ask.

Jim Urbina, his design associate, bubbled over with stories. In fact, I made several late changes after meeting with Jim and with Tony Russell over dinner. In this book, as in all books, there are a lot of good tales that get left on the cutting room floor. There just wasn't room to explain how Jim gave Tony the nickname Guy Lombardo.

Bill Coore and Ben Crenshaw are, simply, the best company in golf. They know more about golf and golf courses than the rest of us will ever know, and they have the knack of conveying their knowledge in vivid Southernese. To them and to the members of their talented crew—Dave Axland, Jim Craig, Jeff Bradley, and Dave Zincand—I am indebted for the time and care they spent to help me understand what they were trying to accomplish at Bandon Trails.

I tip my hat to Shoe, or Bob Gaspar, whose smile I look forward to seeing every time that I arrive at Bandon Dunes. To Dan Cunningham, thanks for the umbrella on a cold and nasty day. To Sam Dunn, a great friend on and off the golf course, I am indebted for an early and thoughtful reading of the manuscript, as well as his company on many a memorable round at Bandon.

Grant Rogers, the director of instruction at Bandon Dunes, led me on several golf adventures. I thought I appreciated links golf, but when I met Grant, I realized that I was a mere neophyte while Grant is far down the road toward enlightenment. More than anyone, he helped me see the outer dimensions of links golf, and to understand the joys to be experienced at Bandon Dunes.

Hank Hickox, the general manager of Bandon Dunes, and Marla Taylor, his assistant, run one of the best and busiest golf resorts in the world, but every time I've needed anything—whether it's a photograph or a fact, or even a dry pair of socks—they have instantly come through. I don't mean to say that I've gotten preferential treatment; it is second nature to them to make sure that every guest at Bandon feels well cared for.

For showing me around Old Macdonald, I am indebted to Jim Urbina and Ken Nice. Tom Doak not only answered pesky questions but generously provided the hole-by-hole notes that are an appendix to this book, adding depth and detail for the reader. C. J. Keurscher, Bill Anderson, and Wood Sabold gave me reports from the field; George Bahto and Karl Olson, members of the advisory design panel, helped me understand some of the intricacies of the design process. Brad Klein shared his notes, photographs, and trenchant comments, and also — editor that he is — saved me from numerous errors.

Finally, thanks to Jeff Neuman, who is the kind of editor that every writer wants. He is deft and diplomatic, thorough and tactful, enormously knowledgeable about both golf and publishing. He helped me bring the fuzzy parts of the book into clearer focus and made it possible—since he was always there as a safety net—to explore the full potential of the story.

If it sounds as though I have had a wonderful time writing this book, I have. I've met exceptional people who have accomplished exceptional things. At some point during the writing I realized that an objective narrative was never going to capture what had happened at Bandon; somehow or other, a more subjective truth had to spill over onto these pages, a truth that is the sum of the dreams and aspirations and plain hard work of those named here, people to whom I extend sincerest thanks, and without whose testimony this book would never have gotten off the ground.

Appendix:
Old Macdonald Hole by Hole
by Tom Doak

Hole No. 1, Double Plateau   This is my favorite opening hole that we've ever built. There is an ocean of fairway to hit at, but several choices on where to go. Straight up the middle is fine, but a drive up to the plateau on the right or wide to the left gives a better look at the green surface, and some strong hitters may even risk the bunkers to try and drive it up near the front of the green. No matter which way you go, getting your second shot onto the front left or back right plateau when the flag is there is an excellent shot. Precedent: National Golf Links No. 11, Yale No. 17.

Hole No. 2, Eden   This par-3 hole into the wind is based on the 11th at St. Andrews, judged by many in Macdonald's day as the ideal short hole. The green is defended by a deep revetted bunker at the front right (the Strath bunker) and another fearsome bunker left, with just enough fairway in between that a carefully judged running approach can be played. The green has a severe back-to-front pitch, so playing over the bunkers is never a safe option. Precedent: St. Andrews No. 11, National Golf Links No. 13, Mid Ocean No. 3.

Hole No. 3, Sahara   A short par 4 up and over a huge dune ridge, based on the old 3rd hole at Royal St. George's in England, which in Macdonald's day was a blind par 3. The safe line to the right requires only a 150-yard carry, but you can get near the green with the drive if you dare to flirt with the big tree on the left. The green is enormous for a short pitch yet it is still sometimes hard to get close to the hole, especially when the hole plays downwind. Precedent: Royal St. George's No. 3, National Golf Links No. 2.

Hole No. 4, Hog's Back This hole is based on the par-4 17th at Lundin Links, Scotland. The tee shot is up onto a narrow ridge that falls away sharply to both sides—a perfect drive will either stay up or kick forward for extra yardage, but anything less will kick away to the side, leaving a very long second shot down the valley toward the green. There is a small plateau on the left of the green that's very hard to hold; when the flag is on that side, 4 is a great score. Precedent: Lundin Links No. 17, National Golf Links No. 16.

Hole No. 5, Short Our shortest hole plays to one of the biggest greens on the course, but the green target is divided into several distinct areas and it is essential to find the right one to avoid a circus lag putt. The right-hand hole locations are especially severe because of the deep bunker to that side. If in doubt, miss toward the center of the green and take your chances from there. Precedent: Royal West Norfolk No. 4, National Golf Links No. 6, Chicago Golf Club No. 10.

Hole No. 6, Long The longest hole on the course plays directly into the summer wind, so three solid shots will be required to get home. The dominant bunker 100 yards short of the green is modeled after Hell bunker on the 14th hole at St. Andrews, Scotland, and should be avoided at all costs. The green is also modeled after the 14th at St. Andrews, with a steep rise at the front right making it difficult to pitch from that side; a running approach might be more successful here. Precedent: St. Andrews No. 14, National Golf Links No. 9.

Hole No. 7, Ocean This stout par 4 into the wind is not modeled after any particular Macdonald hole, but we were sure that Macdonald would have moved heaven and earth to site a green on the dune ridge overlooking the Pacific. Between the elevation change and the prevailing wind, the second shot will play much longer than the yardage, and it is best to hedge to the left as any shot to the right of the green will tumble well back down off the dune. Precedent: none.

Hole No. 8, Biarritz A long par 3 playing from a high tee by the ocean down to a wild green with a deep swale running through the middle of it. When the flag is at the back, many players may opt to land just in front of the swale and let the ball run through it and up to the hole; when the hole is in the front of the green, it's a much shorter shot, but your ball must stop quickly to avoid running down into the bottom. The original version of this hole was built by Willie Dunn at Biarritz, France, but today a hotel sits where the green once did. Precedent: Yale No. 9, Piping Rock No. 9.

Hole No. 9, Cape   A sharp dogleg to the right, with bunkers and gorse on the inside corner keeping you honest on the tee shot, but if you play away from the corner you may be left with a fairly long approach to a narrow target that runs a bit away from you. This hole is based on Macdonald's 14th hole at National Golf Links, though we substituted the gorse and bunkers in place of a pond that guards the dogleg at National. Precedent: National Golf Links No. 14, Chicago Golf Club No. 14.

Hole No. 10, Bottle   As at Macdonald's 8th hole at National Golf Links, two sets of fairway bunkers narrow the driving zone, forcing you to make a carry to the left side of the fairway or funnel into a narrow area on the right side of the hole. The second shot is one of the most difficult on the course, with the green sitting well up above the fairway and not much room through the back; chipping from the base of the green for your third is the best way to avoid a big score, while par is a great score. Precedent: Sunningdale (Old) No. 12, National Golf Links No. 8.

Hole No. 11, Road   The line of the fairway and green here are almost identical to the famous Road hole at St. Andrews. Although the tee shot is visible instead of blind, a long drive down the very right of the hole opens up an angle to the green; any approach played from the left or center is threatened by the deep revetted bunker at the left and a bank falling away at the back right. Precedent: St. Andrews No. 17, National Golf Links No. 7, Piping Rock No. 8.

Hole No. 12, Redan   The most imitated hole in the world is the par-3 15th at North Berwick, Scotland, known as the Redan, after a Crimean War fortress in Russia that was in the news when it was built. The plateau green runs away from a high shoulder at the right front to the back left, with a deep bunker guarding the left flank of the green. Our Redan is a bit different; the left bunker does not come across the front of the green as far as would be typical for the hole, but the bank of the green feeds short balls out to the bunker. Only a straight shot or a controlled fade will work here. Precedent: North Berwick No. 15, National Golf Links No. 4, Chicago Golf Club No. 7.

Hole No. 13, Leven   One of Macdonald's favorite short par-4 holes was at the old Leven Golf Club, whose course has since been split in two; the hole is now the 16th at Lundin Links, Scotland, a few miles south of St. Andrews. The hole is almost drivable, but the green falls away dramatically from the base of a big dune at its front left, down toward the right; so you would like to play your second shot from the right-hand side back up into the slope. Precedent: Lundin Links No. 16, Chicago Golf Club No. 5, National Golf Links No. 17.

Hole No. 14, Maiden   This short par 4 climbing up to an elevated green is named after the famous Maiden at Royal St. George's, the largest dune on any of the Open championship links. The original Maiden hole was a blind par 3 over the dune, which Macdonald sharply criticized; however, he admired the size and scale of the hill. The green has elevated wings at the left and back right that demand a precise approach; the nature of the approach can be altered by driving well out to the right so that the green lays out from front to back. Precedent: none.

Hole No. 15, Westward Ho!   This long par 5 plays back into the setting sun to a green up on the primary dune overlooking the ocean. The heaving contours of the fairway are like ocean swells; the key shot is the second, which must either get past a deep bunker on the right or be aimed safely short and left of it, which makes the uphill third shot much more difficult. The green is sharply two-tiered, so the correct length of the approach is paramount. Precedent: National Golf Links No. 18.

Hole No. 16, Alps   Macdonald's 3rd hole at National Golf Links was not just an homage to the Alps at Prestwick but an improvement on the hole. Instead of making the approach over a dune completely blind, his arrangement of the hole allowed a long drive down the right to get a peek at the green while allowing a way around the dune for short hitters trying to play the hole in only three installments. Our version is faithful to Macdonald's hole, except that we left a narrow open approach for blind shots from the left instead of building a bunker all the way across that line as at Prestwick and National. Precedent: Prestwick No. 17, National Golf Links No. 3.

Hole No. 17, Littlestone   One of Macdonald's most daring ideas came from the par-4 16th at Littlestone, England. The hole in his day was a long dogleg to the left, but Macdonald imagined an alternate fairway among the dunes on the direct line to the hole, which would enable daring players to cut the corner and get home in two. His version of the hole was the par-5 4th hole at Lido Golf Club, Long Island, a great course that closed its doors in the Depression. On our 17th, driving over a small wetland yields an open approach to the green, but the carry is so long that most players will have to be content with playing away to the left off the tee and taking a three-shot route home. Precedent: Littlestone No. 16, Lido No. 4.

Hole No. 18, Punchbowl Many greens on Scottish links were hidden away in natural bowls between the dunes. Macdonald had a very stylized version of this concept, with a huge green surrounded by small hills sweeping down from left to right; our home green is an outsized version of the Macdonald concept, so that the scale and drama of the course will stay with you right until the last putt is holed. Precedent: Chicago Golf Club No. 12, the Creek No. 6.